Holy Women of Twelfth-Century England

STUDIES IN RELIGION

SHARON K. ELKINS

Holy Women of
Twelfth-Century England

The University of North Carolina Press

Chapel Hill & London

© 1988 The University of North Carolina Press
All rights reserved
Manufactured in the United States of America

Library of Congress Cataloging-in-Publication Data
Elkins, Sharon K.
Holy women of twelfth-century England / by Sharon K. Elkins.
p. cm.—(Studies in religion)
Bibliography: p.
Includes index.
ISBN 0-8078-1775-9
1. Monasticism and religious orders for women—England—History.
2. Hermits—England—History. 3. England—Church history—Medieval
period, 1066–1485. I. Title. II. Title: Holy women of 12th-
century England. III. Series: Studies in religion
(Chapel Hill, N.C.)
BX4220.G7E45 1988   87-26128
271'.9'0042—dc19   CIP

92 91 90 89 88   5 4 3 2 1

To Steve

CONTENTS

MAP, CHART, AND TABLES

ACKNOWLEDGMENTS

In the process of writing this book, I have received aid and counsel from many people, including the following, to whom I wish to express my thanks: Pamela Barz, Constance Berman, Laurence Breiner, Caroline Walker Bynum, Penny Schine Gold, Joan McCarthy, Mary McLaughlin, Jo Ann McNamara, Thomas Rossi, and Mary Skinner. I am especially grateful to Giles Constable, under whose tutelage this project originally began. I appreciate the assistance I have been given by the staffs of the following libraries: the Bodleian, Oxford; the British Museum; Lambeth Palace; Episcopal Divinity School; Pope John XXIII National Seminary; Weston School of Theology; Wellesley College; and, above all, Widener Library of Harvard University. Wellesley College generously provided me with a grant to aid in the publication of this book and a leave during which I did much of the manuscript research. The Cistercian Press graciously allowed me to include in a revised form material from two of my articles which it originally published. Certainly this book would never have been written without the encouragement my parents gave me to read and reflect; through a happy coincidence, its publication date is my father's sixty-fifth birthday. Above all, I wish to thank Stephen Marini for his encouragement, inspiration, and love during the many years this project has taken. Other friends and mentors too numerous to name have also given assistance. For all the help I have received from so many, I am deeply grateful.

INTRODUCTION

THE TOPIC

During the mid-twelfth century, women's opportunities to lead a religious life multiplied dramatically in England. In 1130, a woman in England might enter one of the eight surviving preconquest royal abbeys, or she could join one of several new monasteries for women that some bishops had recently begun in their dioceses. But in all of England, she had only about twenty religious communities to choose between, probably all of them observing the Benedictine Rule. And only a woman from a well-to-do or influential family enjoyed even these limited options; lower-class women were virtually excluded from religious life.

A woman of the next generation had far greater possibilities, for by 1165 England had more than one hundred houses for religious women. In the thirty-five years between 1130 and 1165, approximately eighty-five houses for religious women were begun, an average of more than two new communities a year. Not only were there more monasteries; there also was greater variety in the forms of religious life. Although most religious women in 1165 still followed the Benedictine Rule, they interpreted this rule in varying ways; some followed the elaborate customs of new religious orders, like the Cistercians, the Gilbertines, or the Order of Fontevrault. Women also were included in the Hospitaller, Premonstratensian, and Augustinian orders. And no longer was the monastic life restricted to women with financial resources. Even the poorest of women could become "lay sisters," servants fully incorporated in religious life.

Although the foundation of new houses was more concentrated in the middle years of the twelfth century, the entire period between 1100 and 1200 was a time of intense growth and change. In twelfth-century England, approximately 120 new communities for religious women were established, increasing the total number of houses close to a thousand percent. While the English situation was not unique—women on the Continent also flocked to new monasteries with varied institutional arrangements—this percentage of increase was unparalleled. By 1200, the religious houses of England could accommodate more than three thousand women.[1]

After 1200, the expansion ended as abruptly as it had begun. Having formed about seventy Benedictine monasteries in the twelfth century, nuns began just three additional ones before the modern period. The women who modeled themselves on the Cistercians established approximately twenty-four houses by 1200; later they founded only three more. The majority of the female Augustinian communities originated in the twelfth century. All the Gilbertine, Hospitaller, Fontevrauldine, Arrouaisian, Cluniac, and Premonstratensian houses for women started then as well. Without question, the twelfth century was the apex of enthusiasm for women's religious life in England.[2]

This book recounts the stories of the women and their monasteries in this period of unparalleled expansion. No one before has chronicled these years of innovation. Eileen Power began her *Medieval English Nunneries* with the year 1275, several decades after the period examined here. David Knowles devoted only six of almost eight hundred pages in his *The Monastic Order in England, 940–1216* to the history of female monasticism.[3] Although specific monasteries are treated in *The Victoria History of the Counties of England* and in regional journals, the histories of the individual houses for women have never been integrated and interpreted. The renewed interest in medieval women makes the study of this English situation particularly germane.[4]

THE SOURCES

Of all the factors in a growth of such magnitude, the most fully documented is the financial component. A rich array of economic charters survives in original manuscripts and later transcriptions.[5] Critical editions of many of these charters have been published in regional journals and monographs. Even though its texts are not always reliable, the *Monasticon anglicanum* remains an invaluable assemblage of economic charters. David Knowles and R. Neville Hadcock have provided an indispensable guide to primary sources in their *Medieval Religious Houses of England and Wales*. Despite the varying quality of the articles in *The Victoria History*, these volumes also aid the locating of financial records.[6]

Economic charters reveal more than a monastery's wealth. Although written to protect a community's right to its property, such documents often include parenthetical remarks of another nature, such as why the donation was made, who else in the family had granted property to the

community, or what relationship the donor had to a woman in the monastery. Often the most informative asides are in the foundation charters,
the records of gifts given when a church was consecrated and a religious
community formally begun.[7] Cumulatively, these chance references make
it possible to tell the story of the expansion.

While relying heavily on economic charters, this study attempts to
utilize all the surviving evidence about religious women and their communities in twelfth-century England. In addition to the financial documents, there are letters to nuns, poems composed in their honor, rules
detailing their daily lives, and rituals observed in their houses. Particularly informative are the extensive Gilbertine sources: the *vita* of Gilbert,
the early-thirteenth-century manuscript of the Gilbertine Rule, and a
letter about an episode involving a nun in the Gilbertine priory of Watton. Monastic documents alone, however, are not sufficient to present
female religious life in the twelfth century, for many holy women lived as
hermitesses and anchoresses without formally recognized religious houses
and rules. No other source compares in vividness with the twelfth-century *vita* of one such woman, Christina of Markyate; another anchoress
whose life is well-documented is Eve of Wilton.[8]

Because of the surviving records, this study unavoidably gives more
extensive treatment to some women and communities than to others.
Since the sources better reveal *how* women were able to undertake religious life than *why* they did so, the questions I have best been able to
address concern the process whereby change occurred. How could wom-
en's opportunities for religious life transform so radically in only one
generation? What accounted for the regional variations, especially the
distinctive patterns of monastic life south and north of the Welland
River? What kind of financial support did the women receive? From
whom? How were their communities organized, and what was their
relationship to the rest of the church?

While many episodes can be recounted, still many lacunae remain—so
many that Sally Thompson has written an article entitled, "Why English
Nunneries Had No History: A Study of the Problems of the English
Nunneries Founded after the Conquest." Thompson laments the sparsity
of documents, which she credits in part to the nuns' lack of financial
resources.[9] Because there are gaps in the record—particularly a dearth of
evidence about daily life in the houses—there is a temptation to fill in the
missing pieces with material from other countries and other periods.
Since little evidence survives about life in English priories in the Order of
Fontevrault, for instance, one might introduce evidence from the French

houses of that order. Or mid-thirteenth-century rules might be assumed to represent mid-twelfth-century customs.

I do not think such interpolations are warranted. Although incorporating later or earlier documents would give greater balance to this story, I have attempted to draw an accurate picture, not an anachronistic one. Although I refer to developments on the Continent that are essential for understanding the English situation, I wish to provide a regional study of women's monastic life that is specifically English. The history of the religious life, and of women's religiousness in particular, profits from a strict observance of the boundaries of time and place.

THE MONASTERIES

Typically, monastic studies treat together houses of one religious affiliation. For instance, Knowles and Hadcock categorized the religious houses in England according to the religious order with which they were affiliated: Benedictine, Cistercian, Augustinian, Premonstratensian, and so on. Because of this convention, and because religious did (and do) consider their order important for their identity, I have continued to use these traditional labels. For instance, the six tables that summarize my conclusions about the founding dates of the priories also list the probable orders to which they belonged.

However, I have organized this book in another way, dividing the communities along two axes: one chronological and one geographical. This approach highlights distinctive patterns north and south of the Welland, and before and after 1165. It also avoids many of the problems that have plagued historians of female monasticism, especially the dilemma of deciding the affiliation of individual houses. Often a monastery's religious order is not mentioned in the twelfth-century documents. While in part this silence may reflect the more fluid arrangements before Pope Innocent III imposed order on the monastic world early in the thirteenth century, even later records often fail to mention a house's affiliation. Sometimes the first reference to religious identity is in the records of the dissolution of monasteries in the sixteenth century. An additional difficulty in categorizing houses of women comes from the fact that many women were connected only informally to male religious orders. How, for example, should houses of women who adopted Cistercian customs but who were not officially Cistercian be labeled?[10] Treating the monasteries according to their founding dates and their regional locations avoids this quagmire while still permitting a discussion of the problem of religious identity.

The chronological and geographical division has other reasons to recommend it as well. Grouping together religious communities that are usually considered separately reveals remarkable parallels not discernible before. Most striking is the finding that so many religious houses for women also included men. Generations of scholars have written about "double monasteries," ones that included women and men in their communities; but double monasteries have been treated as a peripheral phenomenon. Considered alongside other monasteries, however, these houses do not appear as anomalous as formerly assumed. Indeed, approximately one quarter of all the new foundations for women were actually for women and men. In certain regions and during certain decades, *most* of the new religious establishments for women also included men.[11]

The scholars who employ the term "double monasteries" have suggested reasons for the existence of these houses. But the discovery of so many English houses for both sexes challenges all the theories proposed for double monasteries. Because of the diverse circumstances that led to the foundation of these houses, the least satisfactory explanation is one made during the nineteenth century—that all such monasteries could be traced to a single place of origin. For instance, Varin argued that all double monasteries had Irish roots. However great Celtic influence may have been in twelfth-century England, it does not explain the preponderance of monasteries for both sexes.[12]

Closer to the twelfth-century situation are the functional explanations proposed for such monasteries, such as the theory of A. Hamilton Thompson who argued that the "ideal was not the coordination of the sexes in one house. . . . It was the provision for communities of nuns of a permanent staff of clergy vowed to religious life, who could perform for the sisters services from the performance of which they themselves were debarred."[13] Yet this explanation fails to account for the popularity of such arrangements in particular regions and periods. Other traditional institutional forms, such as all female houses with hired chaplains and male servants under the abbess's control, were more common and convenient ways to provide the essential sacramental and economic services.

An ideological justification offered for such houses has considerable merit, but it too fails to explain adequately the twelfth-century developments. Considering double monasteries in all times and places, Mary Bateson proposed that "double monasteries arose in many countries and

at many times as the natural sequel to an outburst of religious enthusiasm." In her opinion, the elasticity of organization tolerated in the period
of enthusiasm was soon abandoned in face of the need for rules and
regulations, "more practical and less ideal conceptions," which resulted
in highly structured double monasteries.

Part of Bateson's theory fully accords with the pattern in England:
there was a development from fluid forms to more rigid institutionalization. However, her explanation of why the sexes associated with each
other does not correspond with the evidence preserved in the twelfth-
century records. Bateson believed that in periods of "spiritual renewal,"
a "purer form of chastity" was sought.[14] This desire sometimes led to
virgines subintroductae or *mulierum consortia*, when a chaste man and
woman slept naked side by side to prove their conquest of temptation.[15]
Twelfth-century men and women appear to have dwelt together for practical reasons rather than to test their chastity. Precisely why they cooperated with each other is a major theme of this book.

Because of its deviation from the standard interpretations of "double
monasteries," the English situation poses a basic question about the heu-
ristic utility of the term "double monastery" itself. Although modern
scholars have accepted the phrase, it was not used by twelfth-century
advocates of monasteries for both sexes. The term is not only anachronistic; it may even be misleading. Viewed on a continuum with all the
other religious houses of the twelfth century, "double monasteries" were
not as distinctive as the phrase implies. In twelfth-century England,
"double monasteries" were only one of many arrangements in which
celibate men and women affiliated with each other. A variety of institutional forms for both sexes were common, ranging from small hermitages with women and men, to female daughter houses of male abbeys, to
monasteries with a dozen women and three men, to large houses with
full contingents of both men and women. This book contends that the
terms "double" and "quasi-double" are disfunctional because they encourage the study of such houses in isolation from other monasteries. I
have avoided using these terms in order to integrate better the histories
of all the monasteries for women.

THE WOMEN

In order to analyze this expansion, I have tried to treat as many religious
women as possible. Anchoresses have typically been studied separately

from nuns,[16] but I have chosen to describe both the eremitic and ceno-
bitic forms of religious life together because English women experienced
them concurrently. As a result, it has become apparent that in the early
twelfth century, the two groups were not as distinct as has often been
assumed, for small monasteries sometimes resembled hermitages. Also,
by the late twelfth century, both groups had undergone similar processes
of transformation, resulting in greater institutionalization.

Although I have included information about all types of religious
women, I have chosen not to relate the parallel history of male monasticism. Hopefully, other scholars will wish to compare and contrast the
male and female expansion in the twelfth century, but I have aimed at
providing a companion to Knowles, who already has treated the houses
for men. While Knowles was able to avoid discussing female religious in
his book on male monasticism, however, it has not been possible for me
to rule out all discussion of men. Unlike their male counterparts, nuns
could not avoid contact with the opposite sex, for they needed sacramental services from priests. Ipso facto, nuns and anchoresses had to associate with male religious. Since feminist studies have attuned historians to
issues of sexism, it is neither possible nor desirable to ignore the limits
church and society imposed on religious women. Male religious could be
independent of women, but female religious could not be independent of
men.

For several decades, scholars have claimed that even though female
religious required the sacramental services of priests, male religious hesi-
tated to fulfill that function for them. In the 1930s Herbert Grundmann
argued that the reluctance of thirteenth-century Franciscans and Cistercians to supervise female religious drove many women to join heretical
groups. Since Grundmann, scholars have extended his conclusions back
to the twelfth century, with the claim that male religious—the men particularly suited to aid religious women—tried to eschew all responsibility
for nuns.[17]

According to the documents I have examined, however, this conclusion of Grundmann and his followers does not apply to the English
situation. As mentioned above, many communities of women included
male religious as well. Also, more than *half* the new monasteries for
women were founded with the aid of male religious. The prominence of
men in the lives of these women may reflect the nature of the surviving
documents, for men wrote the records and women's opinions are rarely
recorded. Perhaps men did not choose to relate accounts of more independent women; perhaps such women were unable to succeed in a

church and society led by men. Whether or not more radically independent female communities existed, the religious women who appear in the surviving documents found and cooperated with religious men who aided and befriended them.

Since so many new monasteries for women were founded in such a short period of time, it might be assumed that women were being forced to enter monasteries because they were unable to marry. However, nothing in the evidence that survives supports this contention. It does seem likely, though, that both male and female monasticism was able to flourish because England itself was prospering. Hollingsworth estimates that between 1086 and 1193 the population in England grew by 72 percent, from roughly two million in 1086 to almost three and a half by 1193. Studying the evidence from epidemics, Hollingsworth concludes that "the main period of population growth was from 1143 to 1175, rather than in the thirteenth century." Although some have questioned his conclusion that the increase was most pronounced in these middle years, the century as a whole was undisputably a period of growth. In a time of rising population, women would have been less pressured to marry and reproduce—and they may have been encouraged to opt for celibacy. Equally important was the financial prosperity of the twelfth century. Even though there were more people, the introduction of crop rotation created a surplus of food. In such relatively peaceful and affluent times, female religious could seek and find support.[18]

To introduce this unparalleled moment in the history of women in the church, I commence with the situation in the closing years of the eleventh century, before the expansion began. During the period of the conquest, several of the ancient abbeys for women had given refuge to Anglo-Saxon noble ladies fleeing from the Normans. The first problems these nuns faced were practical ones: how to survive under Norman rule and whether to permit some women to leave and marry. In trying to adapt to their new situation, the women in the ancient royal abbeys were subject to competing advice; some men, like Archbishop Anselm, encouraged them to adopt new religious ideas, and others, like the monk Goscelin, reminded them of their ancient splendor. Very few hints existed that a major change would soon occur.

ABBREVIATIONS IN
TEXT AND SOURCES

Christina	Talbot, *Christina of Markyate*
CRR	*Curia Regis Rolls*
EETS	Early English Text Society
FOF	Walker, *Feet of Fines*
Institutes	"The Institutes of the Gilbertine Order"
LC	Goscelin, "The Liber confortatorius"
MO	Knowles, *The Monastic Order in England*
Monasticon	Dugdale, *Monasticon anglicanum*
MRH	Knowles and Hadcock, *Medieval Religious Houses*
PL	Migne, *Patrologiae series Latina*
R. Ben.	*Revue Bénédictine*
RRAN	*Regesta regum anglo-normannorum*
VCH	*Victoria History of the Counties of England*
Vita	"The Life of St. Gilbert of Sempringham"

PART ONE

Origins (1066–1130)

Houses of Women Religious in Twelfth-Century England

CHAPTER 1

Royal Abbeys and Episcopal Priories

At the time of the Norman Conquest, little tangible evidence remained of the halcyon days of female monasticism under the Anglo-Saxons, when great abbesses had hosted councils and swayed ecclesial opinion. The renowned monasteries with their royal abbesses ruling over both nuns and monks—the communities that Bede made famous in his *Ecclesiastical History*—had either been abandoned or converted into monasteries for monks alone. Of the monasteries that had formerly housed nuns and monks, women retained only one, Barking in Essex; and it had been refounded for nuns alone in the late tenth century. This sole surviving remnant of earlier days bore little resemblance to the powerful abbey Abbess Ethelburga had ruled in the seventh century.[1] None of the monasteries for women founded since then approached the prominence of the earlier ones.

Women had not been entirely ignored in the revival of monasticism in ninth- and tenth-century England under Dunstan and his co-workers. The kings and queens of those two centuries had founded six abbeys for women—Wilton, Shaftesbury, Winchester, Romsey, Amesbury, and Wherwell—all in Wessex, in southwest England. More recently, early in the eleventh century, Ednoth, bishop of Dorchester, and his sister Aelfwen, wife of King Athelstan, had established Chatteris Abbey. Still, despite their illustrious founders, these new houses did not have the prestige of the earlier royal abbeys for women and men. Nor were they as important as the ninth- and tenth-century abbeys founded for monks. Bishops and other ecclesiastical leaders came from the revitalized male monasteries, but nuns could not assume comparable roles in the late Anglo-Saxon reform of the church.[2]

The eight female abbeys that still existed after the conquest were neither wealthy nor influential enough to demand immediate attention from the Normans. According to the assessment of the incomes of fifty-four monasteries in the Domesday Survey of 1086, Wilton, the wealthiest female abbey, ranked fifteenth, with less income than fourteen monasteries for men. The picture was not completely bleak; Wilton, Shaftesbury, Barking, and Romsey abbeys had gross annual incomes of between

£246 and £135, more income than half the monasteries for men. But the other four houses for nuns—Winchester, Amesbury, Wherwell, and Chatteris—were among the poorest third of all monasteries; Chatteris was one of the poorest of all, with an income of only £20 a year. Less wealthy than their male counterparts, the monasteries for women were outnumbered as well: there were five times as many houses for monks as for nuns.[3]

The preconquest monasteries for women that passed under Norman rule were neither financial nor ecclesiastical centers. To the conquerors and conquered alike, nothing presaged the transformation to come in the next century. Yet to understand the change that did occur, it is necessary to consider the state of female monasticism shortly after the conquest. The surviving records reveal several aspects of religious life in those years: pressing issues that confronted the women, competing monastic ideals proposed for them, and an increasing involvement of the episcopacy in their affairs. Even though the monasteries for women were not great centers of power, they could not be totally ignored.

NUN OR REFUGEE? (1066–1100)

The monasteries for nuns were burdened in the years after the conquest with a serious problem: what should they do with the refugee women who had entered them to escape the dangers of war? The number of Anglo-Saxon royalty known to have fled to the ancient abbeys in the unsettled decades after 1066 is impressive, especially since the records are sparse for the years around the conquest. Wilton Abbey received Edith, the widow of Edward the Confessor; Gunilda, the daughter of Harold; and Mary and Edith (later renamed Matilda), the daughters of Queen Margaret of Scotland and descendants of Edmund Ironside. Edith, Edward the Confessor's widow, was also temporarily at Wherwell Abbey, perhaps along with her mother-in-law. Christina, Margaret of Scotland's sister, became a nun and later abbess at Romsey Abbey; she was joined there for some years by her niece Edith/Matilda. A chronicle states that in 1086, after the death of King Malcolm of Scotland, Christina and her sister Margaret had been consecrated as "spouses of Christ" at Newcastle upon Tyne in Northumbria, so an otherwise unknown monastery may have existed there and served as a refuge in the far north.[4]

Once more peaceful times returned, the abbeys that had dealt with the influx of royal refugees faced a vexing problem: several of these noble women wished to leave religious life and marry. However necessary the Anglo-Saxon women had found these monastic havens in troubled times, they did not want to remain there once the violence of the conquest was over. Moreover, Norman leaders, seeking to wed women of the old aristocracy in order to cement their claims to rule, knew desirable spouses were in the monasteries. Since some of these women were eager to leave, the episcopacy decided to mediate.

In one of only two of Archbishop Lanfranc's surviving letters that concern nuns, he tried to resolve this complicated issue. Sometime between 1077 and 1089, Lanfranc wrote to Bishop Gundulf of Rochester, "As to those who as you tell me fled to a monastery not for love of the religious life but for fear of the French, if they can prove that this was so by the unambiguous witness of nuns better than they, let them be granted unrestricted leave to depart." Lanfranc's ruling was not meant to affect the status of professed nuns and oblates, children given by their parents to a monastery: "Nuns who have made profession that they will keep a rule or who, although not yet professed, have been presented at the altar, are to be enjoined, exhorted and obliged to keep the rule in their manner of life." Only the refugee women were free to leave. And even they had to reach a decision promptly: "Those who have been neither professed nor presented at the altar" were to be sent away "until their desire to remain in religion is examined more carefully." Lanfranc accepted the political reality that women needed sanctuary in times of war; yet since asylum was not the same as profession, in a peaceful time only professed or oblated women were to remain in the abbeys.[5]

Although Archbishop Lanfranc had intended to resolve the refugee dilemma permanently, years later it still remained. At the turn of the century, Lanfranc's successor, Archbishop Anselm, judged the most celebrated case when Edith/Matilda, the daughter of Queen Margaret of Scotland, sought permission to wed King Henry I. Even though Matilda had continued to live in monasteries long after Lanfranc's ruling, she was able to convince Anselm that she should be allowed to marry. Such a position must have been difficult to maintain years after Lanfranc's letter. Indeed, Anselm's biographer, Eadmer, presented a detailed account of this case precisely because "quite a large number of people have maligned Anselm saying, as we have ourselves heard them do, that in this matter he did not keep to the path of strict right."[6]

To prove that political pressures had not swayed Anselm, Eadmer summarized the debate about whether Matilda was an oblate. Eadmer admitted that "many believed that she had been dedicated by her parents to

God's service as she had been seen walking abroad wearing the veil like the nuns with whom she was living." But Matilda, arguing her own case before Anselm, vehemently denied this assumption by recounting what had happened some years earlier when her father Malcolm had seen her veiled. Malcolm had "snatched the veil off" and, "tearing it in pieces," had "invoked the hatred of God upon the person" who had placed the veil on her.

Although this episode proved that she was not an oblate, Matilda also needed to explain why she had worn a veil for years. Euphemistically labeling it a "little black hood," she insisted that her aunt, the abbess, had placed it on her head to protect her "from the lust of the Normans which was rampant." Most importantly, Matilda denied that she had ever consented to wear the veil. Tolerating "the hood" in fear of her aunt, Matilda said that whenever she was out of her aunt's sight, "I tore it off and threw it on the ground and trampled on it and in that way, although foolishly, I used to vent my rage and the hatred of it which boiled up in me." Despite Lanfranc's time limit for remaining in asylum, Matilda won her freedom by convincing Anselm and an ecclesiastical assembly that she had stayed against her will and was neither a professed nun nor an oblate.[7]

Though persuaded by Matilda, Archbishop Anselm was not always so understanding. A few years earlier Anselm had written a letter to an anonymous nun to prevent her from leaving monastic life. Resorting to morbid reflections to deter her, Anselm reminded this woman, who wanted to marry a certain count, that she had once loved another count, now dead: "Go now, sister, place yourself with him in the bed in which he now lies. Gather his worms to your bosom; embrace his cadaver. Kiss his nude teeth, for now his lips have been consumed by rot. Certainly he does not now attend to your love by which he was delighted while living, and you fear his putrid flesh which you then desired to enjoy." Anselm followed this gruesome image with a warning that the count whom the woman currently wanted to marry might also die. Rather than lament this possibility, Anselm declared that it would be a blessing if it prevented the nun from having sexual intercourse. For if she consummated their union, he wrote, "You will damn not only yourself and that man to eternal death but you will also generate a great and detestable scandal in the church of God."[8]

Anselm directed these macabre ruminations to a woman who thought she could legitimately leave her monastery on the grounds that she had entered with false illusions: she had been promised an abbacy that had never materialized. Anselm countered that even if others had lied to her, she could not lie to God, to whom she was now bound by vows. Anselm warned that her departure and projected marriage would be "an example odious to God, to all his saints, and to good men"; it would be potentially harmful to the religious life; and "if so great an evil will be born through you, you should be certain that it would have been better for you if you had not been born."[9]

Nor was Anselm any more tolerant of Gunilda, a daughter of Harold. In Anselm's view, after having lived in a monastery, Gunilda had thrown aside "the habit of holy conversion." Anselm warned, "It is impossible for you to be able to be saved in any way unless you return to the rejected habit and proposition." Gunilda's contention was that she was neither a professed nun nor an oblate, and hence she should be free to leave. Without disputing her assertions, Anselm still refused to let her leave: "For although you have not been consecrated by the bishop nor have you read a profession before him, nevertheless this alone is clear and undeniable profession in that in public and in private you wore the habit of the holy proposition; by that you have affirmed to all seeing you that you are dedicated to God no less than by reciting the profession." Anselm argued that "many thousand people of both sexes . . . before there was the now customary profession and consecration of the monastic proposition . . . declared by their habit alone to be of this proposition." His conclusion was unambiguous: "You are therefore without excuse if you desert the holy proposition which long ago you professed by habit and conversion of life even if you have not recited the now customary profession and have not been consecrated by the bishop."[10]

No wonder Matilda insisted that she had hated the "little black hood" and had worn it only against her will. After Lanfranc's verdict, women who freely remained in the monasteries and wore a religious habit were no longer permitted to leave even if they were neither professed nuns nor oblates. Extending Lanfranc's judgment, Anselm declared that if a woman willingly lived and dressed as a nun for years so that people thought that she was a nun, then she was in effect a nun. The monastic habit, long the symbol of profession, had become a substitute for it as well.

THE HEROIC IDEAL (THE 1080S)

The religious women from the late eleventh century whose stories have survived lived in the wealthiest preconquest abbeys—Wilton, Shaftesbury, Barking, Romsey, and Winchester. Norman women increasingly joined the Anglo-Saxons there. Muriel, a poet from a rich Norman family, and Eve, the daughter of a "most powerful" Dane, became nuns at Wilton Abbey.[11] Within a few decades of the conquest, women with Norman names—Eulalia, Beatrix, and Alice—were abbesses of Shaftesbury and Winchester.[12] Still, Norman leaders only slowly transferred their allegiances to the English houses. In the early decades after the conquest, women from the best-known Norman families continued to enter abbeys on the Continent.[13]

Less important to the new rulers, the female houses escaped the turmoil many monasteries for men experienced after King William imposed on them abbots of his own choosing. Only one disturbance is known that required episcopal intervention. In the late 1080s, Archbishop Lanfranc instructed Bishop Maurice of London to go to Barking Abbey: "When you have heard both sides of the dispute, order the abbess to be an abbess and the prioress a prioress. Let each behave as befits her station and as the *Rule of St. Benedict* commands." A power struggle was occurring, occasioned perhaps by the installation of a successor to Abbess Aelfgyva, who died in the late 1080s. Lanfranc told Maurice to insure that both the abbess and prioress were respected: "Let the nuns, clergy and laity both within the convent and beyond serve and obey them."[14] Friction between Norman and Anglo-Saxon factions in the monastery may have exacerbated this dispute; or men may have been resisting the female leaders. Whatever the cause, the lack of any other recorded conflicts suggests that the nuns adjusted well to the new political leadership.

What inspired English nuns to choose and persevere in the religious life? No women's writings survive to give first-hand information. The closest we can come to an insider's view is from the pen of Goscelin of St. Bertin. A Flemish monk who had come to England as part of the court of Bishop Hermann of Ramsbury shortly before the conquest, Goscelin of St. Bertin spent the last two decades of the eleventh century traveling around England collecting, collating, and rewriting the *legendae* of many Anglo-Saxon saints. Around 1080, while residing at Wilton Abbey as a chaplain for the nuns, he revised a life of St. Edith, a tenth-century royal nun of that abbey. About 1087, after visiting Barking Abbey, Goscelin composed lives of its royal women—Ethelburga, Wulfhilda, and Hildelitha. The other abbesses whose *legendae* he provided—Milburga, Werburga, Sexburga, Ermenilda, and Mildred—had ruled monasteries that no longer accepted nuns, having become houses for monks alone; however, these abbesses also exemplified Goscelin's ideal of powerful women overseeing vigorous abbeys. Knowing Goscelin well, late eleventh-century nuns would have heard these saints' lives and been inspired by the models of sanctity he proposed.[15]

Goscelin's purpose was to celebrate the Anglo-Saxon saints in the face of criticisms made by "rash ranters" and "to defend powerfully the truth against the teeth of the insolent."[16] The "rash ranters" were the conquering Normans who failed to appreciate insular heroes and heroines. To convince the Normans to honor these Anglo-Saxon saints, Goscelin described noble women who had skillfully governed their royal abbeys and were virtuous in ways the Normans could admire. If late eleventh-century nuns could also be drawn to such models, they would be encouraged to perfect their own managerial abilities and increase the prestige of their monasteries.

Three of the lives Goscelin composed in the 1080s are representative of his ideals—the lives of St. Edith of Wilton, St. Wulfhilda of Barking, and St. Werburga of Ely. C. H. Talbot, an editor of Goscelin's writings, has criticized Goscelin's renditions as having "little or no historical value, for the simple reason that he had no records at his disposal, and in such cases he padded out his tenuous statements with a great deal of rhetoric and pious exhortation."[17] Talbot is correct, but Goscelin's interpolations actually provide greater insight into late-eleventh-century values than an accurate life of a tenth-century woman would. By freely espousing his values, Goscelin revealed his assumptions.

Goscelin's rhetorical flourishes were particularly pronounced in his earliest female saint's life, that of Edith of Wilton. In a preface dedicating the work to Archbishop Lanfranc, Goscelin blended winsome flattery and propaganda. Lanfranc was "our Bezalel," the craftsman who had received the gifts of the Hebrews in order to construct the temple in Jerusalem. Goscelin described St. Edith of Wilton as a precious gem whom Lanfranc should not overlook in his search for riches to build a new Jerusalem.

Attempting to overcome Lanfranc's well-known disdain for Anglo-Saxon parochial traditions, Goscelin reminded Lanfranc that his predecessors in the see of Canterbury had supported Edith's cult, in part because she was from their own archbishopric. During Edith's life, after her death, and even until "the present moment," people "from near and far" had benefited from her intercessions, a sure sign of Edith's favor with God. Although Edith's cult was widespread and effective, Goscelin was presenting this treasure in a newly polished form since he had been unable to find a sufficient description of her among the "rustics." Goscelin concluded his plea to Lanfranc, "Therefore we hand over to your patronage a pearl not to be cast before swine, a lamb not to be mangled by wolves, a dove not to be torn apart by ravens."[18]

Elaborate introductions like this are typical of Goscelin's style, more revealing of literary conventions than historical realities. However, Goscelin included details about the nuns of Wilton Abbey that he probably learned during his stay with them. For instance, Goscelin related that "often by revelations [Edith] is seen among the sisters as if still living in the body." Goscelin informed Lanfranc about these appearances in order to convince the archbishop that Edith's cult was still potent, but Goscelin's comment also reveals the nuns' sense of continued protection by their deceased abbess.[19]

Goscelin composed fourteen lengthy metric poems about St. Edith in which his perspective is most clearly revealed. Goscelin saw monastic life as a regal affair, the intersection of the heavenly and earthly hierarchies; each poem placed Edith's mundane activities in a heavenly sphere. Her innocence, virginity, humility, and love of Christ proved that she had participated from earliest childhood in the heavenly choir of virgins. Although earthly royalty attended her childhood oblation to Wilton Abbey, the ritual was more a cosmic event, celebrated by angels and even the stars, with Mary leading the virgin Edith to Christ in a flower-filled bridal chamber. Edith's dedication of the oratory to St. Denis, which she had built at Wilton, was also a celestial ceremony, attended by cherubim and the heavenly host. Goscelin even compared Edith's care of her monasteries to a new heaven and a new age. Praiseworthy on earth for her royal lineage and her abilities as abbess, Edith continued after her death to intercede for her followers, to whom she sometimes still appeared.[20]

Goscelin never altered this pattern of female sanctity in his later saints lives and *legendae* for the office. For Goscelin, the seventh-century Werburga of Ely exemplified the same virtues as the tenth-century Edith of Wilton even though their lives were actually quite different. Beginning his life of Werburga with a complicated five-hundred-word genealogy, fully one-sixth the total composition, Goscelin emphasized "the holy root from which this holy branch," Werburga, had sprung. Following his standard repertoire of aristocratic virtues, Goscelin described Werburga as a woman who had lived like a nun even when she was a child sur-

rounded with riches in the palace of her father King Weulfhere. Goscelin showed Werburga governing her monasteries with wisdom and pru-
dence, educating by her example, and exemplifying love, kindness, gen-
erosity, patience, peace, and joy.[21]

After these platitudes Goscelin turned in the second half of the life
to Werburga's cult. Werburga's family background, virtuous character,
and abilities as an administrator already established her sanctity, but
her miraculous intervention confirmed it. Local townspeople kept her
memory alive in part because of two miracles she had worked: in one,
she had confronted an unjust judge, and in the other she had both protected crops from ravenous geese and restored to life one goose unfairly
slaughtered. A further sign of her sanctity was her corpse which, after
remaining uncorrupt for two hundred years, crumbled to prevent the
impious Danes invading England from touching it. Admired in life as an
able royal abbess, Werburga deserved continued veneration after her
death.[22]

Goscelin also shaped St. Wulfhilda of Barking's life on the paradigm of
the heroic noble abbess, even though in reality she had deviated markedly from the norm. Wulfhilda's genealogy was not particularly illustrious; but rather than change the stereotypical pattern, Goscelin emphasized what little aristocratic background Wulfhilda had. Goscelin treated
Wulfhilda like the other royal abbesses, who had rejected royal suitors in
favor of asceticism, even though Wulfhilda's "suitor" could better be
described as an abductor. King Edgar first sought Wulfhilda when she
was a girl receiving an education at Wilton. Later he hosted a great feast
where he tried to persuade Wulfhilda to marry him; after she escaped
from him through a narrow opening in the privy, the king still pursued
her. In her final close escape, she fled to the altar at Wilton Abbey,
leaving the sleeve of her garment in her pursuer's hand. Since King Edgar
had so relentlessly sought Wulfhilda, Goscelin had to dramatize her decision for monastic life. But even Wulfhilda's intriguing biography did not
entice Goscelin to vary his pattern, to provide an alternative model.
Goscelin could more readily ignore Wulfhilda's uniqueness than tamper
with his ideal.[23]

Goscelin dedicated his *legendae* to the Norman bishops who could
promote the veneration of the saintly abbesses. But the nuns still living in
Wilton and Barking abbeys would have been his most receptive audi-
ence. Already the prime exponents of St. Edith's cult, the women of
Wilton would have been eager to use the new version of her *legenda*.
In composing the life of Edith, Goscelin would have considered these

women, whom he knew personally since he had been their chaplain. A familiar visitor to Barking Abbey, Goscelin could also address those nuns directly. And even though nuns no longer lived at Ely, which since the tenth century had been for monks alone, Werburga's story would also have appealed to nuns as much as to the Norman churchmen for whom it ostensibly was written.

By highlighting the lineage of the saintly abbesses, Goscelin emphasized the importance of aristocratic nuns, whether they were the refugee Anglo-Saxon royalty or members of the new nobility. Only women of high birth could fully emulate the models Goscelin proposed. But practical abilities and worldly talent were also essential virtues. Although Goscelin glorified a regal model of monasticism and encouraged the nuns to dream of their ancient splendor, he wanted the nuns to manage wisely in order to make these dreams a reality.

COMPETING SPIRITUALITIES (1090–1110)

Whereas Goscelin praised earlier abbesses, two religious men from the Continent found qualities to admire in one late-eleventh-century house. Shortly after Goscelin left Wilton Abbey, Muriel and other women there were acclaimed for their poetry by two monks, Serlo of Bayeux and Baudri de Bourgueil. Because Muriel's own writings have not survived, the two poems these monks wrote in her honor provide the only information about her and the other versifiers at Wilton. But independent verification of Muriel's existence comes from 1113, some years after her death, when nine canons from Laon visiting Wilton Abbey were proudly shown her grave near Bede's.[24]

Although their poems are more trustworthy indicators of Baudri's and Serlo's views than of Muriel's actual attributes, they reveal that she had considerable fame. Claiming that Muriel's reputation was proclaimed "at the crossroads" and held in high esteem "among us," Baudri de Bourgueil began his poem composed in her honor with a rather backhanded compliment: he had heard that when Muriel recited her poems, her honeylike words sounded like those of a man even though spoken with the voice of a woman. Baudri also praised Muriel's wealthy background and attractive appearance; he mused that since Muriel's "seemly form" was pleasing to men, her devotion to virginity was all the more laudable. In an intriguing assessment of the varying effects of education on women of different social classes, Baudri assured Muriel that since she was a women of high social standing, the education she had received had benefited her. Such was not the case for lower-class women: "Much learning will often soften harsh girls, but much learning will make your heart very tough." One wonders if this nun of Wilton Abbey was pleased with praises of her appearance, class, and manly words, but these were the attributes Baudri admired.

Baudri ended his poem with a curious plea: in order to continue their correspondence, Baudri asked Muriel to exchange poems confidentially with him. Since Baudri assured Muriel that he would write only about virginity and that he primarily sought her criticism of his verses, one wonders why he made this request for secrecy. Poetic convention was partly the cause. Perhaps Baudri also hoped to increase the sense of intimacy such an exchange would foster. Baudri told Muriel that if she accepted his request, they could write as if they were friends, as if she were his daughter.[25]

If Muriel responded to Baudri's request, her answer has not survived. But she apparently enjoyed the exchange of literary productions, for the monk Serlo of Bayeux wrote that Muriel had pleaded with him to send her a song. Serlo said that he was responding "with trepidation," since he feared the judgment of the accomplished versifiers among whom Muriel lived and to whom she would show his composition. Perhaps Baudri's request for secrecy also reveals some hesitancy about exposing his verses to these other critics. In any case, Serlo and Baudri reveal that Wilton Abbey was a literary center where Muriel and other nuns wrote and recited verses that they exchanged with other monastic poets.

Although Serlo called the poem he sent Muriel a praise of virginity, it more closely resembles a lengthy deprecation of married life. In line after line, Serlo lamented the lot of the married woman, still under the penalty imposed on Eve in Gen. 3:16; like Eve, married women suffered pains in childbirth and were dominated by their husbands. Even the rare woman fortunate enough to have a gentle, supporting husband was still in a position of servitude and had to endure the constant labor of children. Only virginity could free a woman from these penalties.

Although Serlo basically elaborated on claims familiar in female monastic literature since the fourth century, his poem reiterated that in choosing monastic life, nuns were in part rejecting what seemed a less desirable option: the married life with its ceaseless labors. The only unusual statement in Serlo's long discourse concerned the dilemmas a wife faced: if she was adulterous, she risked the attacks of her husband; if chaste, she was considered rude, crude, and ignorant. Compared to the difficulties of married life, the yoke of the cloister was light indeed; in Serlo's view nuns were free simply to wait through their brief time on earth for the rewards of virginity that would come to them in eternal life.[26]

In the words of a modern scholar, Serlo "depicts the tranquility of the nun, through not her spiritual ecstasies."[27] Even if these poems reflect the reputation of Wilton Abbey more than the reality, certainly this was not the type of spirituality universally revered in the late eleventh century. Archbishop Anselm proposed another ideal in the letters he wrote to English nuns around the turn of the century. Inspired by monastic reforms at his own monastery of Bec, Anselm hoped to transplant its spirituality to English monasticism. Emphasizing a renewal of scholarship and interior prayer, Anselm had little interest in the type of poetry Baudri and Serlo lauded.

In his greetings to the abbesses of Wilton and Shaftesbury after his election to the archbishopric, Anselm acknowledged that their abbeys lived in strict conformity with the Benedictine Rule. But Anselm wanted more than the daily rounds of prayers: he instructed the abbesses to pay closer attention to the interior lives of their nuns, to the nuns' minds as well as their actions. Mere vocal prayer was not enough; the women had to be attentive to the content of the readings, psalms, and prayers. With the warning that salvation was not guaranteed to all who simply lived by the rules in a monastery, Anselm advised the abbesses to monitor closely the actions, words, and even the smallest thoughts of their nuns.[28]

In two other letters to English nuns, Anselm also raised the topic of the interior religious life. Addressing the nun M., Anselm advised her always to strive more diligently for ever-greater perfection. Anselm offered similar advice in a more admonishing tone to the nun Mabilla; instead of simply abiding by the minimum rules and requirements, which allowed frequent visits to her relatives, Mabilla should long to please God in all things.[29]

Another of Anselm's concerns was the loyalty of the nuns of Romsey to local traditions and their veneration of one of their patrons. In the only known time in his archbishopric when nuns were rebellious, Archbishop Anselm sent Archdeacon Stephen in person to Romsey Abbey with instructions to make Abbess Athelitz and her nuns curtail a local cult. Anselm wrote that the "deceased," apparently their patron Earl Waltheof, was not to receive the office and honors due only to saints.[30]

It is not known how the women responded to Anselm's insistence that they end this local cult, nor how they reacted to his plea that they not only follow their rule but also adopt his spiritual practices. Muriel and the other nuns of Wilton must have found Anselm's admonitions strikingly different from their correspondence with Serlo and Baudri, and from the ideals Goscelin had lauded in the previous decade. Goscelin's hagiography was more likely to encourage poetesses like Muriel, proud of her lineage, than the kind of nuns Anselm sought.

Still, the ability of the women at Wilton to attract international attention in the years after the conquest speaks to the healthy survival of Benedictine monasticism. The renewal of monastic fervor was still in the future; the focus on interior prayer and asceticism had not yet transformed female religious life. But the women had weathered the crisis of the conquest; and within their well-disciplined communities, some of them were devoting themselves to literary productions that attracted notice even outside the boundaries of England.

THE BISHOPS' INITIATIVE (1090–1130)

Monks like Goscelin, Serlo, and Baudri encountered no interference from the new rulers of the state when they addressed nuns and proposed their ideals, for the Norman barons paid little attention to female monasticism. As seats of ecclesiastical power, monasteries for men were of immediate concern to the Normans. William the Conqueror founded new abbeys for men and appointed abbots of his own predilection to head older monasteries. But William adopted no similar policy toward the nuns. He did not establish new monasteries for women, impose any foreign abbesses, or tamper with existing endowments. Perhaps the relative poverty of the preconquest abbeys of women convinced him they could safely be left intact.[31]

William's barons followed his lead. Active proponents of female monasticism in Normandy, they did not transfer their allegiance to England. Indeed, at least one Norman found that his desire to appropriate the nuns' possessions overpowered any inclination to help. Sometime before the Domesday Survey of 1086, Robert Marmion expelled the nuns from Polesworth Abbey, a ninth-century foundation, and seized their property. A few of the displaced nuns settled at Oldbury, a manor that had belonged to their abbey, where they eked out a subsistence living too meager even to be listed in the Domesday Survey.[32] Another group of nuns living at a church in Chichester lost their dwelling to canons, who were introduced to serve the cathedral of Chichester when it became the seat of a bishopric in 1087.[33] Apart from these two dispossessions, however, English nuns basically were left alone.

Even when the nuns had difficulties, the Normans did not intervene. Because of the dilapidated state of their seventh-century abbey, Minster in Sheppey, the nuns had left and settled in the manor of Newington. They found no peace there, however, and had to flee when one night their cook attempted to strangle the prioress in bed. The women had no viable alternatives but to return to the ruins of Minster.[34]

Judith, William's niece, is the only Norman layperson in the first decades after the conquest known to have founded a new monastery for women, and her motives were not totally commendable. Judith began Elstow Abbey, providing it with land in three vills, as an act of reparation for betraying and abetting the execution of her husband Waltheof, earl of Huntingdon.[35] Only one other baron is known even to have aided nuns. Robert de Montgomery, earl of Sussex, gave additional property to women living at the manor of Lyminster, so that by the time of the Domesday Survey, Lyminster had more income than half the preconquest abbeys for women.[36] Neither guilt nor piety moved other Norman nobles to alienate their newly acquired fortunes to support nuns. The surviving preconquest abbeys remained perforce the centers of female religious.

The second generation of Normans showed little more concern than their predecessors for female monasticism in England. Between 1090 and 1130, only one layperson, once again a woman, is definitely known to have founded a new monastery for women. In 1120 Emma, daughter and heiress of the lord of Redlingfield, began Redlingfield Priory. Although her husband, Manasses, count of Guisnes, joined Emma in making the grant to nuns, the donation—the manor of Redlingfield and the parish church there—was part of Emma's inheritance.[37] Before 1124, in Northumbria, Robert de Umfraville I, one of the Norman barons favored by King Henry I, may have begun the priory of Holystone, but its early history is obscure.[38] In the early years of the twelfth century, barons gave some additional property to a few of the abbeys, especially to Barking, Shaftesbury, and Romsey.[39] But monasteries for men continued to receive most attention and property.

In the entire sixty years after the conquest, at most three lay people increased the number of English foundations for nuns. In this period of lay neglect, only the Norman bishops were active founders of new houses. The preconquest abbeys were concentrated in the old center of Wessex, so only a few dioceses had monasteries for women. Several bishops decided to rectify this situation. Accustomed to the Norman practice of having monasteries under the ordinary's control, the bishops sought to duplicate this pattern in England.[40]

The initiative was taken by Gundulf, a Norman monk of Bec whom Lanfranc elevated to the see of Rochester in 1077. Accepting a weak diocese long dependent on Canterbury, Gundulf received moral and economic support from Lanfranc and later from Anselm. To invigorate his see, Gundulf began two monasteries. The one for men originated when Gundulf decided to rely on monks instead of canons to serve his new cathedral. During his years as bishop he oversaw the growth of the monastery at Rochester from twenty-two monks to more than sixty. Gundulf also founded a monastery for women, "because loving both sexes, he aimed to be useful for the piety of religious of both sexes." In 1090 Gundulf built a church at his episcopal manor of Malling and then gave the property to nuns. Later Gundulf supplemented his initial endowment with some additional rents and tithes for use in decorating the church.[41]

Because Gundulf taught the nuns, provided them with material necessities, and performed spiritual services for them, he was said to care for both their "interior and exterior" needs. Overseeing the "spiritual mothers" as their prior or guardian (*priores vel custodes*), Gundulf did not appoint an abbess until 1106, sixteen years after the foundation of Malling Abbey and just two years before his own death. When he finally installed an abbess, she was to share authority at Malling with a prior, and Gundulf required a series of commitments from her. Avice, the first abbess, swore that she would be faithful and subject to the bishop of Rochester and his successors and that neither she nor anyone else would dissolve that subjection. The remainder of her oath clarified what this subjection meant: without the bishop's counsel and permission, no nun was to be received, no land given or transferred, and no prior appointed or removed. Although Malling henceforth had an abbess, her authority was severely limited.[42]

Several other bishops also founded monasteries for women. Around 1100, Archbishop Anselm, a monk himself, began a priory at Canterbury when he installed nuns in the parish church of St. Sepulchre there.[43] Another Norman bishop, William Giffard of Winchester, began St. Margaret's Priory at Ivinghoe in a manor that had long been part of his see's endowment. William Giffard's involvement in female monasticism partly reflected general changes in his attitude toward monasticism in his years as a bishop. A canon of Rouen appointed by King Henry I to the see of

Winchester, William Giffard began his episcopacy in conflict with the monks there, and he ended it by becoming a monk himself shortly before his death in 1129.[44]

At least three other bishops began houses for nuns. Before 1122 a bishop of London gave a manor and some land to establish the priory of Stratford at Bow; quite possibly the bishop was Maurice, the Norman appointee of William the Conqueror.[45] Some time before 1150, nuns were installed in the episcopal manor of Brewood in Staffordshire, apparently with rights in the church of St. Mary there. (This house is often called Brewood Black Ladies to distinguish it from another foundation known as Brewood White Ladies.) The founder of Brewood Black Ladies Priory was probably Roger de Clinton, bishop of Coventry and Lichfield.[46] Finally, around 1130, Archbishop Thurstan—a native of Bayeux, a favorite of King Henry I, and a renowned supporter of monasticism—established a priory for women, St. Clement's, York.[47]

Malling Abbey and the five priories of Canterbury, Stratford at Bow, St. Margaret's, Brewood Black Ladies, and St. Clement's, York, were not originally large or wealthy, nor did they become so. Most remained little more than a manor house with an attached church. The foundation charter for St. Clement's, York, provides the most detailed record of possessions: Archbishop Thurstan gave to the nuns the land on which their buildings were constructed, some land for building a guest house, several other plots of land, 20s. a year from the archbishop's fair at York, the tithes from nine mills and an orchard, payments from another mill, and the services of a man valued at 6s. 8d. a year.[48] St. Clement's illustrates the common practice of bishops, who assigned tithes and other revenue of their see to augment the income of the nuns they had installed in episcopal manors.

Only Gundulf is known to have personally ruled his monastery without benefit of a female head, and only he founded an abbey. Perhaps the other bishops chose to found priories instead of abbeys to emphasize that the female leader was only a prioress, not an imitator of the powerful abbesses of earlier days. These bishops would also have supervised their creations, in line with the Norman models they knew. One of Thurstan's successors as archbishop felt his authority at St. Clement's, York, was so entrenched that he could, on his own, make the nuns subject to another monastery instead of to him. Even though the nuns of St. Clement's successfully resisted this transfer, persuading the pope to override it, the attempt reveals how extensive the archbishop's claims might be.[49]

For the nuns, subjection to a bishop might be onerous at times, but it had potential advantages. Bishops were powerful patrons who guaranteed their monasteries the support the preconquest abbeys could not find from the laity. Some already established monasteries even sought the protection of bishops. Chatteris Abbey, for example, had become destitute by the time of the Domesday Survey, which lists its gross income as twenty pounds a year. "A most discreet man" then sought to have Chatteris removed from subjection to Ramsey, the abbey of one of its founders, and placed under the care of the nearby bishop of Ely. According to the register of Chatteris, the bishop agreed, not out of consideration for his own gain, but "so that the father of souls would be even the father of things," one to whom in any necessity the daughters could run and receive aid. The account in the register of Chatteris, written after King Henry I agreed to the transfer, may reflect later attitudes. Nonetheless, the bishop of Ely does appear to have aided the house. Although Chatteris remained poor, the bishop helped it acquire more land and obtained its release from the wardage of 6s. 7d. due each year.[50]

Chatteris Abbey was not the only one to receive episcopal help. In 1130 Archbishop William de Corbeil, a canon and former prior of St. Osyth's, "reedified for Benedictine nuns" the ruined monastery of Minster in Sheppey to which nuns had returned after the attempted murder at Newington.[51] Also, Abbess Athelitz of Winchester Abbey complained when the king expelled Bishop William, an indication that she valued the bishop's support. When Athelitz wrote to Archbishop Anselm lamenting the king's decision and William's departure, Anselm comforted her with the assurance that exile for the cause of justice would increase the bishop's esteem in the eyes of God.[52]

By 1130, nuns in eight monasteries—Malling, Canterbury, Stratford at Bow, St. Margaret's, Brewood Black Ladies, Chatteris, Minster, and St. Clement's, York—were connected with bishops who had either founded their houses or become principal benefactors. The bishops' espousal of female monasticism was not solely a result of their commitment to women in religious life. Powerful men who had come to England on the invitation of the Norman rulers, these Norman bishops founded monasteries as part of their aggressive campaign to increase the prestige and vigor of their dioceses. Several of them were monks themselves; and all of them saw advantages in having monasteries under their control. Whatever their motives, during the sixty years when the laity gave little support, the bishops almost doubled the number of monasteries for women in England.

While Goscelin encouraged women in the preconquest abbeys to imi-

CHAPTER 2

The Eremitic Life

Apart from the few bishops who started new monasteries for women, the leaders of church and state, busy tightening their hold on the recently conquered land, paid little attention to women who sought lives of prayer and chastity. Neither aided nor impeded by the Norman barons, some women on their own began religious lives outside monastic walls. Although they did not enter communities comprised of other likeminded women, these innovators did not act totally on their own, for they often joined with religious men for mutual inspiration and aid.

Some of these women who began religious life without institutional support were called *inclusa*; others were labeled *anachoreta*, and still others were styled *reclusa* or simply *virgo*. How best to translate these terms is a difficult question. However logical it might seem to transliterate *anachoreta* as "anchoress," *reclusa* as "recluse," and *inclusa* as "enclosed one," these English derivatives are somewhat misleading. "Anchoress" and "recluse" have come to have a technical meaning—a permanently enclosed religious woman. But in the early middle ages, the technical meaning for "anchoress" was not yet fixed, for the terms "anchorite" and "hermit" were used as synonyms. As Ann Warren explains in her excellent study of English medieval anchorites, "To be an anchorite or a hermit was to withdraw (*anachōrein*) to the desert (*eremus*)." The terms gradually become more distinct: "during the Middle Ages the word *hermit* continued to express the general meaning initially sustained by both words, but the word *anchorite* became more restricted in use. . . . The anchorite was *inclusus/inclusa* or *reclusus/reclusa*, enclosed and stable with limited access to the world."[1]

Were these early twelfth-century "anchoresses" like the enclosed women later in the century, or were they more like the hermitesses of earlier years? Although by the late twelfth century the ways of life of the hermitess and the anchoress had diverged, nothing in the sources establishes that these early twelfth-century women had undergone the strict enclosure ceremony or made the permanent vows that set apart later anchoresses. Hence, although I follow convention in transliterating *anachoreta* as "anchoress," I do not mean that these women were necessarily like the later recluses, dwelling in their tiny anchorholds for their entire religious lives. In order not to imply more than the documents reveal, I use the word "hermitess" whenever the sources permit, for this more inclusive term can mean both women who were strictly enclosed in their small cells and women who were free to depart.

Rather than give a collective biography of these women, I recount their individual stories, for their lives varied significantly. Some of them followed the monastic hours; others did not. Some were literate and devoted much time to reading; others could recite only a few prayers. But one characteristic is mentioned consistently in the surviving sources: these women had relationships with other like-minded people, and usually these companions were men. Because of their importance in the lives of these women, this chapter devotes special attention to these spiritual friendships.

The women who moved away from their families in order to spend their lives in prayer may have been inspired by the legends of the hermits and hermitesses of early Christianity. Since at least the fourth century, Christians had valued solitude as a place free from the normal demands of society where one could pray without interruption. Like Elijah, John the Baptist, and Jesus during his period of temptation, these women and men sought the spiritual challenges of "the desert," where they could confront in a stark manner the forces of good and evil.

But why at this particular point in time, in the years after the conquest, did women revive this form of religious life? To answer this question, I remain with contemporary accounts instead of interpolating explanations from other places and times. Because several of the hermits and hermitesses had Anglo-Saxon names, they may reflect a reappropriation of the Anglo-Saxon and Celtic eremitic heritage in the face of imported Norman ideas of monastic spirituality. Certainly some of the women were inspired by the eremitism flourishing during the latter part of the eleventh century in the wildernesses of France and Italy. Indeed, Eve of Wilton was so enamored of Continental examples that she moved to France when she decided to become "an enclosed one" (inclusa). Since Eve of Wilton is the first postconquest woman known to have become an enclosed one, I begin this chapter on the eremitic life with her story.

EVE OF WILTON

Most of the information that has survived about Eve of Wilton is contained in a letter (the *Liber confortatorius*) Goscelin sent to her around
1082–83, a couple years after she had left Wilton Abbey at the age of
twenty-two to become an enclosed one in France.² In 1065 Eve's immi-
grant parents, her Danish father and Lothringen mother, had given her
as a seven-year-old child to Wilton Abbey. As a friend of Eve's parents
and occasional chaplain at Wilton, Goscelin attended the reception ceremony for the young Eve. Years later in his letter he reminded Eve about
that rich liturgical event: "There, among the fourteen virgins, with glit-
tering tapers as if with celestial lights and torches, you, trembling, the
next to the last, approached to the Lord's nuptials, with the crowd sol-
emnly expectant." Goscelin remembered that he had wept, "touched by
the dew of heaven," when Eve had put on the "sacred dress, that humble
habit, the pledge of faith."³

The year Eve was received at Wilton Abbey, 1065, turned out to be the
last year of the reign of Edward the Confessor and his queen Edith.
Wilton Abbey was a favorite monastery of that royal couple, partly because the queen's namesake, St. Edith of Wilton, was buried there, and in
the last days of King Edward's rule it still retained some of the ancient
splendor Goscelin would later evoke in his lives of the royal abbesses.
Only one month after her own reception, Eve witnessed the pomp of the
dedication of a new stone church at Wilton in honor of St. Edith, a
project dear to Queen Edith. On that occasion, Goscelin positioned himself near Eve to give her symbolic interpretations of everything, from the
censing by the bishop to the fish served at dinner. According to Goscelin,
Eve herself had participated in ceremonies where heaven became almost
discernible on earth.⁴

Two months after the dedication at Wilton, Eve attended another lavish event, the dedication of a new church at Westminster. But Edward the
Confessor died just two weeks later and Wilton Abbey became a bleaker
place. Eve and Goscelin saw each other less frequently since there were
fewer festivals at which to socialize. During most of Eve's teenage years,
Goscelin lived nearby, at the monastery of Sherbourne, and he occasionally celebrated mass at Wilton, but they only rarely talked face to face.
Eve still confided in him, now primarily by letter. With the death in 1078
of Bishop Hermann and the consecration of a bishop less favorably
disposed to Goscelin, he began the perambulations during which he

wrote the Anglo-Saxon saints' lives. Henceforth Eve and Goscelin would have had even fewer opportunities to meet.[5]

Around 1080, not long after the time Goscelin began his travels, Eve left Wilton Abbey to live as an enclosed one on the Continent. She may have been frustrated with developments at Wilton Abbey as much as inspired by reports of the hermits and hermitesses in France. Certainly the monastery had changed during her fifteen years there: first losing its royal patrons and then accepting Anglo-Saxon refugees. It may have already begun to be the literary center that later in the century acquired fame as the home of Muriel and the other poets. Goscelin's departure from the area may have been another catalyst for Eve's decision. In any case, Eve, accompanied by a companion,[6] left Wilton abruptly, without even telling Goscelin beforehand. From her midtwenties through her midforties, Eve lived at Saint-Laurent de Tertre in Angers, in a neighborhood with other eremitic men and women. According to Goscelin, Eve resided in an eight-foot cell and communicated with the outside world through a tiny window. She was literally an enclosed one.

Because Goscelin praised Wilton Abbey in his writings and remembered fondly his days as a chaplain there, it is not surprising that he voiced objections to Eve's move, especially since she had not even consulted him. How could he, a leading advocate of Anglo-Saxon monasticism, approve such innovation? In the *Liber confortatorius*, which he sent to Eve shortly after she had settled at Angers, Goscelin began with a criticism of her decision. Although Goscelin's attitude is predictable, the intense emotional tone he employed is unexpected. This letter reveals the deep affection Goscelin, in his midforties, had for this twenty-five-year-old Eve.

"Oh dearest light of my soul," Goscelin called Eve in his letter to her. "Behold, while I write, the raging sorrow cannot be ignored." Recounting "the beginnings of love," Goscelin reminisced about festivities they had shared, letters they had exchanged, and times he had preached at Wilton Abbey. Saying that he was unable to bear the rupture of their deep spiritual bond after so many years, Goscelin cried out for mercy like the Psalmist. He reminded Eve of their affection [*dilectio*] and perpetual love [*caritas*] when they were together at Wilton. "I spoke to you, I was exhorted by you, I was consoled by you." Together they had "panted" for the love of Christ. Writing in an attempt to be "present with an inseparable soul" even during this "torment of separation," Goscelin poured out his feelings for Eve.[7]

Moving from this praise of their love, Goscelin began to accuse Eve of

betraying their friendship. "If God is love it would seem holier to undertake the commendation rather than the contempt of love. . . . Yet you
decided to offend in love. Therefore let the strength of your profession be
praised, but bewail the cruelty of your silence." Examining the history of
the church for people who suffered the loss of loved ones, Goscelin
concluded that not even saints like Martin and Benedict had been so
badly treated. Of course, saints had suffered losses, with Mary sorrow-
ing at the cross the prime example. But Goscelin informed Eve that
Christianity neither demanded nor lauded the separation of loved ones.
"Yet you have left weeping many mothers of Wilton, many sisters, many
parents, and others with us."[8]

After this impassioned lament for friendship lost, Goscelin began to
justify Eve's becoming "an orphan of Christ . . . dwelling in solitude . . .
far from her native land seeking her true native land." Goscelin reflected,
"All temporal things have their time: a time of war and a time of peace,
a time of separation and a time of union. . . . We have had our times.
We saw each other enough; we conversed enough, we feasted and ban-
queted, were solemn and joking enough in the Lord, if in any way anything of love is able to be enough." To grieve too intensely for their
friendship was to focus too exclusively on temporal delights that by their
very nature are brief. Goscelin reasoned that even if their love had inspired them with a greater longing for Christ, life was so short that,
under optimal conditions, they still could not have had much more time
together.[9]

While Goscelin had lost the woman he called the joy of his life, he
recognized that Eve had given up everything, all her "sweet acquaint-
ances, numerous friends, charming letters, her pious abbess, earnest
teacher, agreeable sisters, and diverse enjoyable things." Her sorrow
must outweigh his, for he knew that nothing caused her greater grief
"than separation from friends and loved ones." The only consolation
Goscelin could imagine for such loss was heaven. If Eve prayed constantly to Christ for her friends, "for the temporal plagues which I suffer
in your absence, I may possess eternal joy with you." Presenting paradise
as the place where friends could be together forever, Goscelin assured
Eve that in the next world she could receive "a true mother, true sisters,
true parents, and inseparable friends in the true fatherland."[10]

In the final pages of his letter, Goscelin envisioned a heaven that would
more than compensate for the sufferings of this life. In that heaven,
community and friendship were central. There the earthly families would
unite again, under the guidance of their respective saints: St. Dionysius

with the inhabitants of Gaul and Paris, St. Martin with those of Tours, St. Augustine of Canterbury with the Britons, and St. Edith with the sisters of Wilton. Eve, with a perfectly mobile body, would then be free to go wherever she willed, with whomever she wanted. In the heights of heaven she could visit with Edith and the chorus of sisters, or she could descend to the new earth and visit her transformed cell at Wilton, or the one in Angers, made into a palace worthy for God's grace. There at last she and Goscelin would be reunited in everlasting joy.[11]

Since Eve had abandoned the safe, the familiar, and the friendly, Goscelin came to see her as another model of heroism, one quite different from the abbesses he extolled elsewhere. When Eve was younger, Goscelin said, he had imagined he would nurture her in heaven: "I used to presume that . . . I could refresh you in paradise, in the lap of God." Now, however, their roles had reversed: "Now this I hope, that I may deserve to be worthy to see you happy in the bosom of father Abraham." Formerly her spiritual mentor, Goscelin now besought Eve for aid. After reflecting on her decision, he had become convinced that Eve had chosen a praiseworthy alternative to life in the royal abbey.[12]

EVE AS AN ENCLOSED ONE

When, in his *Liber confortatorius*, Goscelin recalled the past he and Eve had shared, when he expressed his emotions, he drew on personal experience. But when he treated her life as an enclosed one, Goscelin was only surmising. Whether or not Eve shared the perspective of her former friend, his writings reveal some contemporary explanations for undertaking the eremitic life in the late eleventh century.

When Goscelin thought of Eve's life, battle images came to his mind. Eve was in the army of Christ, prepared to fight the demonic, eager to engage in cosmic battle during her short time on earth. Once the martyrs had fought external enemies, but Eve's internal struggles against carnal desires, evil thoughts, and temptations were real battles as well.[13]

Being a woman did not hinder Eve in this spiritual warfare. In Goscelin's view, God was especially able to confound His enemies when He acted through women, as He had with Deborah, Jael, and Judith. Although Christ denied the prize "to no sex, no state, and no condition" of person, in this life God often chose to triumph through those the world ignored as lowly and contemptible. To emphasize that women were effective warriors in the cosmic battle, Goscelin recounted the victories of saintly women. Like Sarah, Eve could conquer evil spirits; like the martyr Perpetua, she could overcome the devil. By being patient under torture, a woman, St. Blandina, had converted many to Christ. In Spain a female captive had through faithful service inspired a barbarian king to erect a magnificent church. To be a warrior in Christ's army, Eve did not need to overcome any limits resulting from her gender; since she was a powerful woman, she better revealed God's rejection of the world's false values.[14]

The other words that repeatedly occurred to Goscelin when he thought of Eve's new life were "poor," "small," and "little." Goscelin imagined that Eve would be beset with tedium in a tiny eight-foot cell. He feared the devil would taunt her, telling her that she was but a youth, unable to last for eighty to a hundred years in such a constricted space. To help Eve resist these thoughts, Goscelin suggested that instead she think of herself as a plant lying dormant in winter, from which new life would come. The most positive imagery Goscelin could devise for Eve's tiny cubicle was that of a refuge, quiet and safe, free from "anger, quarrels, dissensions, contentions, emulations, envy, jealousy, scandal, homicide, the passion of flesh, and the furor of war."[15]

Except for its greater deprivations, Goscelin thought Eve's new schedule was much like her old one at Wilton, which followed the monastic hours with regular times for the psalter and sacred readings. Since Eve lacked the spiritual conversations that once had nourished her mind, Goscelin recommended an extensive program of devotional readings: Augustine's *Confessions* and the *City of God*, the life and writings of St. Anthony, the histories of Eusebius and Orosius, and Boethius's *Consolation of Philosophy*. Goscelin knew Eve's training when he recommended this list of authors, further testimony to the literary skills of the nuns of Wilton Abbey. One deviation from typical monastic practice was Goscelin's suggestion that Eve receive the viaticum daily. Although nuns typically received the consecrated host less than once a month, Goscelin thought that Eve, deprived of the daily mass celebrated in the monastery, should commune more often.[16]

The *Liber confortatorius* is the last preserved record of Eve and Goscelin's friendship. But Eve does not pass from view. Around 1125 the poet Hilary composed a piece in honor of Eve, an enclosed one who had recently died. In his poem, Hilary relates details about this Eve that correspond exactly with Goscelin's Eve: she had been born in England, the daughter of a "most powerful" man and a woman named Oliva; she had been given as a child to *Clintonia* [undoubtedly Wilton] where she remained for a long time serving God. Hilary had also heard things about Eve at Wilton that Goscelin never mentioned: even at Wilton, Eve had lived "in a cell" and had practiced strict asceticism; she never quarreled, did nothing disgraceful, fled everything impure, was intent on God alone during the offices, and was quick to weep. Hilary claimed Eve had amazed the abbess and sisters there, women who were common and ordinary in their spiritual practices. Eventually Eve "withdrew from the women with whom she had first lived" and, crossing the sea, sought a solitary place where she could be "fully vacant" for the service of God.[17]

Nothing in Hilary's poem contradicts what we know from other sources about Wilton Abbey and Eve's early life there. Indeed, Hilary confirms that, however gifted the poets were, Wilton Abbey was not noted for spiritual fervor. If Hilary's information is an accurate supplement to Goscelin's history, Eve retired from community life to a small cell some years before she finally moved to the Continent. Although Hilary does not mention Goscelin, it still remains likely that Goscelin's departure helped provoke her decision to leave Wilton.

Hilary's poem continues Eve's biography past what Goscelin knew. At some point she moved to Saint-Eutrope, near the priory of Lévière. Hilary claimed that Eve gained fame from her constant prayers, virtual abstinence from food and drink, and disinterest in worldly things. In only one way were Eve's deprivations less harsh than Goscelin had imagined: her life was not devoid of human friendships. "There Eve lived for a long time with the companionship of Hervey." Formerly a monk of Vendôme, Hervey also had left his monastery to become an enclosed one (inclusus).[18]

In case anyone might be suspicious of such a friendship, Hilary explained, "This love [dilectio] was not in the world but in Christ." Hilary praised "the wondrous love [amor] of such a man and such a woman, which all approve and discover without reproach." Theirs was "a worthy and pleasing companionship [societas]" that nourished their piety and was free of anxiety. They inspired each other to aim for heaven, where they would reign with their creator. In this friendship, Eve was the elder; "rightly Eve was followed in the way by Hervey." But "Hervey led her by words and work [verbum et opus]," a reference presumably to his priestly role. Hervey celebrated mass, by which Eve "was given refreshment in mind and body." When she died in her late sixties, Hervey was left "dejected with a great desolation."[19]

Still another source confirms that Eve spent her last years in the company of Hervey. In 1102 Geoffrey, abbot of Vendôme, addressed a letter "to the servant and the handmaid of God, Hervey and the enclosed one Eve." Geoffrey's letter is a traditional exhortation to a virtuous life, outlining the glories of heaven and the dangers of hell, so it provides little specific information about Eve and Hervey's life together. However, since the letter was written two decades before Hilary's poem, it reveals that Hervey and Eve had enjoyed their friendship for many years. Moreover, Geoffrey's letter indicates that he approved of their relationship, for he began it with a friendly greeting and included in it a praise of love that conquerors fear: "Who is perfect in love, let them not fear."[20]

During her almost seventy years of life, Eve had experienced many changes, often ones she herself had initiated. The royal ceremonies of Wilton Abbey before the conquest were far removed from the austere life of prayer and fasting at Saint-Eutrope. Yet certain constants remained: she still recited the office, received nourishment from mass, and spent time with the "sacred readings" that Hilary called Eve's food and drink. Her early training at Wilton had prepared her for life as an enclosed one. Goscelin was right that in many ways Eve's new life was simply a more rigorous version of her earlier one. But one continuum Goscelin had not imagined remained central in Eve's life: she continued to have intimate friendships. Much as Goscelin had loved Eve in her youth, Hervey loved her in her maturity. In both her asceticism and her close relationships with religious men, Eve became the prototype for early twelfth-century English hermitesses.

CHRISTINA OF MARKYATE AND HER ACCOMPLICES

Goscelin exhorted Eve and Hilary eulogized her, but neither tried to portray her personality. An anonymous monk of St. Albans Abbey, on the other hand, wrote a remarkable *vita*, or life, of another eremitic woman, Christina of Markyate, in which he recorded not only her actions but also her thoughts, fears, and hopes. Beginning the *vita* during her lifetime, the monk dedicated it to an unknown prelate whom Christina "revered . . . more than all the pastors under Christ." The monk so intently desired to present an accurate and full portrait that he dined with Christina at her priory and plied her with questions. Many of the details he could only have learned from Christina herself.[21]

Like other medieval *vitae*, Christina's blends perception and reality; visions are reported as if they were as real as the food Christina ate. Although intending to be reliable, the monk shaped his account so that it would please the unknown prelate and edify the other monks at St. Albans who were interested in Christina's story. Even though his interpretation cannot be distinguished from Christina's narration, this *vita* reports enough of Christina's private thoughts and personal opinions to give an unparalleled view of the inner life of a hermitess.

Given other options, Christina probably would not have become a hermitess. Unlike Eve, who chose to leave Wilton Abbey, all Christina had originally intended was to join a monastery. About 1111, when she was in her early teens, Christina had accompanied her parents, merchants from Huntingdon, on a visit to St. Albans Abbey. Inspired by the demeanor of the monks, Christina pledged her virginity to God, offering as a sign a penny at the altar. "Grant me, I beseech Thee, purity and inviolable virginity whereby Thou mayest renew in me the image of Thy Son." This vow to virginity became pivotal for Christina. Indeed, the most common designation the monk used for Christina was *virgo*, not *inclusa* or *anachoreta*, terms he employed for Alfwen, another woman in Christina's *vita*.[22]

Although virginity is central in the monk's account, he gives little theoretical interpretation of its significance. In fact, the treatment of virginity's spiritual importance is so minimal that in a recent study Thomas Renna has argued that the monk focused only on "the negative side of virginity (as the abstinence from sexual sin)" and thereby typified a trend in twelfth-century monasticism "to reduce the status of virginity and chastity among the principle monastic attributes." Renna rightly notes the scant attention in Christina's *vita* to the motives for virginity—a virtue that fourth-century *vitae* described as the "true *philosophia*, . . . a symbol and a summation of all virtues."[23] In a meeting with Prior Fredebert of the Augustinian canons in Huntingdon, Christina argued that she should be allowed to remain a virgin, despite her family's opposition, for "if many mothers of families are saved, . . . certainly virgins are saved more easily."[24] But such comments are few.

However, despite the lack of theoretical statements about virginity, the *vita* repeatedly reiterates the supremely practical value of this virtue. For only Christina's secret vow to virginity enabled her to undertake a religious life in the face of serious obstacles. According to the *vita*, those who opposed Christina's plans for a religious life sensed as well as she did that the best way to destroy her resolve was to force her to have sexual intercourse. Her first major trial came, according to the *vita*, when Christina was seventeen years old: Bishop Ralph Flambard tried to seduce her, and when she resisted, he then tried to rape her. After she escaped, the bishop determined to marry her against her will to a man named Burthred, for "the only way in which he could conceivably gain his revenge was by depriving Christina of her virginity, either by himself or by someone else, for the preservation of which she did not hesitate to repulse even a bishop."[25]

Christina's determination to remain a virgin infuriated her parents, who wanted her to marry Burthred. When Christina resisted her parents' wishes, they besieged and beguiled her until they finally drove her to consent to a betrothal. Confronted in church, Christina was pressured into agreeing that she would marry Burthred in the future. Henceforth, many people believed her public betrothal outweighed her youthful secret vow to virginity. But Christina rightly saw that if she could preserve her virginity, she could still retain control over her future.[26]

Much of Christina's *vita* concerns the incessant attempts of her parents to get her to consummate her betrothal to Burthred. They plied her with alcohol, gave her love potions, and sent Burthred into her bedroom in order to force Christina to have sex with him. When Christina foiled her family's efforts, her mother "swore that she would not care who deflowered her daughter provided that some way of deflowering her could be found." According to the author of the *vita*, virginity in itself was not so objectionable to Christina's family. What they wanted was to profit from a daughter with "such comeliness and beauty, . . . so intelligent, so prudent in affairs." They imagined that if Christina turned her mind to "worldly pursuits" she would enrich and ennoble "not only herself and her family but also all her relatives." "So keen were they on these advantages that they begrudged her a life of virginity."[27]

Hence virginity had a pragmatic value for Christina. Only her virginity saved her from her family's plans for her future. No wonder Christina said that her greatest fear was that she would be forced to have sexual intercourse with Burthred. On one occasion, her parents sent Burthred into Christina's bedroom, and she hid from him behind a curtain, "faint with fear" because in her mind "she saw herself already dragged out in their midst, all surrounding her, looking upon her, threatening her, given up to the sport of her destroyer."[28] For women like Christina who sought independence from an arranged marriage, virginity's fundamental importance was not its spiritual qualities but its guarantee of freedom.

Christina's parents' violent opposition to her desire to remain a virgin forced Christina to ally with religious men. None of the men who aided Christina had any obvious reason to concern themselves with her welfare. One of the first was Sueno, a canon "advanced in age" in the

Augustinian priory in Christina's hometown of Huntingdon. "Conspicuous for his good life, and influential in his teaching," Sueno had seen Christina by chance when she was a small girl and had thereafter talked with her about the glories and difficulties of preserving virginity. When Christina confided to Sueno her secret offering at St. Albans, he "confirmed the virgin's vow before God."[29]

There was often tension in Sueno and Christina's relationship. Christina supported Sueno even when rumors reached her of his sexual misconduct; her loyalty strengthened him "in the pursuit of holiness." However, when Sueno heard about Christina's public betrothal to Burthred, he became convinced that she had renounced her vow to virginity and he "accused her of feminine inconstancy," a judgment for which he later begged Christina's forgiveness. After these difficulties, they renewed their friendship (amica familiaritas), and Sueno became an active advocate of Christina's cause. He pleaded for her with his own unsympathetic prior, Fredebert; he undertook a secret mission to Burthred on her behalf; and he "prayed to Christ day and night for the afflicted maiden's deliverance." When Christina's parents, relatives, and bishop were trying to force her to consummate her betrothal to Burthred, Sueno was "her only comfort."[30]

An even less likely ally was Eadwin, a man "leading a religious life in solitude" whom Christina bribed her parents' servants to bring her "by stealth." After one brief conversation with Christina, Eadwin promised to help her. Eadwin sought advice in person from Ralph d'Escures, the archbishop of Canterbury. Then Eadwin plotted Christina's escape and found her a hiding place. Disguised as a man, Christina fled on horseback, and for the next six years, she hid with those in eremitic life: two years with the anchoress Alfwen and four with Eadwin's relative, the hermit Roger.[31]

The first woman known to have aided Christina in her escape from her parents was the "venerable enclosed one," "the anchorite" Alfwen, who welcomed her with joy at Flamstead. "On the same day she put on the religious habit," and Alfwen concealed her in a dark chamber, "hardly large enough . . . to house her." Sitting in the small enclosure, Christina frequently recited verses from Psalm 38 that seemed particularly appropriate for her:

> My friends and my companions shrink from my wounds,
> even the dearest of them keep their distance;

men intent on killing me lay snares,
others, hoping to hurt me, threaten my ruin,
hatching treacherous plots all day.
But I am like the deaf, I do not hear,
like the dumb man who does not open his mouth.

"This she repeated often, lamenting at one moment her own weakness and blindness, at another the violence and guile of her parents, friends, and relatives, who were seeking her life."[32]

Christina's *vita* includes very little about the two years Christina remained with Alfwen, probably because their relationship ended unpleasantly. Alfwen frequently communicated with Roger, Eadwin's relation, a hermit who lived two miles away at Markyate. Formerly a monk of St. Albans, Roger had become a hermit a few years earlier, after completing a pilgrimage to Jerusalem. Roger's servants visited Alfwen often, and he was said to love her very much on account of her holiness. When Christina for some reason had to leave Alfwen, Roger offered to bring her to his hermitage at Markyate. Although Alfwen opposed Roger's plan, Roger had Christina brought to him anyway; but "in order that there might be no excuse for Alfwen to accuse him before the bishop of being a cause of dissension," Roger intended never to speak with Christina directly or see her. After the move, Alfwen fades from view, probably unhappy with the succeeding events.[33]

If all religious had been as helpful as Sueno and the hermits, Christina would not have had to resort to desperate ploys like a thirty-mile horseback journey dressed as a man and six years of hiding in cramped quarters. But churchmen were her bane as well as her cure. Bishop Ralph Flambard had initiated her troubles; Sueno's superior, Prior Fredebert, refused to honor her secret vow of virginity.[34] Particularly problematic was Christina's inability to get her own bishop, Robert Bloet of Lincoln, on her side. After initially favoring Christina, Robert reversed his judgment; according to Christina, Robert had bowed to pressure from her parents.[35] Robert's decision prevented Christina from living as a religious until his death in 1123, when she was in her midtwenties.

By a remarkable coincidence, an independent confirmation of Robert's opposition has survived. In an early version of his *De Gestis Pontificum Anglorum*, written around 1125, William of Malmesbury recounted, "The manner of [Robert Bloet's] death had been foretold him in an ambiguous prophecy by a holy hermit named Roger, who dwelt in the forest near St. Albans, and led an austere life, seldom heard of in our times." According to William, "On a certain occasion, the bishop . . . demanded why [Roger] harboured a virgin who, having forsaken her suitor for the sake of celibacy, had sought refuge with him. The hermit gave a fitting reply, when the bishop broke out, 'Bold and insolent is your answer; your cowl alone sustains you.'" Roger retorted that the bishop himself would one day "sorely wish to have one, and words shall be wanting to you in which to ask for it."[36]

William interpreted Roger's remark as prophetic, for Bishop Robert died suddenly and unexpectedly, with no chance to be clothed in a religious habit. Expunged from later versions of the *De Gestis Pontificum Anglorum* along with the other hostile remarks about Bishop Robert, the anecdote confirms both Robert Bloet's opposition and the fact of Christina's refuge with Roger. It also indicates that the bishop suspected Christina was there but was unwilling or unable to violate her shelter.

When Christina was finally able to live openly as a religious, she had depended on the aid of religious men and women for seven years. Men were her main supporters—Canon Sueno, the hermits Eadwin and Roger, and the archbishop of Canterbury, Ralph d'Escures. Other religious men were her chief enemies, especially the Bishops Robert Bloet and Ralph Flambard. Although Alfwen was the only known female supporter, her aid was given at a critical time when Christina first fled her home with her family and bishop in pursuit.

Why did some people help Christina and others cause her endless trouble? It has been suggested that Anglo-Saxons backed Christina against Norman church leaders. Eadwin and Alfwen are Anglo-Saxon names; Roger spoke Old English; Roger's disciples had Anglo-Saxon names. If these hermits and the anchoress saw themselves as preserving Celtic eremitism in the face of the Norman invasion, they would have had additional reason to side with Christina.[37]

But ethnic loyalties cannot be the main factor, for Normans, like the archbishop of Canterbury, also were among Christina's supporters. What most clearly united Christina's accomplices was their immunity to her parents' power. The hermits and anchoress were outside the structures of her parents' society; the archbishop was above their sphere of influence. Christina's enemies, on the other hand, were local church leaders—the bishop of Lincoln and the head of her hometown Augustinian priory. Such men succumbed to the pressure Christina's parents exerted; they had little sympathy for a young woman's wishes, however holy. Their assessment of political realities is understandable. What remains remarkable is the number of people who intervened on Christina's behalf simply because they believed she had a right to religious life.

FRIENDSHIP AND VIRGINITY IN CHRISTINA'S *VITA*

Virginity was central to Christina's identity, yet to preserve it she had to depend on friendships with men. The men who encouraged her, helped her escape, sheltered her, and instructed her had no official responsibility for her. All acted out of friendship and respect for her character and vocation; affection and admiration encouraged them to support her in the face of opposition and threats. Christina both needed and desired these friendships with men.

And so the very alliances that enabled her to preserve her virginity also threatened it, for the close friendships Christina formed with men unavoidably exposed her to sexual temptations. The author of Christina's *vita* was sensitive to this dynamic and repeatedly discussed it, especially in his treatment of her relationships with the hermit Roger and Abbot Geoffrey of St. Albans (discussed below). Although he revealed little about the relationship between Alfwen and Christina, he recounted in detail the effect Christina and Roger had on each other.

Despite the fact that Roger supposedly had determined not even to look at Christina, on the very night she arrived at his hermitage, he glanced at her during prayers in his chapel. At that moment Christina also was assessing Roger's "bearing and deportment" for signs of holiness. "And so they saw each other, not by design and yet not by chance, but, as afterwards became clear, by the divine will." As a result, "the fire . . . which had been kindled by the spirit of God and burned in each one of them cast its sparks into their hearts by the grace of that mutual glance; and so made one in heart and soul in chastity and charity in Christ, they were not afraid to dwell together under the same roof."[38]

During the four years Christina lived with Roger, she hid during the day in a tiny room adjoining his cell and nightly prayed with him in his chapel. Commenting on this relationship, Christina's biographer admitted, "If they had not had a glimpse of each other, neither would have presumed to live with the other in the confined space of that cell." Nor did they openly reveal their friendship. They concealed their activities even from those who dwelt with Roger, for "they feared scandal to their inferiors and the fury of those who were persecuting the handmaid of Christ." In the cramped quarters of the cell, stifling hot in summer and too small for adequate clothing in winter, Christina sat silently on a rock, unable even to leave "to satisfy the demands of nature," for "even when she was in dire need," she "would rather die in the cell than make her presence known to anyone at that time."[39]

"Through their dwelling together and encouraging each other to strive after higher things their holy affection [*sanctus amor*] grew day by day, like a large flame springing from two brands joined together." Under Roger's tutelage, Christina learned "contemplative meditation" and other "heavenly secrets," such as how to be "on earth only in body," with the mind "fixed on heaven." Roger gave her instruction, "first by word, then by example."[40]

The motives for Roger's decision to aid Christina were complex. Originally he intervened because Christina's reputation impressed him and heavenly signs persuaded him. During her years with him, he responded to her spiritual gifts. When he eventually decided to designate her as his heir, her holiness had inspired him. In welcoming a woman hiding from her parents and her betrothed, Roger showed his willingness to take risks. When he knew he was about to die, Roger decided to leave his hermitage to her. Roger had several disciples, including five hermits who lived with him when Christina was there. But Christina was his "Sunday daughter [*sunendaege dohter*], because just as much as Sunday excels the other days of the week in dignity so he loved [*amare*] Christina more than all the others whom he had begotten or nursed in Christ."[41]

If Christina was to succeed him, Roger needed to find her a patron. Like Eadwin six years earlier, Roger went to the top; "at length he bethought him of Archbishop Thurstan of York, for he was a helpful promoter of such holy vocations." Beyond the sway of Christina's wealthy family, Thurstan responded positively to Roger's request. Arranging for a secret interview with Christina, Thurstan promised her that he would annul her marriage and confirm her vow to virginity, but only after the death of Robert Bloet, the bishop of Lincoln who had decided not to honor Christina's secret vow. When Roger died in 1122, Thurstan remembered Christina, but since Robert Bloet was still alive, Thurstan decided to provide Christina a hiding place with a certain cleric, "a close friend of his."[42]

After all these trials, Christina still was not safe. The cleric friend of Thurstan's developed an intense sexual attraction for Christina, and she too was tempted. Unable or unwilling to conceal his desire, "the wretched man, out of his senses with passion, came before her without any clothes on and behaved in so scandalous a manner that I cannot make it known, lest I pollute the wax by writing it, or the air by saying it." Pleading with Christina to have pity on him, the cleric persisted in his entreaties until he was frightened by a dream in which Mary Magdalene reproached him.[43]

Christina concealed her passion, while she tried futilely to cool her lust with fasts of raw herbs and water, nights without sleep, scourgings, and constant prayers. Even after 1123, when Bishop Robert Bloet's death enabled Christina to return to Roger's hermitage, "she unwillingly felt its stings" until she had "the consolation of an unheard of grace": Christ came to her "in the guise of a small child," and for an entire day let himself be not only "felt but also seen." Holding Christ in her arms, the maid "gave thanks, and pressed Him to her bosom. And with immeasurable delight she held Him at one moment to her virginal breast, at another she felt His presence within her even through the barrier of her flesh." Envisioning herself mothering the infant Christ—suckling him and feeling him within her womb—quenched her sexual desires. "From that moment the fire of lust was so completely extinguished that never afterwards could it be revived."[44]

Christina's most complicated relationship was with Abbot Geoffrey of St. Albans, the monastery where she had first pledged to undertake a life of virginity. When Abbot Geoffrey became acquainted with Christina, she had already inherited Roger's hermitage and was living there with other women. Christina initiated the relationship by sending Geoffrey a warning revealing that she knew something he was thinking. For the next twenty-three years, until Geoffrey's death, Christina and Geoffrey had a friendship that inspired them, pleased some, and scandalized others. Christina's preternatural powers, treated at some length in her *vita*, were often focused on Geoffrey. Christina foreknew when Geoffrey was to visit Markyate, which he did frequently. She could describe in absentia the abbot's actions, conversations, and even his dreams, so that he "could not offend God, either in word or deed, without her knowing it instantly in the spirit." Awed by her gifts, Geoffrey "heard her admonitions, accepted her advice, consulted her in doubts, avoided evil, bore her reproaches."[45]

Just as personal relationships with hermits led her to adopt their way of life, her friendship with the abbot directed her to cenobitism. At Geoffrey's urging, Christina publicly confirmed her vow to virginity in 1131 at St. Albans before Bishop Alexander of Lincoln. In preparing for her public profession of virginity, Christina fretted about her answer to the question of whether she was a virgin: "For she was mindful of the thoughts and stings of the flesh with which she had been troubled, and even though she was not conscious of having fallen either in deed or in desire, she was chary of asserting that she had escaped unscathed." Virginity no longer was simply a pragmatic issue. Christina wanted perfect virginity, total purity in body and mind.[46]

After Christina decided to remain at Markyate—refusing offers to join Marcigny or Fontevrault or to head Archbishop Thurstan's new monastery at York—Abbot Geoffrey helped her gain legal possession of the site. In 1145, in Geoffrey's presence, Bishop Alexander of Lincoln consecrated a church at Markyate, the final stage in the conversion of Markyate from a hermitage into a Benedictine priory with Christina as head (*magistra*).[47] Exactly what effect this transformation had on the lives of Christina and the women living with her is unknown, for the *vita* does not cover events after 1142. Before Markyate became a priory, the women—called *virgines* or *puellae* in the *vita*—were not strictly enclosed, for they occasionally left the hermitage, sometimes to visit nearby St. Albans Abbey, and Christina left Markyate sufficiently often to have a special tunic for such occasions. But after the establishment of Markyate Priory, the women may well have been more strictly enclosed.[48]

Sometime after Markyate was formally established as a priory, a psalter of Christina's, which had originally been composed for her before 1124, was altered to bring it more in line with St. Albans's calendar, a further indication of Markyate's continued connections with St. Albans. Christina's psalter also gives additional evidence of her preoccupation with virginity. Two distinctive features of this psalter are the large number of female saints included in the calendar and the prominence given the life of St. Alexis. As one of its editors, Pächt, notes, "No story can have impressed Christina's contemporaries as a more perfect metaphor of her tribulations than the legend of Alexis, the homo Dei." Much like Christina, Alexis was forced to marry but managed not to consummate the union; instead he left his spouse for a life of virginity. The prologue to the life of Alexis, "epitomizing its content and proclaiming the glorification of the chaste life as its principal theme," is extant only in this particular psalter.[49]

Despite the potential threat to their chastity, the relationship between Christina and Geoffrey was not solely concerned with practical matters like the establishment of her priory. Calling Geoffrey her "spiritual friend," "dearest one," "most intimate one," "her heart," and especially her "beloved [*dilectio*]," Christina "cherished him with great affection and loved him with a wonderful but pure love." In countless ways Christina revealed her affection. For instance, when Geoffrey was supposed to go on a mission to Rome, Christina wanted him to stay home near her instead. Praying that Geoffrey would be released from the mission, Christina, while "rapt in ecstasy," saw herself in the presence of Christ. There she saw Geoffrey, "encircled with her arms and held closely to her breast." Fearing that "since a man is stronger than a woman, he would free himself from her grasp, she saw Jesus . . . closing her hands with His own loving hand" in a grip that strengthened hers and enabled her to keep her friend with her. When Geoffrey finally was excused from the burdensome journey, he was further convinced of the power of Christina's love.[50]

Christina sometimes worried about her friendship with Geoffrey. But, according to her biographer, her only concern was whether it was possible or proper to love another person more than oneself, "at least in matters that pertain to the love of God," for "if anything, she was more zealous for him than for herself." Christina learned that she should not try to place another before herself in God's love after she had a vision in which she was on Jesus' right and Geoffrey on His less worthy left. Accepting this one limit, Christina prayed constantly for Geoffrey's enlightenment and well-being. During her periods of deepest meditations, she was delighted that "there came to her, at such moments, the remembrance of her beloved friend." When Geoffrey celebrated mass at Markyate, Christina received the eucharist, and often "was so rapt that, unaware of earthly things, she gave herself to the contemplation of the countenance of her Creator."[51]

Others were less confident than Christina about the wisdom of this friendship. Some people accused Christina of being too motivated by worldly, material desires, for Geoffrey provided Christina with goods from his abbey. Others felt she loved Geoffrey with an earthly love, not a spiritual one. According to the *vita*, no one had questioned Geoffrey's goodness or Christina's virtue before their relationship blossomed; but "when their mutual affection in Christ had inspired them to greater good, the abbot was slandered as a seducer and the maiden as a loose woman." Complaining because the friendship was attacked "with gossip, poisonous detractions, barbed words," Christina's *vita* compared her accusers to those who had "despised the disciples of Christ because they took women about with them." Christina's reaction to the criticisms was to light a special candle each Sunday as an offering to God, "to enlighten the abbot and put an end to the shamelessness of her detractors, whom she pitied."[52]

In the more than fifty years covered in her biography, Christina relied on many friendships with religious men. She could neither prevent the rumors or avoid totally the risks of seduction, for the preservation of her virginity paradoxically depended on close relationships with men. From the time she visited St. Albans Abbey as a child until she became the confidante of its abbot and head of her own monastery, Christina was inspired and aided by religious men. Women were important too, especially Alfwen who first hid her and Christina's own disciples at Markyate. But men were her main mentors, and they were the ones who gave form to her religious life. Christina adapted and was able to carry out her commitment to virginity in many contexts. Both in her friendships with men and her versatility, Christina exemplifies the life history of many other religious women of her time.

EREMITIC WOMEN AND THEIR MALE COMPANIONS

Christina's reasons for adopting an eremitic life were different from Eve's; Christina would have preferred to be a nun, whereas Eve was not satisfied at Wilton Abbey. Their distinctive histories warn against sweeping generalizations about why women became hermitesses. People in twelfth-century England valued the life of prayer, asceticism, and chastity; what set apart the hermits and hermitesses was their decision to lead such a life without the benefits of a formally established religious community. The uniqueness of each story is further exemplified in the lives of the other known hermitesses.

A chance encounter was the decisive factor in Matilda of Wareham's decision to undertake an eremitic life. John, abbot of Ford, tells of Matilda in his *vita* of Wulfric of Haselbury, the priest who in 1125 left his parish to become an anchorite. Sometime after Wulfric had settled as an anchorite at Haselbury, Matilda, a woman from West Saxony beginning a pilgrimage "across the sea," stopped for a rest there. Wulfric's serving boy noticed Matilda and led her to Wulfric, since all morning the ascetic had been looking for someone he called "his sister." Not his sister by blood, Matilda was to become Wulfric's sister by her style of life. When Wulfric predicted, "You will serve God in the profession of an anchoress [*anachoretica*]," Matilda abandoned her plans for a pilgrimage.[53]

According to John of Ford, Wulfric's prediction concerning Matilda's future was detailed and precise. First Matilda would serve as a cushion maker in Wareham for two and a half years so that she could prepare nearby a narrow dwelling. Then she would move into her prepared place and remain there for fifteen years as an anchoress. After that, she would die. Convinced by Wulfric, Matilda felt she was "no longer ignorant of the order and mode and time and place" of God's plan for her. And all proceeded as Wulfric had prophesied, with Matilda even dying in her sixteenth year as an anchoress.[54]

After she settled near Wareham, Matilda found a handmaid, Gertrude, to help her acquire necessities. Matilda then introduced Gertrude to the eremitic life. Becoming Gertrude's mentor, Matilda encouraged her to endure pain and hunger; when Gertrude complained about a toothache, Matilda chastised her for murmuring. Matilda told Gertrude that she herself never moaned even when her jaw felt as if it were breaking into pieces, for she welcomed pain as a reminder from God that her days were numbered. After Matilda's death, Gertrude, formerly the handmaid, inherited the site, imitated Matilda's austerities, and eventually was buried with her in the same tomb. Undertaking the ascetic life because of an anchorite's prophecy, Matilda herself engendered Gertrude's vocation.[55]

Eremitic individuals sometimes influenced their siblings. Christina of Markyate's sister Margaret joined her at Markyate. In the north of England, Godric of Finchale inspired his sister Burchwine. After Godric had tried many occupations and traveled extensively, he decided to become a hermit. Before 1128, perhaps as early as 1110, he settled at Finchale, near Durham, where he remained until his death in 1170. Sometime during those years Godric was joined there by his sister Burchwine, who, "disregarding all secular things," convinced him to let her live a solitary life with him.

Godric welcomed his sister, who "from her mother's womb had remained a virgin and uncorrupted, always devoted to God." He "constructed a certain secret cell which was somewhat removed from his own oratory, in which the virgin devoted to God lived." In order to become a hermit, Godric had acquired permission from the bishop and received instruction from another ascetic. But Godric alone assumed responsibility for his sister; "and therefore he showed Burchwine by example the ways to God." Like Godric, Burchwine wore a hair shirt and subjugated her body with fasts and prayers. "There was nothing of the good which she on her own knew or learned that she did not strive to fulfill." Once Burchwine had received instruction, "she rarely visited her brother's oratory," unless by chance a priest was present to say mass. Normally Burchwine knelt when she heard her brother signal the hours for the divine office and said as much of the office as she knew. After her death, Burchwine was buried at Durham, and Godric prayed for her until he was assured of her salvation through a vision of her between two angels.[56]

Living near each other, these individuals could communicate in person, but sometimes written references survive about their relationships. During the first decade of the twelfth century, several women were living holy lives in an informal community under the supervision of a certain Robert. In a letter Archbishop Anselm wrote at their request, he named six of them: Seit, Edit, Thydit, Lwerun, Dirgit, and Godit. Anselm called these women "his most loved sisters and daughters," but he reserved his most generous praise for "his dearest friend and brother" Robert, "whom God inspired so that he would have care of you according to God, and so that daily by word and example he would teach you how you ought to live." Anselm assured Robert that God would reward his willingness to care for and love these handmaids (*ancillae*).

To aid this little community, Anselm offered practical spiritual advice. In a masterly summary of the mental technique in which thoughts are countered not by confrontation but by substitution, with good desires introduced to drive out perverse ones, Anselm told them how to overcome evil thoughts and desires: they should refuse to entertain them even long enough to combat them. Anselm lauded the form of life these women were leading; his only warning was to worry as much about their desires as about their actions, since God would judge a person's will.[57]

In his *Vita Wulfstani* (*Life of St. Wulfstan*), William of Malmesbury also described a relationship between "a holy priest named Dunstan" living near Brumeton and a female recluse (*reclusa*) living in the same village. William commented, "This woman was inferior to no man in sanctity." Seeing the priest and the recluse rivaling each other in goodness, William concluded, "you would not know whom you prefer": the priest excelled "by teaching doctrine [*instruendi doctrina*]"; the woman "by submitting to discipline [*parendi disciplina*]." This spiritual friendship flourished sometime between 1095, the year of Wulfstan's death, and 1124 to 1143, the period when William provided his version of Wulfstan's life. William happened to mention the pair only because they had a vision of Wulfstan in the choir of heaven.[58]

Matilda, Gertrude, Burchwine, the recluse of Brumeton, Margaret, and Alfwen were mentioned only parenthetically in the biographies of more famous people. Still, these women and the six friends of Robert supplement the richer information preserved about Eve and Christina. The eremitic life spread through personal example and inspiration.

Friendships influenced all of these individuals; personal bonds, not institutional affiliations, linked these men and women for there were no official reasons to enter or remain in these relationships. The men who recorded these friendships were unanimously positive about them, even when they admitted that others were suspicious.[59]

Although the friendships were mutually edifying and inspiring, the men frequently were said to offer instruction to the women. In part this reflected the background of the men, all of whom had received training in the religious life. Roger, Hervey, Goscelin, and Geoffrey had monastic experiences on which to draw; Sueno was a canon; another ascetic had taught Godric. Hervey, Goscelin, Geoffrey, Wulfric, Dunstan, and Sueno were priests. But once the women had been initiated into religious life, they too were said to offer spiritual guidance: Eve led Hervey, Christina advised Geoffrey, and Matilda had her own disciple Gertrude. The women were all noted for their ascetic abilities. Indeed, in their enthusiasm for strict discipline, the women rivaled even their more famous companions.

Apart from praising the women's ascetic rigors, the sources rarely mention what other kinds of spiritual prowess the women exemplified. While the recluse of Brumeton is said to have had a vision (of Wulfstan in heaven), only the *vita* of Christina provides any details about spirituality. Christina is said to have had numerous visions. When praying, at times Christina felt something like "a little bird fluttering gently with its wings within her breast." At other times she perceived light: "when her mind roamed freely," she saw sometimes one, but often three, lights radiating with equal splendor and brilliance. "Sometimes she saw Evianus (though not in the flesh) lightly caress her face and mouth with his first and middle finger. . . . Whichever of these signs she saw, it meant her prayer was granted. For these visions were not imaginary or dreams: she saw them with the true intuition enjoyed by the mystics."[60]

Christina also had corporeal visions, in which people seemed to appear in the flesh. Sometimes her visions were of Christ himself, but Christ often preferred "to comfort His spouse . . . through His holy Mother." When Christina worried whether she could withstand her parents' threats, when she tried to cool her sexual passion for the cleric friend of Thurstan's, when she wondered whether she would inherit Roger's hermitage, when she fretted about her purity, when she wanted to know whether her brother would die: on all these occasions Christina felt Mary was the one who responded to her plea. Most often Christina saw Mary as the Queen of Heaven. Sometimes "a voice" spoke Mary's will; other times Mary sent her infant son or angels with a crown of virginity for Christina. On occasion Mary even appeared to Christina's companions on her behalf. All these experiences seemed real to Christina, although sometimes she said she did not know "whether she saw these things in the body or out of the body."[61]

One might surmise that the other women had similar experiences to Christina's. Certainly twelfth-century women on the Continent—like Hildegard of Bingen—are famous for mystic visions. But rather than overgeneralize about these women, it seems wise to emphasize their distinctiveness: their lives and motivations varied, although all were committed to chastity, strict asceticism, and prayer. Perhaps true differences are reflected in the varied terms used for these women in the sources: the *reclusa* of Brumeton; the *inclusa* or *anachoreta* Alfwen; the *anachoreta* Matilda; the *inclusa* Eve; the *virgo* Christina. Some of the women called recluses and anchoresses were probably strictly enclosed; the anchoress Matilda appears to have remained for fifteen years in the narrow dwelling she constructed. Those labeled "enclosed ones" may have already adopted the way of life that later in the twelfth century had definitely become ritualized and regularized. But certainly not all eremitic women were so restricted, for both Christina and Burchwine occasionally left their abodes.

The lives of these women challenge one assumption sometimes made about eremitic women, for they demonstrate the eremitism was not a solitary form of religious life. Christina hid with Alfwen, shared a cell with Roger, gathered other women at Markyate, and was close to Abbot Geoffrey. After Eve left Goscelin and her sisters at Wilton, she settled beside Hervey. The recluse of Brumeton had her priest mentor; Burchwine was with Godric; Matilda moved near Wareham after Wulfric's prophecy and trained her handmaid Gertrude; six women lived with Robert. Whatever term one chooses for such women, certainly in the first part of the twelfth century, they did not live alone.

PART TWO

Expansion (1130–1165)

CHAPTER 3

Male Religious and Female Monasticism in the South

Eremitism was one of the earliest signs of the monastic revival among women. In the first third of the twelfth century, male monasticism had already entered its period of expansion, with the number of English monasteries for men approximately doubling, from around 75 houses to around 155. Female monasticism did not begin a similar increase until 1130. In the early years of the century, apart from the houses for nuns that some bishops founded, the eremitic movement was the only evidence of a religious renewal among women.

In the middle third of the century, women and men both began numerous new monastic foundations. The number of houses for male religious doubled again, to more than 300 houses. But the percentage of increase for female houses was even greater: from 20 houses to more than 100 in the thirty-five years between 1130 and 1165.

Not only did monasteries for women multiply more rapidly than monasteries for men in these middle years of the century, but the process whereby some of these women's houses came into being was also distinctive, for several of the monasteries for women were founded with the aid of religious men. Female religious played no discernible role in the creation of new monasteries for men; hence, David Knowles in his *Monastic Order in England* could tell the story of the expansion of male monasticism without referring to nuns or sisters. But male religious—hermits, monks, and canons—were active on behalf of women.

Many of the new communities for women that male religious helped establish had already begun before the men became involved. Women who were leading religious lives came to the attention of monks or hermits, who then encouraged and aided the transformation of the women's communities into priories. When monks facilitated the formal establishment of a monastery for women, they often made the new foundation dependent on their own monastery. Although a parent monastery usually retained ties with a "daughter house" of its own gender, the fact that monks were willing to assume responsibility for houses of nuns is striking. Moreover, that monks in even the richest and oldest abbeys of England accepted women's communities as affiliates of their own monasteries challenges the platitude about monks' reluctance to aid women.

Women profited from the support of these wealthy abbeys. At the beginning of the period of expansion, there were so few monasteries for women, and the few that existed were relatively so poor, that they were apparently not able to create daughter foundations for women or for men. Only one female house, Farewell Abbey, is known to have established a daughter house, and these two monasteries did not remain connected for long. (See discussion to follow.) In this situation, female religious could definitely benefit from the aid men offered. But male support had its price, which women had to weigh against the advantages of the men's help.

FEMALE DAUGHTER HOUSES OF MALE MONASTERIES

Christina of Markyate is the best-known example of a hermitess who transformed her community into a priory as a result of the encouragement and aid of religious men. The process was a slow one, with a quarter of a century passing between the time Christina settled with Roger at his hermitage and the formal establishment of Markyate Priory. In 1131, eight years after Christina had inherited Roger's hermitage, she finally made publicly the vow to virginity she had taken secretly in her youth. Although for many years she accepted gifts of rents and tithes from Abbot Geoffrey of St. Albans in order to construct and repair buildings at Markyate, only in 1145 did she receive possession of the property from the canons of St. Paul's, London, the actual owners of the site where the hermit Roger had settled. The charter of transfer describes Markyate as an estate enclosed by ditches and adjoining woods. Having acquired the property, Christina had Bishop Alexander of Lincoln consecrate a church there, the final stage in the establishment of Markyate as a priory.[1]

Since the canons of St. Paul's had owned the property, they expected some recompense for their donation. The nuns of Markyate were to pay the canons three *solidos* a year. In addition, each of the nuns had to swear "faithfulness and indemnity" to the canons; all future heads of Markyate, called mistresses (*magistrae*) in the charter, were to make a similar oath. The nuns also agreed that henceforth they would elect a new mistress only with the assent of the canons. Since earlier the monks of St. Albans had been the primary supporters of Christina, in establishing Markyate as a priory she further enmeshed her community in a network of relationships with male religious.[2]

Abbot Geoffrey had been a primary influence in Christina's decision to adopt the Benedictine way of life, and he was also instrumental in the decision of another group of women to do the same. Around 1145, the year Markyate was established, hermitesses living at Sopwell, in the neighborhood of St. Albans Abbey, accepted Abbot Geoffrey's urgings that they convert their hermitage into a Benedictine priory. The fullest account of this process is in Matthew Paris's *History of the Abbots of the Monastery of St. Albans*, written almost a century after the event. According to this account, "Around 1140, next to the woods which is called 'Eywoda,' not far from a river which broadens there, two holy women, having made an extremely poor dwelling from the branches of trees woven together with pieces of bark and twigs, had begun to lead a life of vigils and prayers, under marvelous abstinence." Like many other holy women who acquired fame, these women were known for their asceticism. "Enervating their bodies with bread and water, they continued felicitously their new religious life with irreproachable chastity" for several years.[3]

These women came to the attention of Abbot Geoffrey about a decade after he had befriended Christina. Drawn by "their commendable way of life [*conversatio*]" and "persuaded by divine prophecy," Geoffrey "judged it suitable to construct there a little dwelling for the women." Once he had aided them, Geoffrey then encouraged the women to accept regulation. After they were joined by others, "he constituted a way of life under the order of Saint Benedict" and gave them "veils in the custom of nuns."

Abbot Geoffrey's patronage benefited the women. "Inspired by the grace of God," Geoffrey increased the "spiritual and temporal" assets of Sopwell; he also provided the nuns with a cemetery for their own use. But he imposed restrictions as well. "Guarding the reputation and well-being of the nuns, having made there a house, he declared them to be enclosed there, under lock and doorbolt and the seal of the abbot." He further specified that no more than thirteen women were to live at Sopwell Priory, and the permission of St. Albans Abbey was required before any maidens (*virgines*) were received. According to Matthew Paris, Abbot Geoffrey, not the women, initiated this process. Geoffrey's own sense of divine will spearheaded the transformation, not any pressing need of the women who had lived on their own "felicitously" for several years.[4]

About the same time, women were installed in Kilburn Priory through the intercession of religious men. Shortly before 1140 "the three girls [*puellae*] namely Emma, Gunilda, and Christina" received from Abbot Herbert of Westminster and his prior Osbert of Clare "the hermitage that Godwyn had built at Kilburn, with all the land of that place." In addition to the land and church at Kilburn, the women received from the monks of Westminster Abbey a rent of thirty *solidos* a year and two "corrodies." [Later the corrodies were defined as bread, ale, wine, mead, and a pittance (the daily allotment of vegetables).]

Whether the women had already begun a religious life before they received this endowment at Kilburn is not known. What is remarkable, however, is that the monks of Westminster were willing to support women instead of the men they had formerly aided. One of the corrodies given to the women had previously been held by Ailmar, a hermit in Westminster's care. From the perspective of the abbey, the three women were the successors to Ailmar and Godwyn, the builder of the hermitage. Westminster Abbey did not intend to sever any ties with Kilburn just because it had introduced women there. "Lest its rights be harmed by anything rash or its rule by anything perverse," Westminster Abbey retained "subjection and jurisdiction" over Kilburn.[5]

In return for their priory the women of Kilburn became subject to a master as well as to Westminster Abbey. At the transfer, Abbot Herbert of Westminster appointed Godwyn the "master (*magister*) of the place and guardian (*custos*) of the girls as long as he lives." After Godwyn's death, with the consent of the abbot of Westminster, "the convent of girls will choose a suitable senior who will preside over their church." At least by the thirteenth century, a prioress of Kilburn shared authority there with this master or guardian, who had explicit responsibility for "the possessions and things of the church." Emma, Gunilda, and Christina gained material goods and spiritual services; in return, they became subject to male religious.[6]

About 1160, some hermitesses living at Ling entered a similar arrangement with another wealthy abbey, Bury St. Edmunds. Since Abbot Hugh of Bury St. Edmunds wanted everyone in the future to know that he had "rationally and orderly" installed women in Thetford Priory, he left a detailed account of the transfer. According to Abbot Hugh, Bury had long held the cell of St. George at Thetford, but through the death one by one of its occupants and the dissipation of its goods, Thetford had become so diminished that it seemed more like a deserted house than a place for religious men. By 1160, only two men remained, the canons Folcard and Andrew. They complained to Abbot Hugh that the poverty was so intolerable at Thetford that they neither could nor wanted to remain.

When Hugh objected that to desert a place where religious had lived for such a long time would be scandalous, Folcard and Andrew pleaded with Hugh to give Thetford to certain women leading a religious life at Ling in Norfolk with only a few possessions. The canons reasoned that if the sparse possessions of these women were combined with those at Thetford, the place could be relieved of its poverty and recalled to a proper religious rule.[7]

Abbot Hugh described his response to their suggestion: "We desired greatly the improvement of Thetford but nevertheless we drew off from receiving so suddenly in that place those women [*foeminae*], for by this they were called." To justify his hesitancy, Hugh explained that it was "partly because they were women, whose sex was not customary in that place, but primarily because we had nothing certain concerning their life and customs." Although Hugh originally intended to delay his decision until much later, "men of great name and our dearest friends" interceded for the women so persistently, day after day, that Hugh reconsidered.

The list of men who pressed the women's cause included prominent laymen and clergy. William Turbe, bishop of Norwich, commended the way of life of the women in the strongest of terms, "for he had known them as if they were his own disciples": they had received "from his hand the habit of religious and from that reception had lived religiously in his parish." Although these women were known simply as *foeminae*, they clearly wore habits and had already been consecrated to religious life. Jeoffrey, archdeacon of Canterbury and the keeper of the king's seal, interceded on their behalf. William of Camera, sheriff of Norfolk and Suffolk, spoke for the women since "he had known them both under the religious habit and before they had received it," and he had even sustained them with his alms. "And there were many others" who of their own free will interceded for the women, "too many to signify by name" in the charter.

Pressured by these intercessors, Abbot Hugh agreed to the transfer. Andrew and Folcard "standing there still, not only not recanting but pleading with good will that it be done," swore to abjure all their rights in Thetford. Hugh then ceded Thetford, with all its movables and everything in pasture, pannage, arable lands, and rents, "to the often men-

tioned nuns, into the hands of their prioress Cecilia." Hugh added everything the abbey held in the village of Thetford, including two parish
churches and rights in a field.

As in the other transfers, obligations accompanied the benefits. Because Thetford had been "a member" of Bury "up to this day," and since
its loss would be like cutting a limb from the body, Prioress Cecilia swore
"faith and obedience" to Bury "as to the mother of her church." Their
"spiritual father" remained the bishop of Norwich, who had given the
women their habits. As a sign of the relationship between the two monasteries, the nuns agreed to pay the monks four shillings a year; and
Prioress Cecilia offered, "without sorry or fraud," a faithful promise that
"no work nor counsel, either by her or any other person" would scheme
to deprive Bury of what it was owed. This link was made visible in Bury's
weekly grant of supplies to the nuns.[8]

From these remarkably well-documented cases, the circumstances that
led three of England's wealthiest, oldest, and most prestigious Benedictine abbeys to support female daughter houses appear to have been strikingly similar. Eremitic women living an ascetic life in small communities
became known to religious men—Abbot Geoffrey, the hermit Roger, the
canons Andrew and Folcard. Living outside monastic enclosures, the
hermit and two canons were ideally placed to meet such women. For a
variety of motives, including their own desire to be rid of a dilapidated
cell, the men brought these women to the attention of the abbeys with
which they were associated. As a result, the abbeys oversaw the formal
establishment of the hermitages as priories dependent on the parent
house.

Whether the women's lives changed appreciably after these transfers is
hard to discern. Even after the communities became priories, they remained small and poor. If the women had not followed the Benedictine
Rule before, a new regularity was introduced into their schedule. Change
must have been most apparent at Kilburn and Thetford, where a prior
was installed; sometimes called guardian or master, this man assumed
roles the women would have performed otherwise. Their new depen-
dency on powerful abbeys had repercussions for the women. Nuns often
had to consult the abbeys on the election of the prioress, reception of
nuns, appointment of a prior, alienation of property, and expansion of
the priory. In addition, the nuns all made annual payments to the parent
abbeys in acknowledgment of the subjection of their priories. Whatever
effect the transformation had on the day-to-day life of the women, they
were henceforth fully integrated with established forms of monastic life.

RELATIONSHIPS BETWEEN MONASTERIES FOR
MEN AND THOSE FOR WOMEN

St. Albans, Westminster, and Bury St. Edmunds were not the only abbeys
to aid women. By 1160 the abbot of the Augustinians at Darley had "the
care of the virgins whose house he had constructed about a mile from the
canons" at King's Mead Derby. Because of the abbot's role in founding
Derby Priory for women, Walter, bishop of Chester, exempted it from
episcopal obligations and assigned responsibility for the nuns to the abbot. In a confirmation charter, Bishop Walter wrote, "we give to that
abbot [of Darley] freedom to consecrate virgins whose care we commit
to him."[9]

The surviving documents often focus on the subjection of the daughter
house to its parent abbey. Around 1160 William of Waterville, abbot of
Peterborough Abbey, founded St. Michael's Stamford for up to forty
nuns "living regularly in religion and piety." The nuns owed Peterborough one half mark of silver annually for their convent (*coenobium*) and
another ten *solidos* for their church.[10] According to other charters, the
abbot and chapter of Peterborough supervised the appointment of the
prior, who was responsible for the material possessions of Stamford. The
monks also had to be consulted and give their permission before the
ordination (*ordinatio*) of the prioress and the reception of nuns. "Indeed
these nuns and the arrangement of all their affairs in every mode are at
the pleasure of the lord abbot and chapter, so that the monastery of
[Peterborough] will not suffer the detriment of anything on account of
the increase of [Stamford]." When Abbot William granted the women of
Stamford two other churches, these were also held in return for an annual payment to Peterborough Abbey.[11]

The ties between a monastery for women and its parent abbey were
similar whether it was hermits, canons, or monks who had facilitated the
foundation. The women were given possession of residential buildings
and a church, and additional revenue came from rents, tithes, other
churches, or direct subsidies of food. Only Peterborough Abbey envisioned a large dependent daughter when it prepared Stamford for forty
nuns. The other priories were small houses for just a few women.

Whether the communities were large or small, positions of leadership
were clearly defined. In addition to a prioress, most houses also had a
prior who had responsibility for the church and its possessions and who
sometimes supervised the entire priory. Like Stamford, each daughter
house was subject to its parent monastery, which typically was consulted

on the selection of the prior, the election of the prioress, the reception of
nuns, or the acquisition and alienation of property. Women who received
the aid of a neighboring monastery traded independence for material
benefits and protection.

If this subjection was onerous to the women, the sources give no hint
of it. On the contrary, when a zealous clerical friend of the women of
Stamford tried to increase their independence, the women complained.
In a letter to Richard, the archbishop of Canterbury, the nuns of Stamford repudiated certain privileges their clerical friend had obtained for
them in Rome. The nuns had sent the cleric to gain a general confirmation of their possessions; but "beyond commandment and conscience,
nay against the common will of our chapter," the prioress of Stamford
wrote, this cleric had secured for the nuns the free election of their
prioress. Calling this new privilege "pernicious and hurtful," the prioress
complained that it was contrary to the intentions of their founders and
that "the abbot and convent of [Peterborough] have conceived a rancor
against us and indignation, deservedly."

The nuns of Stamford had further "incurred the indignation of our
lords the abbot and convent" for failing to mention that they owed
Peterborough an annual fee for two churches. "Desiring therefore . . . in
humility and all kind of satisfaction, fully to reconcile the grace and
favor of our lords and founders to us," the nuns of Stamford asked the
archbishop to remove from their privileges all the sources of discord.
"Restore the fullness of the former love and favor of our lords; because,
without them, we are not able to live; without their suffrages our church
is not able to stand, nor the order there instituted to be observed."[12]

The plea of the prioress of Stamford for the restoration of Peterborough's support is an eloquent testimony that the nuns believed they
benefited from their relationships with a parent monastery. The women
welcomed the men's aid even though it resulted in their subjection to a
parent abbey. This English material suggests that women were eager to
trade independence for support, despite some modern assumptions that
such bargains were onerous. And certainly this material challenges the
thesis that male orders were reluctant to supervise religious women.[13]
The abbots of St. Albans, Westminster, Bury St. Edmunds, Darley, and
Peterborough decided to found monasteries for women and to retain
responsibility for their daughter houses. St. Paul's, London, also assumed
control over Christina's priory at Markyate. The monks and canons of
these abbeys not only agreed to this ongoing relationship; some of them
moved to the daughter houses to serve as priors.

In addition to the monks and canons who founded priories for nuns, some religious men accepted women into their own monasteries and then made them their heirs. The first known occurrence of this practice was at Blithbury Priory. Early in the twelfth century, a layman, Hugh de Ridware, gave a site on a river to the monks Saxe and Guthmund to form a religious community. Sometime before 1148, Bishop Roger Clinton confirmed the monks' possession of Blithbury. But in another, presumably later, charter, Hugh de Ridware gave the same site to a different group: "to the monks Guthmund and Saxe and to the nuns dwelling there." After this, only nuns are referred to in the records of Blithbury; monks are not mentioned again.[14]

Similarly, around 1150 Roger de Scales and his wife Muriel gave Blackborough Priory to "the brothers there serving God." When their son William received the religious habit at Blackborough, Roger and Muriel added more land for "the brothers." Sometime later Roger's son Robert confirmed his parents' grants and added gifts of his own—but to a different set of recipients. In one charter Robert donated "to the sisters present and the brothers serving God there," in another "to Hamon Wauter and Matilda his mother and all." This reference to both men and women at Blackborough Priory cannot be a simple scribal error, for in both charters the quoted phrase occurs twice. In a presumably later charter, Robert made a grant to "the sisters." Later records mention only nuns or sisters at Blackborough Priory.[15]

Farewell Abbey also began as a monastery for men. Sometime before 1140, Bishop Roger Clinton gave to "the church of St. Mary of Farewell and the canons and lay brothers there serving God the place in which the church is situated, the land which they have assarted, and as much land as they are able to assart." But in the next charter, from around 1140, women were considered the owners of Farewell Abbey: Bishop Roger gave the very same site "to the nuns and women devoted to God at the church of St. Mary of Farewell." The phrasing implies that not all the women "devoted to God" were nuns. For their support, Bishop Roger added a mill, woods, pannage, more land, and six serfs (*coloni*).[16] Originally founded for men, Farewell Abbey was the only female monastery with its own daughter house, Langley Priory.[17]

Blithbury, Blackborough, and Farewell priories show that entire monasteries could be transferred from one sex to another, much like the hermitages of Markyate and Kilburn had been. At Haliwell, women received a portion of a canon's prebend in order to found their priory. Between 1133 and 1150, Robert fitz Gelran, a canon of St. Paul's, Lon-

don, who held a prebend at Haliwell, gave to women the church of St.
John the Baptist there, with three acres of "moor where the spring Hali-
well" originated. Walter the precentor, one of the canons who succeeded
Robert in the prebend, doubled the plot.[18] Within two decades, Haliwell
Priory had attracted "twenty sisters [sorores] veiled and consecrated to
God" who offered continual praises and were "regularly obedient" to
the Lord.

Since it had been founded on a portion of a prebend, Haliwell Priory
was poor. In the mid 1160s, the financial situation became intolerable
when the women were threatened with the loss of the temporalities of
the church of Dunton. Gilbert Foliot, bishop of London, pleaded the
sisters' case. Even though Haliwell had "rightly gained fame," the bishop
pointed out that the place was "narrow and meager" in resources. Without revenue from the church of Dunton, the twenty sisters would not
even have enough food and clothing. The bishop never mentioned any
ongoing relationship between the women of Haliwell and the canons of
St. Paul's, London; it does not seem that the community of St. Paul's
assumed any obligations for the priory established on a former canon's
prebend. Despite the poverty of Haliwell, Bishop Gilbert claimed that the
women were so devoted to the place that they would resolutely remain
there "until death."[19]

Because there was no standard, authorized way for women to acquire
monasteries from male religious, the conveyance took varied forms.
Women, sometimes living as hermitesses, often already in religious habits, moved in with celibate men or accepted monasteries from them.
Despite the variety, some patterns repeatedly appeared. In many ways,
the men determined the form of the continued relationship. Hermits had
one view of what their ties with women should be like; monks in powerful abbeys had other opinions. When women settled with hermits, they
often remained in informal, spiritual friendships for years. When women
acquired monasteries from wealthy abbeys, their priories became dependent daughter houses, under the abbeys' supervision and jurisdiction.
Still another variant was at Blithbury, Blackborough, Farewell, and Haliwell priories, where nuns, sisters, and other women devoted to God
inherited sites from monks, hermits, canons, and lay brothers. If men
determined the type of ongoing bond, the women were adaptive and
innovative partners, able to profit from the offered relationships.

MONASTERIES FOR WOMEN AND MEN

The religious women who accepted the aid of religious men often lived with them as well. As we have seen, the hermitesses were not the only religious women to dwell with men, for several priories included both sexes at an early stage in their history. Other priories had a prior as well as a prioress officially responsible for its well-being. Despite all the interconnections between female daughter houses and their parent abbeys, scholars have considered these priories to be single-sex houses, for women alone. Only monasteries with large contingents of women and men have been labeled "double monasteries."

Four priories in the South, however, have fit the typical, modern definition of a double monastery: a religious house for both men and women where the two sexes dwell in separate but contiguous quarters. As double monasteries, these four houses—Harrold, Chicksands, Westwood, and Nuneaton priories—have been considered anomalous, distinctive from the other monasteries of the South. But they can better be understood on a continuum with the priories already described. In the twelfth century, these four priories were not considered unique, nor were they called double monasteries. Since these houses or their orders began when women received support from religious men, even in their origins these four priories are similar to the other monasteries already examined.[20]

In its early phase, Harrold Priory, in the Order of Arrouaise, was a house for nuns under a prior. Sometime between 1136 and 1138, Sampson le Fort, a wealthy landowner in Bedfordshire, donated some land and the churches of Harrold and Brayfield to Abbot Gervase of the Abbey of Arrouaise in France. Sampson's gift fulfilled the wishes of his kinsman, Hilbert Pelice, one of the first canons of the Order of Arrouaise, for it allowed Arrouaise to establish its first English house.[21]

Nuns were not the focus of the Order of Arrouaise, a newly reformed congregation of Augustinian canons. Nuns were not even included in the Abbey of Arrouaise itself; lay sisters and lay brothers were there, but their purpose there was to aid the canons. In contrast, Arrouaise's first English colony at Harrold Priory was principally for nuns. The foundation grant of 1136–38 says that Sampson gave the site of Harrold to Abbot Gervase "for the sustenance of his sisters the nuns." A confirmation charter mentioned nuns "and those serving God with them." According to an inquest conducted in the 1170s, "his sisters the nuns" were in fact biological sisters of Gervase. These women and a lay brother came from France to begin Harrold Priory, which was placed under the supervision of Canon Hilbert Pelice, the instigator of the project.[22]

Harrold Priory shared many characteristics with the other priories that religious men founded for women. As in other cases, Harrold was created to support women well-known to its originators. In Harrold's early years, personal ties connected the nuns with the men who served them as priors. Hilbert Pelice, the canon who originally wanted an English house, not only agreed to the introduction of the nuns; he even returned from France to serve as Harrold's first prior. A later prior was a biological brother of Gervase of Arrouaise and therefore also a brother of the nuns. Like the other priors discussed thus far, the prior of Harrold was charged with keeping "watch over" the church. Like other parent abbeys, Arrouaise Abbey retained control of its daughter house; the canons of Arrouaise installed the priors and "made arrangements according to their will regarding both the nuns and the things [res] of the church."[23]

The main distinguishing characteristic of Harrold in its early days was that it also included lay brothers, men responsible for "guarding" the nuns there "according to the institutions of the church of St. Nicholas of Arrouaise." The number of men at Harrold Priory increased during the middle part of the century. Between 1150 and 1165, gift formulae refer to a prior, canons, brothers, a prioress, and nuns. Precisely how many men ever were at Harrold is unknown. The increase of men could have been quite small, for with a prior and a brother in the beginning, the addition of just two canons and one other brother would match the gift formulae of 1150–65.[24]

The other three priories in the South that have been labeled double monasteries were in orders that developed their institutional forms outside the region. Hence, in contrast with Harrold, these Southern examples cannot fully reveal the processes that led to their internal arrangements.

Chicksands Priory was earliest, the creation of Countess Roaise, widow of Earl Geoffrey de Mandeville of Essex and wife of the baron of Bedford, Payn de Beauchamp. When in 1150 Countess Roaise decided to endow a monastery, she chose "the nuns serving God under the custody of Gilbert of Sempringham in the church of St. Mary of Chicksands." Her gift was exceptionally generous, one of the largest provided in the entire century. The monastery itself centered around the church of Chicksands. To provide additional residences and income, Countess Roaise granted several dwellings, a demesne plantation, a mill, a second church, a woods, a grange with forty acres, and all the land held by three of her men (which totaled some four and a half virgates plus another sixty acres). To help the nuns maintain their buildings, Roaise even provided the services of a carpenter.[25]

When the countess began Chicksands Priory, her gift was to the nuns under Gilbert of Sempringham's care. (For more on Gilbert, see Chapters 5–7.) Hence, in the mid-twelfth century, Chicksands looked like many other monasteries: it was founded for religious women who were supervised by a male religious. Although, in this case, the man—Gilbert of Sempringham—was not in permanent residence, he was responsible for the nuns nonetheless. At this early date, only a lay brother appears to have aided Gilbert at Chicksands Priory. Later in the century, by 1169/79, Gilbertine canons had been added at Chicksands and they assumed there the same role they had in the other Gilbertine houses, a topic discussed in Chapter 5. The canons may have been added around 1166 when Roaise's son increased Chicksands's endowment with three churches and some chapels. By the century's end, Chicksands Priory was one of the wealthiest Gilbertine houses, able to support 120 women and 60 men. But at its origins, Chicksands resembled other priories in the South.[26]

Families of the highest social standing also founded two priories of the Order of Fontevrault, Nuneaton, and Westwood. About five years after Countess Roaise founded Chicksands, Robert, earl of Leicester, gave twenty-five *librates* of land to Fontevrault so that it would found an English daughter house. The original site at Kintbury was soon exchanged for land in Eaton in Warwickshire, where Nuneaton Priory was constructed. The earl's family remained loyal to his foundation: his wife Amice joined and his daughter Hawise lived there temporarily. Nuneaton was also supported by Earl Robert's son-in-law, Gervase of Paynel, who added a mill to its possessions.[27]

At about the same time, around 1155, the prominent de Say family, not earls themselves but frequently the spouses and heirs of earls, gave land in Westwood in Worcester to "bring together a convent of the nuns of the church of Fontevrault." The endowment of Westwood Priory was generous, including land for the priory, the church of Cotheridge with its appurtenances, land for assarting and for making a park, a salt pit, and other land. The de Says were the third family of wealth and influence to introduce in the South a priory in an order where religious men were responsible for the care of religious women.[28]

By the time Westwood and Nuneaton priories were founded, the Order of Fontevrault was influential and well-respected. In its origin, Fontevrault Abbey was like the English priories examined thus far, in that a religious man began it for women (and men) he knew who were seeking a religious life. Founded around 1100, Fontevrault Abbey was the creation of Robert of Arbrissel, then around forty years old. Earlier in his life, in the last years of the eleventh century, Robert had been a hermit in Angers, a contemporary there of Eve from Wilton Abbey. Eventually, with the encouragement of Pope Urban II and many admirers, Robert became a successful itinerant preacher. Having attracted many followers of both sexes, Robert organized them into a community and provided them with Fontevrault Abbey in what was then a deserted place on the borders of Anjou, Poitou, and Touraine. According to his biography, written around 1117, Robert believed that "women should live with men," but he sought a desert place where they could live together "scrupulously, without scandal."[29]

For the remaining fifteen years of his life, Robert did not remain at Fontevrault. Instead, he continued to preach throughout western and southwestern France. Whether Robert retained authority at Fontevrault is debated, for he left one of the women, Hersende, in charge as prioress when he resumed his travels. According to a second biography of Robert, written shortly before 1120, Robert gave the Order of Fontevrault its permanent form a few months before his death in 1117. Fontevrault was to be a community of men and women under the rule of an abbess. The women, bound by the Benedictine Rule, were to devote themselves to psalmody and contemplation. The men promised to obey "the handmaids [*ancillae*] of Christ" and to assume responsibility for physical and spiritual labors.[30]

When he founded Fontevrault Abbey, Robert of Arbrissel was concerned for his female (and male) followers, much like the religious men in southern England who began priories for women. At Fontevrault Abbey itself, a large contingent of men served the nuns. In a recent examination of the surviving charters of Fontevrault, Penny Gold identified seventy-nine different monks during the period 1100–1149. But in the other houses of the order, the male population may have been much smaller. Certainly in France this seems to have been the case, and in England there is no evidence that the numbers of men were ever very large. Gift formulae reveal that contemporaries regarded Nuneaton and Westwood as primarily houses for women. The most common gift formula was to "the nuns"; less frequently gifts were to "the church" of Eaton or Westwood "and to the nuns there of the Order of Fontevrault." If only a few men were included in the communities, Nuneaton and

Westwood were even more similar to the priories male religious founded for women.[31]

In their internal arrangements, the priories of Nuneaton and Westwood were clearly distinctive in only one way: the prioress held authority over the entire monastery, and the prior was subservient to her. At Fontevrault, Robert appointed an abbess as the superior of the entire community; he even chose a formerly married woman to be the first abbess since he felt that she had the practical, worldly knowledge needed to oversee a large monastery. Other monasteries in the order duplicated the arrangement at Fontevrault, except that their female heads were simply prioresses, since all the monasteries in the order came under the authority of the abbess of Fontevrault herself. The prioress shared responsibilities with a prior, but she was in charge.[32]

With their female heads, Nuneaton and Westwood reveal another type of cooperation between religious men and women—a distinction that came from the French origin of the order. But in most respects they resembled the other priories already discussed in this chapter, and thus they fit nicely into the English environment. At Nuneaton and Westwood, the local officials were the prioress and prior, as at many other monasteries. Like the other monasteries that included men and women, nuns were the larger group. The ordained men at Westwood and Nuneaton acted as priors, provided sacramental services for the nuns, and served as priests for the churches donated to the priories so that the nuns could receive the churches' revenues.[33]

Harrold, Chicksands, Nuneaton, and Westwood priories reveal the same harmonious relationships between celibates of opposite sexes as was seen at Markyate, Sopwell, Kilburn, Thetford, Stamford, Derby, Blithbury, Blackborough, Farewell, and Haliwell priories. Although somewhat larger contingents of men joined the women in these four priories, the differences were those of degree, not of kind. These four priories were distinctive because they were part of federated orders, not because they included men as well as women. To label only these four priories double monasteries belies their fundamental similarity to other monasteries in the region.

Considered collectively, these fourteen priories of the South show that women seeking religious life were actively supported by religious men. Aid took whatever form the men considered best. Monks and canons encouraged women to accept the regulation of a rule. They then included the women in their own monasteries or founded dependent priories for them. Some men devised new religious orders to guarantee that women and men would continue to associate for mutual benefit. Whereas men bound by rules expected women to adopt their way of life, hermits were content to live near hermitesses. For women, the corollary of support was conformity with the men's expectations. Nonetheless, the result of cooperation was an unparalleled expansion of female monasticism and the creation of innovative religious ways of life.

CHAPTER 4

Lay Foundations in the South

Although holy women needed the aid of hermits, monks, and canons, religious men were not the only supporters of female monasticism in the middle of the twelfth century. For the first time since the conquest, large numbers of lay people donated property and money to help women desiring a religious life. In addition to the highest-ranking families of the realm who introduced priories in the federated orders of Arrouaise, Fontevrault, and the Gilbertines, women and men from virtually all levels of society invested in the burgeoning female religious movement.

Statistics reveal the great change in lay involvement. In the first sixty-five years after the conquest, lay people founded only three monasteries for women. Increased interest in female monasticism is first visible in the last years of King Henry I's reign, when lay people started four priories for women. Then a flood of new investment began. The laity established seven priories between 1135 and 1148, another six between 1148 and 1154, and eight more by 1165. They created a total of twenty-five new monasteries for women in one generation, at the rate of almost one a year. These twenty-five priories were in addition to the four in federated orders examined in the last chapter—Harrold, Chicksands, Nuneaton, and Westwood. A transformation was taking place.

Since most of this expansion was during the years of King Stephen's reign, in what is sometimes called a period of anarchy, the political situation may have had a role in the increased participation of lay people. Certainly, the lack of strong royal control permitted women and men to experiment and to devise new institutional forms. The competition for leadership may have encouraged men to found monasteries to further their prestige and indicate their power.

Precisely what other effects a weak monarchy had is hard to determine. As this chapter will argue, the support of female monasticism did not correspond to party lines, nor did it appeal more to one class than another. Both sides in the contest between King Stephen and Empress Matilda invested in priories for women. One of Stephen's most devoted allies, Earl Simon of Northampton, began one priory, and one of Stephen's most ardent foes, Earl Ranulf of Chester, founded another. In addition to barons, large numbers of women and men of far less social standing began new houses. As the evidence will illustrate, the appeal cut across economic and political lines.

In order to characterize this transformation, we will consider two monasteries—Godstow Abbey and Clerkenwell Priory—in some detail. Because these two houses are the best documented, their records permit an in-depth description of the complex network of support that created the upsurge in female foundations. The histories of these two monasteries can then be compared with the surviving evidence for the other twenty-three houses in order to suggest how and why lay people aided holy women.

GODSTOW ABBEY

One of the first new lay foundations was Godstow Abbey, the ruins of which are still visible in the fields near Oxford. Begun in the last years of Henry I's reign, Godstow was consecrated in 1138–39 at a lavish event that was extensively documented in the register of the abbey. Numerous donors were present, bringing a wide assortment of gifts.[1]

Godstow's conception was attributed solely to Edith, the widow of a knight from Winchester and the mother of a son and two daughters. According to a fifteenth-century cartulary of the abbey, Edith, "a lady bore of the worthyest blood of thyse reme," had a vision in 1133. In this vision, she was instructed to go to Oxford and remain there until she received a token from God "how and what wyse she shold byeld a place to godes seruise." After beginning a holy life near Oxford, at Binsey, Edith heard a voice one night telling her to go where the light of heaven "a-lyhtyth to the erthe" and there build a convent for twenty-four "of the moost gentylwomen that ye can fynde." Locating the spot, an island in the Thames, Edith obtained King Henry I's approval for her project and convinced the owner of the site, John of St. John, to grant her the land. Since the first surviving record of Edith's vision was written three hundred years later, it is impossible to know whether Edith felt she was strictly following supernatural communications. But all the evidence indicates that Godstow Abbey was her idea.[2]

At the consecration of the new abbey in 1138–39, Bishop Alexander of Lincoln praised God for making "illustrious [the church] of our times with a new light of holy religion." Since Bishop Alexander had already heard Christina of Markyate's vow to virginity, and since he had already consecrated Harrold Priory, he was well-informed about the "new churches being founded so that every one may bless and praise God in every place in His dominion." Alexander considered Godstow Abbey a sign of the "wondrous operation" of God, where "holy women" in the religious habit lived "under the care and rule of the remarkable matron devoted to God, Edith, who has built the church of this place by her own expense and labor and by collecting alms of the faithful."

If angels rejoice over the saving of one sinner, Alexander reasoned, how much more they must rejoice over the innumerable handmaids of Christ who live the penitential life, who have all their desire for God, who dwell on earth although by their way of life they are in heaven. He continued with his assessment of their ascetic abilities: "These [women] in the flesh, living beyond the flesh, have devoted themselves eternally to their spouse Christ, and crucifying carnal desires in themselves, they either do not know through experience the vices of the flesh, or they have conquered them by resistance."[3]

Edith's project drew the support of many church leaders. In addition to consecrating the abbey, Bishop Alexander promised one hundred shillings from the tolls owed him by the merchants of Banbury Market. Theobald, archbishop of Canterbury, was present at the consecration and gave a hundred shillings. Other bishops who came were Roger, bishop of Exeter, who gave forty shillings of income from two churches, and Roger, bishop of Salisbury, who donated a mill with some land. Walter, archdeacon of nearby Oxford, granted the tithe of his lordship of Cudesland. Monks also attended. The abbot of Westminster gave sixty shillings to Godstow, as did the abbot of Abingdon. Since the abbot of Westminster founded Kilburn Priory for women a year later, he may have been inspired by the enthusiasm for Godstow Abbey.[4]

An impressive group of secular magnates added their aid to this new enterprise. Giving their approval to the project begun under King Henry I, the new royal family came to the consecration. King Stephen gave land worth a hundred shillings and permission to have a fair on the feast of St. John the Baptist, the patron saint of Godstow. Queen Matilda and their son Eustace gave gifts as well. Robert, earl of Leicester, and his wife Amice gave grants worth sixty shillings. Witnessing these events at Godstow may have had an impact on these secular magnates. King Stephen soon established two new monasteries for women, at Higham and Norwich; and a few years later Earl Robert and his wife Amice gave the land to Fontevrault for Nuneaton Priory.[5]

Many people of less standing gave smaller gifts. Miles, constable of

Gloucester, offered twenty shillings. Half a meadow and a bushel of wheat a year came from one man; another gave part of a meadow, while his son added five shillings' worth of land. The citizens and burghers of Oxford gave some land. John of St. John, lord of Wolvercote and Stanton and owner of the place where Godstow Abbey was constructed, gave generously. He provided not only the site but also a parcel of land in front of the church, the second half of a meadow, a mill, and the messuages of two men.[6]

In return for his gifts, John of St. John retained the right of patronage at Godstow Abbey.[7] Other donors sought prayers. And four fathers expected Godstow Abbey to receive their daughters as nuns. One man gave nine shillings in rent "along with" his daughter. Another gave a yardland plus ten acres with his daughter. Two sisters entered when their father gave half a church. Although these women were called "gentlewomen" and came from families of some means, none of them represented the highest ranks of society.[8]

Granted control of the material and spiritual possessions of the monastery, the abbess had extensive rights and responsibilities. With the assent of the archdeacon of Oxford, Bishop Alexander of Lincoln exempted Godstow Abbey from most diocesan obligations; he promised free hallowing of holy oil; he excused the nuns from hospitality obligations; and he assured them that they could freely elect their own abbess. All the power of oversight was thus entrusted to Edith. She was succeeded by her daughter, also named Edith; between them, they held the position of abbess for fifty-one years.[9]

Particularly impressive was the abbess's authority over her chaplains. The abbess herself could select the four or more chaplains needed to serve the abbey. The abbess alone decided whether her chaplains should attend synods and chapters; they were not required to answer to the archdeacon or any other minister. She could correct or dismiss the chaplains without recourse to a diocesan court if she called in a neighborhood priest to hear the complaints. At least by the latter part of the twelfth century, the abbess could also install chaplains of her own choosing in the six or more churches that belonged to Godstow, but these priests were responsible to the bishop for "spiritualities." Some of the chaplains the abbess selected remained at Godstow Abbey for many years, like a certain Walter listed as a witness to charters for at least fifteen years.[10]

By the end of the century, Godstow's possessions included at least six churches and shares in six others. In addition to the income from this ecclesiastical property, Godstow relied primarily on rents and feudal dues. The abbey's possessions included seven mills and tithes from another, a manor with full manorial rights, rents of specified amounts from more than a dozen places, five dwellings, a shop in London, several meadows, numerous plots of land, and a salt pit. The abbess and her hired chaplains and servants could manage such established forms of revenue, which could often be readily collected in absentia. As well as revenue-producing property, the abbey received a few gifts like wood to dry the nuns' herring and the site for a reservoir.[11]

Some of these grants came "along with" women. When women joined the abbey, members of their families, usually their fathers, often made donations to the house. Bringing gifts—usually of revenue-producing land—along with them into the community, the nuns steadily increased their endowment. However, none of the women were accompanied by lavish gifts. A tract of thirty-four acres was the largest entrance donation recorded. Often other members of the family joined women already at Godstow. For instance, three daughters and two granddaughters of Robert, lord of Wytham, were at Godstow; each of them brought gifts of pastureland to the abbey. Although Godstow attracted many daughters or spouses of local lords, no one of baronial status is known to have joined.[12]

Unrivaled within the monastery, Edith exemplified the strong abbess of the mid-twelfth century. On her own, Edith had decided to found the abbey. She had gained royal approval, acquired the site, raised the necessary funds, and received episcopal confirmation. Taking the initiative from the start, Edith became a nun, and as abbess continued to oversee Godstow's spiritual and material operations, even having jurisdiction over the chaplains. Like the monks, canons, and hermits who preferred personally to oversee the monasteries they helped to begin, women could exercise a similar control if the foundress herself, like Edith, undertook religious life.

CLERKENWELL PRIORY, LONDON

Abbess Edith dominated Godstow Abbey, but abbesses and prioresses did not always have such control. When men were the primary agents in the creation of a monastery for women, the female heads of the community rarely ruled as fully as Edith at Godstow. An example of a house with a different distribution of power is Clerkenwell Priory, begun in the early 1140s in a suburb of London. One man decided to establish a

monastery at Clerkenwell, another planned it, and still others faithfully
served it for years.[13]

Clerkenwell Priory was the idea of the layman Jordan de Breiset,
founder of the nearby Knights Hospitaller House of St. John of Jerusalem. However, "chaplain Robert" made the decision to support women
instead of men at Clerkenwell. Jordan de Breiset gave chaplain Robert
fourteen acres "to build a house of prayer and place there an observance
[*religio*] which will be pleasing for the service and supplication of God."
Jordan suggested introducing "grey monks or nuns." Robert chose nuns,
a decision Jordan approved. For their initial endowment, the nuns of
Clerkenwell received ten of the fourteen acres Jordan had given Robert, which they were to hold from Robert as freely as he held it from
Jordan.[14]

The rule of life adopted by the women of Clerkenwell Priory is not
definitely known. Repeatedly called nuns in the charters and referred to
as Benedictines in a papal bull from 1186, they probably followed the
Benedictine Rule. However, according to Hassall, the editor of Clerkenwell's cartulary, Clerkenwell and Haliwell priories seem "to have been
really Augustinian, although in several documents they are distinctly
called Benedictine." Hassall concluded, "The truth seems to be that the
importance attached to the name of the order, in this and other houses of
women, was less than has been generally assumed."[15]

Hassall is correct that in many cases we do not know what rule of life
women followed in their monasteries. Often the first mention of the
order of a monastery for women is at the dissolution under King Henry
VIII, by which time the women may no longer have had the same affiliation as they had in the twelfth century. Even when a monastery's order is
documented earlier, sometimes there is conflicting evidence, as at Haliwell and Clerkenwell priories, which are called both Benedictine and
Augustinian in the records.

Although Hassall accurately defined the problem, his explanation—
that for women the name of the order had less importance than has been
assumed—may not be sufficient. Why would women find their order
insignificant when it shaped their daily routine and gave them a sense of
identity? Another explanation is that the identity of the religious men
connected with the monasteries was sometimes recorded instead of the
order of the women, or that the women adopted some of the customs of
the orders of their male supporters. Thus, the seemingly contradictory
references to Haliwell and Clerkenwell as Augustinian and as Benedictine may reflect two identities. Quite possibly, the women of Clerken-

well and Haliwell were Benedictines, like the vast majority of all women
in monasteries in the South founded before 1165. Yet they also may
have accepted Augustinian customs because Augustinian canons played
a prominent role in their foundation and operation. If so, they were like
the religious women described in the last chapter who adopted the way
of life of their male religious supporters.

Even after the foundation, chaplains had considerable importance
in the organization of Clerkenwell Priory. Far more frequently than at
Godstow Abbey, chaplains witnessed charters, and the same chaplains
repeatedly appeared. The chaplain Robert who decided that nuns should
be given Clerkenwell in the first place may be the same "Robert chaplain" who witnessed five charters from before 1182. Most frequently
named among the other chaplains were two Richards, who witnessed
thirty-six charters between 1152 and 1220; Arnold, who witnessed
twenty between 1185 and 1198; and Radulf, listed on twenty-one charters between 1185 and 1222. In addition to a half-dozen chaplains associated with Clerkenwell for years, there was a larger group of chaplains
who were named less frequently: Walter, Gilbert, William, Hugo, Roger,
Joseph, and more than a dozen other men. Although these men were
called chaplains, since no mention was made of their order, they could
have been Augustinians or secular clergy.[16]

Although the chaplains often witnessed charters, they did not have the
extensive powers of the guardians or custodians described in the last
chapter. The chaplains were witnesses to transactions, but their assent
was not necessary in the acquisition or alienation of property. The prioress herself oversaw the financial activities of Clerkenwell.[17] Yet the chaplains should not be considered mere hirelings. An example of the permanent relationship they could enter with the priory is the agreement made
between chaplain Richard and the nuns. Chaplain Richard, identified in
one charter as "the priest of Willingale," gave all his possessions to the
nuns with the promise that he would serve their church all his life.[18]

A number of "brothers" also associated with Clerkenwell. When a
certain William gave a stone house to the nuns, sometime between 1193
and 1212, he explained that they had admitted him as a brother of the
convent and that after his death he would receive the services typically
given to a brother of the house.[19] A dozen "brothers" of the nuns are
mentioned in the witness lists of charters.[20] Although not as powerful
as custodians or guardians, the chaplains and brothers associated with
Clerkenwell were crucial for its origin and continued existence.

Although male religious served Clerkenwell, the nuns depended primarily on laity for financial support. Two bishops of London, in whose diocese Clerkenwell was located, granted the nuns a chapel, a church, and some land.[21] But most gifts were from lay people. Jordan de Breiset's family continually increased Clerkenwell's endowment. Particularly helpful were the grants of adjoining properties—such as the valley next to the monastery with an old fish pond and garden, and another ten acres in the field where Clerkenwell was built. Jordan's kinsmen also gave another garden, a meadow, other land, and a park suitable for a garden. Jordan's wife Muriel even made donations after she remarried, increasing Clerkenwell's endowment with land, two churches, and two men with their tenements. Muriel's daughter and granddaughter became nuns at Clerkenwell, a further sign of continuing familial loyalty. Provisions were also made for a second daughter to join later in her life if she wished.[22]

Clerkenwell attracted women both from nearby London and areas farther away such as Cambridgeshire, Essex, and Dorset. As entrance donations, Clerkenwell received land, rents, a church, woods, a marsh, and annual payments from the families of some twenty women known to have joined in the twelfth century. Several of the nuns were related: an aunt joined with her niece, another aunt with two of her nieces. Although modest grants were added by King Stephen, King Henry II, King David of Scotland, and the earls of Essex and Chester, women from such illustrious families apparently did not join Clerkenwell. The nuns mostly had Norman names—Rose, Aubrey, Margaret, Avice, Alice, Beatrice, and Juliana—an indication that they were from the new landed families prospering in the region.[23]

Like Godstow Abbey, Clerkenwell was conceived by a layperson, but in contrast to Godstow, Clerkenwell never came under his family's control. Even when kinswomen of the founder eventually joined, they did not assume a leadership position comparable to that of Abbess Edith and her daughter at Godstow. In part the difference reflected the larger number of families involved in Clerkenwell from its inception. Also, it was many years before any of the founder's kinswomen became nuns there. No women at Clerkenwell had the natural claim to leadership that Edith had at Godstow. But another major distinction was the active involvement of male religious, from chaplain Robert who chose to introduce nuns at Clerkenwell to the numerous chaplains and brothers affiliated with the house throughout the twelfth century. Another type of lay foundation is represented at Clerkenwell, one closer to the monasteries that male religious founded, one in which the prioress cooperated closely with religious men.

PRIORIES JOINED BY THE FOUNDRESS OR FOUNDER'S KIN

Often it has been assumed that familial bonds motivated the laymen who founded monasteries for women. Men are thought to have begun priories so that their female kin would have a suitable living. But, in fact, only rarely did the foundress or female kin of the founder join the new monasteries. Of the twenty-nine lay foundations in the South begun between 1130 and 1165, the foundress or female relatives of the founder are known to have joined only six—Nuneaton, Godstow, Clerkenwell, Higham, Wroxall, and Littlemore. The knightly class was most concerned about providing for its kinswomen. Edith, foundress of Godstow, was the widow of a knight.[24] Knights were responsible for the foundation of Wroxall and Littlemore priories. Higham was the only house with royal founders.

Between 1148 and 1152, King Stephen and his wife Matilda helped establish Higham Priory for their daughter Mary and her companions, some nuns from St. Sulpice, Brittany. Sometime earlier, Mary and her companion nuns had entered Stratford at Bow, the monastery a bishop of London had begun early in the century. The royal lady with her foreign nuns had been a disruptive presence at Stratford. "On account of the difficulty of order and a dissonance of custom which they were not able to bear," Mary and her companions were released from Stratford. The nuns of Stratford returned to Mary the manor of Lillechurch that she had given them, and Mary converted it into a priory, called Higham or sometimes Lillechurch, which she governed for a number of years. Stephen and Matilda, who had originally given Mary the manor of Lillechurch, approved her decision to begin a new priory there and granted her a few additional possessions.[25] The abbot of Colchester added to her endowment the church of Higham, in whose parish the priory was located and after which it was often called. Although Stephen and Matilda have traditionally been considered Higham's founders, clearly Mary herself had major responsibility for the new monastery.[26]

Hugh, the lord of Hatton and Wroxall, a knight who had served in the Holy Land under the Earl of Warwick, founded Wroxall Priory. Accord-

ing to a fifteenth-century document, Hugh had been imprisoned in the
Holy Land for seven years when he had a vision of St. Leonard, the
patron saint of a church on Hugh's property in England. St. Leonard
instructed Hugh to "found at his chirche a place of nunnes of Saint
Benets order." St. Leonard then disappeared, but shortly thereafter Hugh
was miraculously transported still in chains to his own land. There shepherds found him and took him to his wife, who recognized him. Supposedly in response to these astonishing events, Hugh built the requested
monastery sometime before 1135. Hugh decided to bring a nun from
Wilton Abbey to instruct the women he gathered at Wroxall Priory, evidence of Wilton Abbey's continued reputation. Sometime later, Hugh's
wife and two daughters became nuns at Wroxall.[27]

Only three monasteries for women in the entire twelfth century were
said to have been built in response to visions, and the tradition at
Wroxall was the most fantastic.[28] While Edith began Godstow after supposedly seeing lights and hearing voices, the knight Hugh's mysterious
journey is a claim so unlikely that it raises serious questions about the
entire story of Wroxall's origin. Since the first records of the vision narra-
tives for both Wroxall and Godstow are in the fifteenth-century car-
tularies of these monasteries, later periods may have amplified twelfth-
century traditions. On the other hand, even if the visions were elaborated
later, it is a striking coincidence that two of the earliest lay foundations
were traced to direct divine inspiration. Perhaps in those early years,
wondrous signs were one explanation given for the increased lay activity.

Although the foundress and her daughters joined Godstow Abbey and
the founder's kinswomen entered Wroxall Priory, both foundations were
ascribed to visions, not to a desire to provide a home for female relatives.
Littlemore Priory, the other monastery joined by its founder's kin, provides little additional information on the motives for such foundations.
The only surviving evidence reveals that sometime before 1154 Robert
de Sandford, a knight of the abbot of Abingdon, gave some land and a
church to create Littlemore Priory, where a few years later a charter
listed his young daughter among the nuns.[29] Therefore, according to the
existing documents, only King Stephen created a monastery explicitly to
provide for a female relative, and she already had been living as a nun
and was the prime mover behind the new foundation. Even in the cases
where members of the founder's family joined, the twelfth-century evidence does not confirm the typical assumption that lay founders were
acting in order to aid their own kin.

OTHER BENEDICTINE PRIORIES WITH LAY FOUNDERS

During the Anglo-Saxon period, kings and queens founded all the monasteries for women. The contrast with the twelfth-century expansion could not have been greater, for the royal family was responsible for only a tiny percentage of the new houses for women. King Stephen was the first Norman king to act when he helped to establish two monasteries for women between 1136 and 1153, seventy years after the conquest.[30] King Stephen's foundations bore little resemblance to the earlier royal abbeys, but they are representative of two types of twelfth-century lay creations in that Higham Priory, the one already discussed, was begun for a relative, and the other—Norwich Priory—was for women already leading religious lives.

In 1136–37, a number of years before Stephen helped establish Higham Priory for his daughter, he also founded a monastery for women, Norwich Priory, but under quite different circumstances. To find Stephen acting at all on behalf of women in 1136–37 is surprising, for in that period, he was still defending his right to rule. Nonetheless, Stephen gave his land in the fields of Norwich, worth twenty-five shillings, along with the adjoining meadow, "to the church of St. Mary and St. John of Norwich and to my nuns there serving God." Stephen clearly specified the purpose of his gift: "I want that on that land they should found their church." According to another record, the nuns were two sisters, Seyna and Lescelina. On land they were said to hold as freely as Stephen had held it, the women built a monastery that they dedicated to St. Mary of Carhowe.[31]

Stephen's actions at Norwich Priory are far more typical of twelfth-century lay founders than his investment at Higham, for laymen often supported women already leading a religious life, like the sisters Seyna and Lescelina. Although little evidence remains about these women in the surviving records, it is clear that such women were able to find sympathetic lay supporters who provided them with a house or a church and some revenue.

One of the first barons to found a monastery for women was Robert Marmion II, who around 1130, with his wife Milicent, responded to the needs of some nuns living at the manor of Oldbury. These women had been driven from the ancient abbey of Polesworth when Robert Marmion's ancestor seized it shortly after the conquest. Robert and Milicent resettled the women at Polesworth, under the prioress Osanna, who then retained Oldbury as a dependent cell.[32]

About a decade later, around 1140, one of the most powerful barons, Ranulf de Gernon, earl of Chester, endowed Chester Priory, in the very years when he was most actively opposing Stephen. Like Robert Marmion II, Earl Ranulf may have been restoring a house that had fallen into ruins, for a monastery is mentioned at Chester in the Domesday Survey. Whether the priory was built on previous foundations or not, Earl Ranulf was aiding particular women whom he knew. Earl Ranulf gave "to the nuns of Chester, our sisters in Christ," certain crofts "for building there a church . . . and for the foundation of their buildings."[33] Neither visions nor the needs of their own kinswomen influenced King Stephen and the two barons in the founding of Norwich, Polesworth, and Chester, but particular religious women whom they knew.

The sisters Seyna and Lescelina, the nuns of Chester, and Prioress Osanna with her companions at Oldbury manor—these were only a few of the women trying to eke out religious lives without sufficient revenue or a formally recognized priory who received help from the laity. In the 1140s, Simon of Senlis, earl of Northampton and one of Stephen's most ardent supporters, provided Northampton Abbey as a more suitable dwelling for nuns who were living at the church of Fotheringhay. Earl Simon gave the nuns and their abbess a church of his own patrimony, St. Mary Delapre, Northampton, where they could resettle, and some additional income from churches, rents, and services. According to some sources, the women were affiliated with the Cluniac order, although precisely how is not clear.[34]

Around 1154, Geoffrey de Clinton, either the treasurer of Henry I or his namesake son, gave 150 acres of his land and a meadow "for founding a cell of the order of nuns." Geoffrey placed the foundation charter for Bretford Priory "in the hand and arrangement of my dearest friend [charissimae amicae meae], the lady Noemi, so that the order and custom" that she had constituted there would be preserved. Some years later, the nuns Noemi and Seburc, with Geoffrey's assent, gave Bretford, which had remained only a cell, to the canons of Kenilworth Priory, a rare instance of a women's monastery's becoming a place for religious men.[35] Still, Bretford is another example of a monastery that a baron created for women he knew who were already leading a religious life.

Religious women also inspired the foundation of the priories of Pinley, Henwood, and Kington St. Michael; in these cases, however, the lay founders were not of baronial rank. Sometime before 1135 Robert de

Pillarton gave the nuns of Pinley all his land in Pinley "so that the order of nuns about to be constituted may be kept there inviolable for all times." Once the priory of Pinley was consecrated, gifts were made to "St. Mary of Pinley and the nuns there serving God."[36] Before 1160 Ketelberne de Langdon gave "the place of Estwell" to "St. Margaret and the nuns regularly serving God at Estwell," the first recorded mention of what was later called Henwood Priory. Until Ketelberne made his donation, the "nuns" must have been surviving with only minimal resources, for Ketelberne gave them not only their site, but also the right to take material from his woods "for making their church, all their workshops, and all their houses," and a place for building a mill.[37] Kington St. Michael was also in an early stage of formation when Robert Wayfer gave land and constituted the place there for nuns.[38]

Similarly, the men considered as the founders of the priories of Flamstead and Cambridge actually only improved the situation of nuns already living there in churches or cells. When around 1150 Roger de Tony gave land, woods, and tithes "to the church of St. Giles and the nuns of Woodchurch of Flamstead," the women already had a cloister, for some of the land Roger donated was described as being "on all sides around the cloister of the nuns," and other land was for enclosing "as if with another cloister." Since the anchoress Alfwen had been at Flamstead with Christina of Markyate in the 1120s, the women whom Roger aided may have been her successors or disciples. These women must have considered Roger's help essential since they called him their founder and made several promises to him of the sort sometimes made to lay patrons: that they would not elect a prioress without Roger's or his heir's assent, that they would not be subject to any other religious house, and that they would limit their number to thirteen unless Roger or his heirs allowed them to expand.[39]

At Cambridge, women acquired their priory in stages clearly delineated in the records. First there was the "cell of nuns newly formed outside Cambridge," to whom Nigel, bishop of Ely from 1133 to 1169, referred when he gave them some adjoining land. By 1138 William de Moyne, a goldsmith, had given "the nuns in the church of St. Mary of Cambridge" two virgates of land, six acres of meadow, and the labor and holdings of four cotters in Shelford. And, finally, between 1159 and 1161, King Malcolm IV of Scotland granted the women another ten acres "for founding their church," the basis of the new priory called henceforth St. Mary and St. Radegund of Cambridge.[40]

Considered collectively, these priories reveal the ongoing processes in which lay founders participated. In small groups, women at Oldbury, Fotheringhay, Flamstead, and Cambridge were trying to survive as nuns in ruined priories, old cells, or poorly endowed churches. Laymen supported these women and founded what became the priories of Polesworth, Northampton, Flamstead, and St. Mary and St. Radegund of Cambridge. Women at six other sites—Norwich, Chester, Bretford, Pinley, Henwood, and Kington St. Michael—were provided with land on which they built their conventual church and priory. In all ten cases, the lay donors aided women already leading religious lives by providing them with land and resources for a priory.

Very little has been recorded about the women who accepted these ten priories. Indeed, that their existence is recorded at all is fortuitous. Lacking the scriptoria of wealthy abbeys or priories in federated orders, these monasteries kept only meager records, and few of these have survived. The range of questions addressed for Godstow Abbey and Clerkenwell Priory cannot possibly be answered for these smaller, poorer priories. Yet, even in the fragmentary documentation, religious women were recorded living in informal arrangements before they found lay donors who provided them with priories.

Similar women have already been described: the hermitesses befriended by hermits, the religious women granted priories by neighboring abbeys, the sisters and nuns who inherited monasteries originally for men. The women who accepted these ten priories were like these other women described earlier. When such women settled alongside hermits, they might continue in an informal way of life for years. If they encountered canons or monks, they accepted priories dependent on or including male religious. When lay people came to their support, the women were provided with land to build small, independent priories. In all these cases, women themselves were the initiators of the new foundations. Half of the lay foundations were begun for women who had on their own undertaken ascetic life in ruined buildings, manor houses, or deserted places.

The backgrounds of these women are unknown. Since so few of the women who joined the better-documented new lay foundations were from illustrious families, it is unlikely that the social status of the women in the less well-documented foundations was high. Except for King Stephen's daughter Mary, none of the identifiable nuns who joined the new monasteries in the South were from the royal or great baronial families. The women with the highest known social status were widows and daughters of knights.

Why laymen responded to these women is not specified in the records, apart from the repeated stipulation that prayers were expected in return for the donations. There is no evidence that the laymen demanded material compensations for their gifts, for the donations were typically said to be free, pure, and perpetual alms. Nor is there any suggestion that the nuns assumed feudal obligations as a result of accepting the grants. When the donors ceded rights over churches to the women, however, they may have accrued some moral advantages. Since the days of Pope Gregory VII late in the eleventh century, lay ownership of churches had been criticized; so when lay people gave churches to nuns, they rid themselves of morally questionable possessions and received at least prayers to compensate for their losses.

Often the laymen seem to have been providing in the least expensive way possible for women they knew who wanted to live a religious life, or for women who had settled on their property. None of the foundation grants were large, and frequently the women were granted little more than a manor house or a church. Indeed, virtually the only surviving information about the remaining priories that lay people founded in the South between 1130 and 1165 is the fact that they were begun in already existing churches or manors. The endowments of Ankerwyke[41] and Polsloe[42] are not known, but the surviving documents suggest that the priories of Wix,[43] Ickleton,[44] Rowney,[45] and Cannington[46] were formed in manors that had churches or chapels attached; and the priories of Wothorpe,[47] Swaffham Bulbeck,[48] Davington,[49] and Goring[50] began in churches.

With the addition of these twenty-five priories founded by laymen, the opportunities for female religious life in the South had altered dramatically. In thirty-five years, the range of options had widened; in addition to the few royal abbeys, there were large houses in federated orders, daughter houses dependent on male abbeys, and more than two dozen small priories begun in manor houses and churches. When lay people were the founders, the nuns themselves remained responsible for their priories, unless religious men became involved at an early date, as at Clerkenwell Priory. Few women oversaw monasteries as rich and influential as Godstow Abbey, but in most lay foundations, the prioress alone ruled. Although the women themselves are rarely portrayed in any detail, many religious women are visible, seeking lives of prayer and accepting whatever aid is offered, with whatever requirements are demanded. In order to lead their holy lives, the women were inventive and adaptive.

CHAPTER 5

Female Monasticism in the North

North of the Welland River, the expansion of female monasticism was even more chronologically concentrated than in the South. In the North, between 1130 and 1165, in just thirty-five years, women acquired forty-six new monasteries, an average of more than one a year. Before women were given these monasteries, they had virtually no options for religious life in the entire region. Until 1130, the North was completely devoid of religious houses for women (except possibly for Holystone and Newcastle priories, which may already have existed in Northumberland).[1] Archbishop Thurstan probably began the first monastery for women when he founded St. Clement's, York, in 1130.[2] Within a generation, the region was blanketed with monasteries.

With no earlier abbeys to provide alternatives, women were limited in their choices to the forms of religious life offered in the new houses. During the first decades of the expansion, the organization of these new monasteries was remarkably homogeneous, for religious men were typically included in them. Between 1148 and 1154, the six years of the most rapid expansion, women were given twenty new monasteries; in at least fifteen, and maybe more, of these new houses, the women lived with a master and/or lay brothers. By 1154 in the North women had many monasteries they might join, but these houses had less variety in internal arrangements than monasteries in the South.

This one type of organization dominated the region for several reasons. One was the vacuum in which the expansion occurred. Had earlier abbeys for women existed, they might have inspired institutional alternatives. Also, male monasticism was only beginning its own resurgence in the North. As David Knowles observed, "If in 1130 a line had been drawn across England from the mouth of the Welland to the estuary of the Mersey, the district north of it would have been found to contain only five abbeys, the cathedral priory of Durham, and two or three smaller houses."[3] Whereas in the South the great variety of institutional forms resulted from the cooperation of monks and hermits in the religious life of women, in the North this was not possible. With so few monasteries for men in the North, women could not depend on support from abbeys, nor were there enough hermits to affect female religious life significantly.

But the homogeneity in the North was not only the result of a lack of alternatives. Female religious were supported primarily by a particular group of lay people—the vassals of the great feudal lords—and this group appears to have had strong preferences about the type of religious houses it wished to establish. A new elite of both Norman and Anglo-Saxon ancestry had been formed when King Henry I distributed the remaining demesne land in the North to men of his own choosing.[4] As these barons consolidated their control of the region, many of them founded monasteries for men—in part responding to the increased enthusiasm for monasticism and in part continuing the Norman custom of lay foundations. Although these new magnates of the North also supported religious women, the women's most ardent supporters were from a slightly lower social group. This class, the vassals of the earls and other barons, preferred to build monasteries for women in which many of the necessary physical and spiritual services were provided by religious men who were full members of the monastery.

These lay founders also revealed a preference for the new monastic orders of the twelfth century, especially the Cistercian Order. The laity in the North could have acted otherwise. In the South, lay supporters of religious women created a solid Benedictine phalanx; in the South, only the barons selected monasteries in the new federated orders, and only they began houses with large contingents of both men and women. In contrast to their Southern peers, the vassals of Northern barons favored new monastic orders and designed monasteries for women that often included men as well.

This chapter explores the religious, economic, social, and political factors that encouraged lay people in the North consistently to back this one type of monastic organization for women. Although few records remain of the holy women who inspired the new foundations, there is considerable documentation on the women who joined the monasteries after they were begun. And there is rich information about the main proponent of female monasticism in the North, the man who helps account for the North's distinctive organizational preference: Gilbert of Sempringham.

SEMPRINGHAM PRIORY

In contrast to the South, where bishops, monks, and canons founded monasteries for women, in the North, only four churchmen began houses for religious women. Three of the churchmen were bishops, and the fourth was Gilbert of Sempringham. After starting a priory for nuns at Sempringham in Lincolnshire in 1131, Gilbert soon established more, so that by 1154, he was responsible for an entire order, with nine monasteries that included not only nuns but also canons, lay brothers, and lay sisters.

According to Gilbert's *vita*, as the son of a wealthy Norman knight and Saxon lady, Gilbert would probably have become a knight himself, were it not for a physical deformity he had from birth. To escape an unhappy childhood in Lincolnshire, Gilbert studied for several years on the Continent in one of the new centers of education. Upon his return to Lincolnshire, Gilbert became a teacher, beginning a school at Sempringham for the boys and girls in the parish. Because Gilbert taught monastic rules of discipline as well as rules of grammar, the *vita* considered that parish school the first sign of Gilbert's future vocation.[5]

Gilbert made the transition from teacher of children to religious innovator after seven years in the service of the bishop of Lincoln. Because Bishop Robert Bloet, who invited Gilbert to Lincoln in 1123, died shortly after Gilbert's arrival, most of Gilbert's stay there was under Bishop Alexander. Although the *vita* minimizes Alexander's influence on Gilbert, the bishop's attitude toward religious women may have had a decisive impact.[6] Alexander let Christina of Markyate live openly as a religious as soon as he became bishop, a privilege denied her by his predecessor, Robert Bloet. Gilbert was part of the episcopal court when Alexander granted Christina this right. After Gilbert left in 1130, Alexander continued to support female monasticism: in 1131 he publicly confirmed Christina's vow to virginity, in 1136–38 he consecrated Harrold Priory, in 1138–39 he spoke eloquently in praise of Edith at his consecration of Godstow Abbey, and in 1145 he consecrated Markyate Priory for Christina.[7]

However, although Bishop Alexander may have inspired Gilbert, it is likely that the influence was mutual. During his time at Lincoln, Gilbert was already in his thirties, a well-educated man, personally informed about eremitic and monastic reforms on the Continent. In 1131, the same year Alexander confirmed Christina's vow to virginity, Gilbert began Sempringham Priory, a gesture in support of female religious even more dramatic than the bishop's. Whether Gilbert sparked Bishop Alexander's sympathy for religious women, or vice versa, both men became leaders in the female monastic movement.

Many years later, Gilbert recalled the early days at Sempringham and what had encouraged him to begin a new religious order there. By the time he left his account—preserved as the introduction to the *Institutes* of his order—the Gilbertines had been shaken by discord, which may have colored his recollections. Still, his first-person reminiscence provides an unparalleled perspective on why priories for women and men became a norm in the North.[8]

When Gilbert returned to Sempringham, he no longer intended to be just a teacher, for he had been ordained during his stay at Lincoln. His original plan was to begin a new monastery for men. As part of his inheritance, Gilbert had two churches in his free possession and rights in several others. As a priest, Gilbert could have legitimately kept these churches, but he wanted instead to give the revenue "to the divine cult and for the sustenance of those choosing poverty for God." A man in his late thirties or early forties, hardly a youthful enthusiast, Gilbert said he originally had had no intention of aiding women.

"But when I could not find men [*viri*] who wanted to submit their necks for the love of God to a strict life according to my wish," Gilbert recalled, "I found young women [*virgines*] who, often instructed by us, wanted to aim without any impediment for divine slavery, disregarding the cares of this world." As Gilbert remembered the events, in his first months back at Sempringham, his preaching had inspired seven women to desire a strict monastic life. The rapidity of their conversion suggests that these women may have already been attracted to such a life, and that they now had found a supporter. In any case, in 1131, with the aid of Bishop Alexander of Lincoln, Gilbert built at Sempringham dwellings and a cloister for the seven women "whom I had stirred up with divine love." Like the religious men who were his counterparts in the South, Gilbert wanted these women to be well-supervised, so he enclosed them in the monastery "afterwards never to depart, according to a plan which I had then."[9]

Gilbert claimed that he had had no grandiose visions for a new order when he began Sempringham Priory for these seven young women: "I was not thinking of adding any more to those living there." The next development occurred when Gilbert decided that it was dangerous to have enclosed women served by secular girls "running here and there," able to do more harm than good. So, following the advice of a Cistercian monk, "the first abbot of Rievaulx who had come by for me and had praised my plan," Gilbert permitted "my serving women themselves to be regulated in dress [*habitus*], in poor food and clothing, and to minister to those enclosed for Christ."[10] The first abbot of Rievaulx was William; sent by Clairvaux to head its new daughter house at Rievaulx, William arrived there in early 1132, just a few months after Gilbert had enclosed the seven women at Sempringham.[11]

Gilbert in essence adapted the Cistercian system of lay brothers (*conversi*) to meet the need he had identified. Just as the Cistercian lay brothers served the Cistercian monks, the Gilbertine lay sisters were to serve the Gilbertine nuns. But in regularizing the serving women into a "lay sisterhood," Gilbert insisted that he was following the wishes of the serving women themselves, who "entreated" him "with great devotion." Only then did Gilbert allow the sisters (*conversae*) "to vow chastity, humility, love, obedience and perseverance in the good, and renunciation of the world, all property, and even [their] own will: indeed all things that are agreed to by religious."[12] In promising so much, the serving women pledged even more than Benedictine nuns, who only vowed stability, obedience, and change of life (*conversatio*).

The success of Gilbert's experiment shows that many poor women were willing to undertake lives of the strictest asceticism. Although Gilbert saw himself as opening monastic life to a class customarily excluded, one might argue that he was taking advantage of the financial needs of these women. However, any woman who chose the Gilbertines for material reasons must have been virtually destitute, for Gilbert ruled that the lay sisters were permitted no more than a pound of coarse bread and two vegetables each day; water was to be their only drink. The lay sisters were to wear contemptible clothing and spend most of their time watching and laboring, with only the rarest moments of quiet.

The lay sisters did not resolve all Gilbert's labor difficulties, for they did not perform strenuous manual labor or agricultural work. Not wanting secular men to have charge of "the possessions of my house and the agriculture," Gilbert organized men in "a similar mode and order . . . as I had commanded for the lay sisters." Gilbert again explicitly acknowledged his dependence on the Cistercian model: "I took for myself male servants, giving them the habit of religious, just as the lay brothers of the Cistercians have."[13] However, Gilbert's lay brothers were quite different from the Cistercian *conversi*, for they were to serve women, not men.

Before the end of the decade, more people wanted to join Sempringham than it could accommodate. So in 1139 Gilbert's feudal lord, Gilbert of Gant, a powerful landholder in Lincolnshire, granted Gilbert three additional carucates of land. This permitted Gilbert to build an enlarged priory at Sempringham for the nuns, lay sisters, and lay brothers.[14] The expansion of his original plan was already well underway.

THE ORIGIN OF THE GILBERTINE ORDER

In 1139, in addition to enlarging Sempringham Priory, Gilbert began a second foundation, Haverholme Priory. The donor of the site was his old friend, Bishop Alexander of Lincoln, who gave Haverholme to the religious women "under the custody and teaching of the priest Gilbert." In the foundation charter, Bishop Alexander emphasized that he was responding to real needs. "Since they did not have a suitable place for their religion, we, inspired by divine grace, have prepared and given to them what is sufficient for this life." Or, again, he said he made the donation because God "illuminated the eyes of our mind and inclined our heart to the needs of his handmaids."[15]

Bishop Alexander gave to Gilbert and the women under his care the island of Haverholme with its appurtenances in meadow, marsh, lands "which are suitable enough for cultivation," water, and all things within the boundary of the island, including two mills. The choice of location clearly was Alexander's, for two years earlier he had offered this same island to the Cistercian monks of Fountains. After erecting some buildings there, the monks had asked him for Louth Park as a site instead. If Haverholme was "sufficient" in Alexander's view, it was not abundant in resources. Not only did the Cistercians reject it; a year after the Gilbertines settled there, a layman added some other lands, saying he feared that otherwise the nuns would lack the necessities of life. Even though Haverholme had only meager resources, Gilbert accepted the site.[16]

In the foundation charter, Bishop Alexander made a curious claim: that the women of Haverholme "seizing on the narrow life, the holy life—namely, the life of the Cistercian religion—strive to keep it, and they do keep it, as much as the weakness of their sex permits."[17] Nowhere else in the extensive Gilbertine records is an assertion made that the nuns sought to live like Cistercians. Certainly Cistercians are frequently mentioned. Gilbert attributed his creation of the lay sisterhood and brotherhood to Cistercian influence. At the beginning of the thirteenth century, Gilbert's *vita* added another claim: that Cistercian advice led to the addition of canons and the final formation of the Gilbertine

Order. But no other Gilbertine source asserts that the nuns were aiming for a Cistercian way of life.

Despite its uniqueness, Bishop Alexander's statement may have validity. Bishop Alexander was a man who would have known Gilbert and his nuns' intentions, not only because he was Gilbert's friend but also because he was donating a site to them. Whereas most Gilbertine records were written after the final formation of the order, the foundation of Haverholme preceded these later developments and could reflect Gilbert's and his nuns' ideas at an earlier stage. After all, Gilbert himself said that the seven women for whom he began Sempringham were willing to accept a strict life, and in the 1130s the "strict" monastic life was almost a synonym for Cistercian ideals. Another indication of the validity of Bishop Alexander's assessment is that it explains so nicely the next phase in the development of the Gilbertine order: Gilbert's attempt to affiliate the priories of Sempringham and Haverholme with the Cistercian order.

As Gilbert explained the chain of events, the enlargement of Sempringham and the foundation of Haverholme had made him uneasy, for "there were not yet literate religious necessary for the care of the women and the guidance of the laity."[18] Gilbert's assertion that literate religious men were "necessary" is a striking assumption. In the long-familiar system of single-sex Benedictine monasteries, abbesses and prioresses had managed on their own to care for their houses. Did Gilbert want other men to provide the type of guidance he had been giving simply because his experiences had been successful? Had the addition of lay brothers to the monasteries created a situation that he felt all-female houses could not handle, for it required that women instruct men? Were the nuns themselves hoping to find other priests with the same skills Gilbert provided? The reason for Gilbert's sentiment is not clear, but, as future events would show, others also felt as he did.

Whatever role the nuns may have had in Gilbert's decision, he wrote "I [Gilbert] went to the chapter of the Cistercians, Pope Eugene being present, a man of great counsel and holiness, so that I might deliver up to their regulation our houses and the handmaids of Christ and our brothers." The year was probably 1147, although the Cistercian documents make no mention of the event. Apparently Gilbert had decided that the best way to provide care for the nuns, lay sisters, and lay brothers was to affiliate them with that powerful order. But, he reported, "I suffered a refusal altogether. Forced by necessity I gathered to me clerics for the regulation and care of the women and men who had given themselves to external labor."[19] From at least the beginning of the thirteenth century, the reason given for the Cistercians' rejection of Gilbert's plea was that Gilbert's monasteries included women.[20] Gilbert himself gave no explanation, curtly describing his encounter there in one sentence, mentioning only Pope Eugene with approbation.

After the Cistercian rejection, Gilbert and the nuns, lay sisters, and lay brothers resumed an independent course. Gilbert added to his monasteries a fourth group, the canons, placing them under the Augustinian Rule. Gilbert did not state in the *Institutes* that the Cistercians had advised him to add canons, although some of his followers made this claim in his *vita*. Rather, Gilbert presented himself as devising on his own the complex Gilbertine organization with its carefully delineated arrangements.

In the surviving records, Gilbert never explains why he chose Augustinian canons instead of other monks or priests to serve his monasteries. In the South, the priors of monasteries for women were often monks; and there would have been more symmetry in the Gilbertine arrangement if the nuns had shared their houses with monks. Yet in this decision, Gilbert perceptively gauged the needs and resources of his region. Only a few older monasteries existed, so there was not a supply of already existing monks to staff his houses. Many of the men who wanted to become monks were joining the new Cistercian houses beginning throughout the northern shires. Because the Cistercians had already said that they would not help him, Gilbert could not rely on monks of that order to serve his monasteries. Gilbert must have realized that he would have trouble finding monks willing to join his monasteries.

But Augustinian canons were already numerous in the region; under King Henry I's patronage, the Augustinians had prospered in England. These canons could easily undertake the type of service Gilbert envisioned. Moreover, regular canons would have found Gilbert's monasteries ideal environments in which to carry out their vocation. Many of the regular clergy in the twelfth century, when monasticism had such a widespread appeal, had come to want a more contemplative communal life. At the same time, these canons understood their vocation as one of teaching, both by word and by example.[21] Sometimes canons felt a tension between these two desires, for how could they both live a contemplative life in a community and actively exercise their priestly and teaching functions? Gilbert's monasteries provided a solution, for there they could balance the active and contemplative life; the canons could live under a rule in a prayerful community and at the same time serve as priests and teachers for the nuns, lay sisters, and lay brothers.

In the remainder of the introduction to the *Institutes*, Gilbert briefly outlined the respective duties of the women and men. Nuns were in charge of all food, clothing, silver, and everything that lawfully (*licite*) pertained to their skills. Four men—the prior, cellarer, and two "illiterates"—were given custody of all the things which by right (*jure*) were given to men, including all buying and selling.[22] Although Gilbert described the assigned responsibilities as if they were the lawful and expected norms, monasteries that included only one gender did not typically honor these divisions. Monks often handled what Gilbert assigned "lawfully" to the women, and prioresses oversaw what Gilbert assigned "by right" to men.

Gilbert was obviously pleased with his new plan, for he did not just add canons to the three groups already present at Sempringham and Haverholme. He also agreed to accept into his new system seven additional monasteries within the next seven years. Between 1147 and 1154, Gilbert received grants from lay people that permitted the establishment of Chicksands Priory in the South and six additional monasteries in the North: Watton Priory in Yorkshire and five new priories in Lincolnshire—Alvingham, Bullington, Catley, North Ormsby, and Sixhills.[23] Through sheer numbers alone, by 1154 his monastic system had become a dominant force in the region.

"CISTERCIAN" PRIORIES

Gilbert did not labor alone in the North. Even between 1130 and 1147, when Gilbert just began Sempringham and Haverholme priories, eight other monasteries for women were founded: four in Yorkshire, three in Lincolnshire, and one in Nottingham. Since Newcastle upon Tyne, Holystone, and St. Clement's, York, possibly were already in existence by 1130, the total number increased from three to thirteen in a little less than two decades. Except for Gilbert's two houses, all the other new monasteries had lay founders. Gilbert was the only founder to experiment with institutional innovations, for his were the only monasteries for women which included men—and until 1147 his included just lay brothers, without any canons.[24]

In one important way, however, the other founders were like Gilbert, for they too were impressed by the Cistercians. Five of the eight new priories that these lay people began between 1130 and 1147 were "Cistercian" houses. Even after Gilbert's rejection at Cîteaux, these lay people continued to found "Cistercian" houses: thirteen more in the next two decades, for a total of eighteen Cistercian priories for women in the North by 1165. The desire of these lay founders to extend the Cistercian model to their female monasteries is understandable given the great popularity of that order. Beginning its first house in England at Waverly Abbey in 1128, by 1148 the Cistercian order had twenty-eight monasteries for men, mostly in the North. Naturally the lay founders of monasteries for women wanted their houses also to be associated with that growing, well-respected order.

Since Gilbert was attracted to the Cistercians and since the appeal of the order was widespread, one might imagine that the existence of eighteen "Cistercian" priories for women was so logical that it could not be controversial. Yet whether these monasteries were Cistercian was debated at the time, and their status has remained a problem of recent scholarly literature.[25] As is often the case for monasteries of women, the first record of the affiliation of some of these houses is from the time of the dissolution under King Henry VIII, an unreliable indication of their identity in the twelfth century. But determining whether these houses were Cistercian is even more complicated, because not until 1213 were Cistercian nuns officially mentioned in legislation of the Cistercian order. The status of "Cistercian" houses for women before that date is uncertain. They do not seem to have been formally in the Cistercian order, nor were they bound by its Charter of Charity, nor were they represented at its general chapter. These English "Cistercian" priories for women were not even begun in the customary Cistercian manner of filiation, for none of them are thought to have been the daughter houses of other Cistercian monasteries.

Yet contemporaries, like Pope Alexander III, certainly considered some of these monasteries for women to be Cistercian, and the nuns themselves sometimes claimed this identity. The advantages of a Cistercian identity were obvious. In addition to the prestige brought from association with this order, a monastery gained financially from the automatic exemption from certain tithes that was granted to the Cistercians. In fact, when one of these monasteries for women is called Cistercian in a twelfth-century document, usually the reference appears in a charter granting economic privileges. For instance, in 1172 Pope Alexander III encouraged the nuns of Sinningthwaite to uphold there with distinction "the monastic order . . . according to God, the rule of St. Benedict, and the institution of the Cistercian brothers." He assured the nuns, "Of course, no one may presume to demand tithes from you on what you produce by your own hands or at your own expense or from the support of your animals."[26] Similarly, in 1177 Pope Alexander confirmed Swine Priory's exemption from the same tithes "just as to the brothers of the Cistercian order," even though some had "evilly" tried to require such a tithe from the nuns.[27]

A case from the end of the thirteenth century illustrates the complications involved in determining whether these twelfth-century houses were Cistercian. In 1270, to help decide whether nuns in five Lincolnshire "Cistercian" monasteries warranted the Cistercian exemption from specific tithes, the abbot of Cîteaux was consulted. Abbot John of Cîteaux wrote emphatically to the dean of Lincoln that nuns in the five priories in question—Greenfield, Gokewell, Legbourne, NunCotham, and Stixwould—were not in the Cistercian order and should not receive its privileges. But Abbot John acknowledged that the nuns wore Cistercian habits, one way in which they clearly asserted a Cistercian identity. And the entire episode illustrates that at least by 1270 the nuns of these five houses claimed to be Cistercians.[28]

To understand the expansion of female monasticism in the North, it is not necessary to determine the exact status of the "Cistercian" priories for women. As the recent articles on Cistercian nuns have argued, it is unlikely that any of these monasteries were fully incorporated in the Cistercian order in the mid-twelfth century. Nonetheless, nuns in these "Cistercian" monasteries probably adopted Cistercian customs, used Cistercian missals, dressed in Cistercian-like habits, and claimed Cistercian exemptions. If so, these houses were similar to certain Cluniac monasteries that were affiliated with Cluny in a general way and influenced by its *horarium*, liturgy, and customaries.[29] One of the new monasteries for women in the North, Arthington Priory, was probably Cluniac in this broad sense.[30] Yet the existence of so many "Cistercian" houses that were not fully Cistercian indicates how complex it can be to describe female houses with terms from male monasticism.

Although their exact status is uncertain, one significant fact about these "Cistercian" houses is that at least half of them included men. Even though the records are often meager for these monasteries, the documents reveal that nine of the eighteen "Cistercian" priories for women also had men. Seven of the nine included lay brothers.[31] The number with men may have been greater, for of the remaining nine houses, four may have had lay brothers and two have left virtually no records. The three other exceptions were the earliest "Cistercian" houses for women in each shire, begun before the advantages of including lay brothers had become clear.[32]

It cannot be merely coincidental that in the North twenty of the twenty-eight monasteries for women that may have included lay brothers were either Gilbertine or "Cistercian." Since Gilbert himself ascribed his addition of lay brothers and sisters to Cistercian inspiration, one way these monasteries for women were like those of the Cistercians was in their adoption of the Cistercian *conversi* system. Even if the nuns were not recognized by the Cistercians, even if they were rejected at Cîteaux like the Gilbertines had been, they could imitate one of the Cistercians' distinctive methods of organizing monastic life.

Lay brothers were not the only men in these "Cistercian" priories for women, for many of them included canons and priors as well. By the mid-1170s, five of the "Cistercian" priories—Greenfield, NunCotham, Stixwould, Swine, and Wykeham—had a master or prior; as did Legbourne, at least by 1200. Typically, these houses also included lay brothers, although the records of Legbourne and Wykeham do not mention *conversi*. Between 1160 and 1181, canons are also recorded at three of the houses, an indication that the priors were Augustinian canons, not monks.[33]

The arrangement adopted apparently was virtually identical to the Gilbertine arrangement. And the reason is obvious. Like Gilbert, these other founders had also been attracted to Cistercian ideals. Unable to obtain official Cistercian affiliation for their monasteries, they too found appealing the plan Gilbert devised after his rejection at Cîteaux. The situation in Yorkshire is particularly revealing. There most of the monasteries with nuns, a master, and lay brothers were "Cistercian," not Gilbertine.

Whether these monasteries also included lay sisters is harder to discern. References to lay sisters are rare in the documents, since they were not mentioned in the gift formulae that identify the other members of the community.[34] Evidence exists for lay sisters at only two "Cistercian" monasteries, and in both cases, the documentation is late. According to the early thirteenth-century constitution of NunCotham, lay sisters were included along with the nuns, master, two chaplains, and twelve lay brothers.[35] Also in the early thirteenth century, lay sisters were at Hutton/Baysdale; they are included among the people permitted burial at the monastery.[36] Although it is possible—even likely—that these Cistercian priories had both *conversi* and *conversae*, the extent to which women of lower social standing were included remains uncertain.

NunCotham seems to have most closely approximated Gilbert's four-fold arrangement. When it was begun between 1147 and 1153, Nun-Cotham may have been for women alone, but at least by 1181 male religious were permanent members as well. In a letter he wrote to Nun-Cotham between 1159 and 1181, Pope Alexander III promised, "None of the brothers or sisters after making profession in that place is permitted to leave from your monastery without the permission of the master and chapter, unless they want to go to a stricter religion." According to the constitution of NunCotham approved by Hugh de Welles, bishop of Lincoln between 1209 and 1235, the priory was to be composed of at most thirty nuns, two chaplains, twelve lay brothers, and an indeterminate number of lay sisters. Although this constitution is from the early thirteenth century, the same groups were already present in the late twelfth century. The master and the prioress shared responsibilities for the monastery.[37]

If Cistercian monks had been able or willing to join predominately female houses, masters and canons might never have become part of these "Cistercian" priories. But Gilbert's experience at Cîteaux and his subsequent decision to add canons influenced the development in the entire region. Lay brothers and canons became full members not only of Gilbert's priories but also of some of these small "Cistercian" houses for women. Women attracted to the Cistercian way of life entered monasteries where lay brothers did much of the manual labor, and where a prior or master shared responsibility for the house with the prioress. Both the Gilbertine and the Cistercian nuns relied on male religious in order to live a monastic life.

OTHER FOUNDATIONS

By 1165, the number of monasteries for women in the North had increased to almost fifty.[38] The canons who joined Gilbertine and Cistercian houses were not the only ones active on behalf of women. Between 1147 and 1160, Premonstratensian canons aided the foundation of three houses for women: Guyzance, Orford, and Broadholme priories.

The Premonstratensian order had its roots in the foundation of Prémontré Abbey near Laon in 1120, which the itinerant preacher Norbert of Xanten began for his male and female followers. Based on the Augustinian Rule, the order was known for its strict austerities, and it quickly spread after receiving papal approval in 1126. Although in its origins it was much like the Order of Fontevrault, the Premonstratensians had a very different history, for they did not follow the plan begun by their founder. After the death of Norbert in 1134, his followers altered the arrangement he had devised. Around 1137, the general chapter of his order ruled that women were no longer to remain in the same communities as the men. Instead, the Premonstratensian sisters were to set up their own religious houses at some distance from the men.[39]

The first English Premonstratensian canonry, Newsham in Lincoln, was begun in 1143, after the legislation separating the women and men. So Guyzance, Orford, and Broadholme priories were all begun after it was no longer permitted to include canons with the sisters. Yet all three houses for women were founded in cooperation with nearby Premonstratensian canonries. Guyzance Priory was created in a church that the canons of Alnwick had owned and that they agreed to give to women. Orford Priory was begun in a church and on some land that a layman had earlier granted to the canons of Newsham. And, similarly, Broadholme Priory was built on land previously given to the canons of Newsham by its founder, apparently because the founder's wife wanted a sister house for her husband's canonry.[40]

Brothers and sisters are mentioned in the earliest charters of Broadholme Priory, even though it was begun after the legislation forbidding monasteries for both sexes.[41] These brothers may have been lay brothers, or Premonstratensian canons and sisters may have continued to associate in the period immediately after the separation decree of 1137. If there was an ongoing relationship between the canons and sisters in these houses, it is unknown.

Augustinian canons not associated with the Premonstratensian order also cooperated in the creation of houses for nuns. Augustinian "canons and nuns" were the original inhabitants of Marton Priory, begun during the reign of King Stephen by the sheriff of York.[42] Grimsby Priory was another house that had some connections to canons, in this case, the nearby Augustinians of Wellow. If the canons played any role in the foundation of Grimsby, it is not documented. But a relationship is likely because the women of Grimsby appear to have adopted the Augustinian Rule, and in the late twelfth century the canons of Wellow assumed they had rights in some of the property of Grimsby. By the mid-thirteenth century, a prior from Wellow was at Grimsby Priory.[43]

The canons who assumed responsibility for religious women might also perform other tasks. Gilbert's canons served at their order's hospital in Lincoln, where they were aided by Gilbertine lay sisters and lay brothers.[44] Gilbertine canons, like other canons, might also live in single-sex communities. In 1150, one of the most powerful men in the region, Eustace fitz John, gave Gilbert two pieces of property: on one he began Watton Priory, for both sexes, and on the other, Malton Priory, for men alone. The purpose of this first Gilbertine canonry is not stated; it may have been designed as a retreat house for canons, where they could have time free for meditation and prayer. Whatever its functions, Malton was only the first of several such Gilbertine priories for men.[45]

The logic of having men with women in monasteries was so compelling in the North that even Benedictine monasteries included them. For many of these houses, the records are later, revealing the situation in the thirteenth century and not necessarily in the twelfth. However, if the later material indicates the twelfth-century situation, of the thirteen Benedictine monasteries for women founded between 1130 and 1165, six had lay brothers and three had priors or canons.[46] Although men were not as universally present as in houses of the new religious orders, for men to be included at all reveals how completely the region was dominated by Gilbert's preferred arrangement.

As Table 4 indicates, in the twenty-three non-Gilbertine priories that may have had both sexes, Gilbert's model was not slavishly followed. Only six are thought to have housed all three groups: nuns, priors, and lay brothers. Most ubiquitous in the religious life of women were the lay brothers. In as many as twenty-eight priories in the North, the nuns were aided by lay brothers, who were present in monasteries of all affiliations.

In all the monasteries for women and men, women outnumbered the men. But the men were not mere tokens. Before the turn of the century, the Gilbertines limited the size of their priories, and in so doing, compiled a list giving the maximum number of women and men at each of their priories. Although statistics of maximum size do not necessarily reveal actual size, they indicate the expected ratio of women to men. In the Gilbertine list, nuns and lay sisters were grouped together, as were canons and lay brothers. Watton in Yorkshire was potentially the largest with 140 women to 70 men. Sempringham was next: 120 women to 60 men. The ratio continued: two women to every man. Malton Priory, for men alone, was to have at most 35 brothers, and the priory serving the hospital in Lincoln was limited to 16 men and 20 women.[47]

This proportion of women to men also existed at non-Gilbertine houses. By the time of its constitution in the early thirteenth century, the Cistercian priory of NunCotham was permitted 30 nuns, 15 men, and an unspecified number of lay sisters.[48] Although most houses were much smaller than the Gilbertine priories, the ratio of women to men appears to have been similar. A typical small monastery of 13 nuns might include 1 to 3 priors/canons and an equal number of lay brothers. In the monasteries for women and men, men comprised one-quarter to one-half the total population.

Women in the North had different relationships with religious men than their sisters in the South. Women encountered fewer hermits and they rarely had dealings with monks. Only rarely were religious men the founders of their monasteries. But men often joined their priories. Like the female members of the monastery, canons and lay brothers made their vows, lived out their lives, and were buried in the monasteries. Even though only a few religious men founded monasteries for women, their cooperation helped women increase the number of monasteries in the North in a single generation from three houses to almost fifty.

THE ECONOMIC, SOCIAL, AND POLITICAL CONTEXT

Gilbert of Sempringham had rightly judged the preferences of his region, for monasteries for nuns, priors, lay sisters, and lay brothers prospered in the North. Gilbert's influence was fundamental, but the Cistercian impact was significant as well, whether encountered directly or mediated through Gilbert. Cîteaux never claimed responsibility for the hybrid form that linked nuns and lay brothers and lay sisters, yet this combination was an adaptation of its *conversi* system. The Augustinian canons' search for an appropriate mission, both pastoral and regular, was another factor in the expansion. And, of course, nothing would have happened were it not for the desires of women, like the first seven at Sempringham, who wanted "to submit their necks for the love of God to a strict life."

Economic realities in the North also favored the fourfold arrangement that Gilbert popularized. In the South, nuns frequently received income-producing property that they could manage on their own: manor houses, feudal dues, rents, and tithes. But in the North, the nuns often acquired either land that required extensive labor or churches that needed the services of priests. An indication that canons and lay brothers were vital, even necessary, is the correspondence between their presence and the type of property that a monastery possessed.

When a monastery acquired a church, it had to provide it with priestly services in order to receive the offerings, tithes, and altar and burial dues. If the monastery included canons, they usually could perform the sacramental functions and gain the church's entire income for the monastery. Between 1170 and 1180, Pope Alexander III wrote to the Gilbertines, "It will be lawful for you to place in your vacant parish churches four or at least three of your canons, one of whom will be presented to the diocesan bishop so that he may receive the cure of souls from him." Responsible to the bishop "concerning spiritual matters," the canons obeyed the Gilbertines "concerning temporal matters and the observance of order."[49]

Lay brothers also performed essential functions, for often the monasteries in the North received extensive grants of pastureland. Although in theory nuns could work the land or herd sheep, it was considered more appropriate for nuns to pray and for lay brothers to husband the land. In almost all cases, priories that owned large tracts of land included lay brothers who could tend it. For instance, the nuns who settled first at Hutton, moved to Nunthorpe, and finally made their home at Baysdale Priory were aided by lay brothers. In addition to other land, Baysdale Priory had pasture for 20 cows and a bull, 200 sheep, 11 swine and a boar, 5 mares and a stallion, 10 oxen and a working horse. Rosedale, another "Cistercian" priory with lay brothers at least by the thirteenth century, acquired in one grant alone pasture for 200 sheep and a team of oxen. Lay brothers were equally useful to the nuns of Benedictine Marrick with their pasture for 80 cows, 500 sheep, 100 wethers, and horses and pigs "without number."[50]

Monasteries with all four groups—nuns, canons, lay brothers, and lay sisters—were able to handle a diversified economy, one that included feudal dues, churches, and agricultural lands.[51] Since their lay brothers could clear land, the Gilbertines could—and did—accept virtual wildernesses in which to build priories. Several Gilbertine priories were established on marshy islands, like Catley Priory, with its woods, fields, meadows, marshes, water mill, and pastureland for 400 sheep.[52] Woodland areas, such as the site of Bullington Priory, were also useful to the Gilbertines.

By the century's end Bullington Priory had varied types of properties, representative of the diversity the Gilbertines could manage. Bullington held at least 175 acres of arable land, 200 other acres, 17 bovates, 20 *seliones*, meadowland, several tofts, and pasture for at least 1,600 sheep. The lay brothers farmed and herded under the canons' supervision. The canons served the fourteen churches Bullington possessed and managed the feudal dues received from three mills and the services of a few serfs.[53]

By the end of King Henry II's reign, the Gilbertine priory of Sixhills possessed a similar assortment of land and dues. With less acreage than Bullington, Sixhills still had more than 139 acres, 48 bovates, woods, meadows, and pastureland. Feudal dues came from six mills, rights in two other mills, the manor of Ludford with all rents and men (for which the nuns owed an annual fee), a complete village (except for six marks annually), and half another village. Canons served nine churches and rights were held in two others.[54]

The non-Gilbertine monasteries that duplicated Gilbertine internal arrangements often had the same types of property as well. For instance, NunCotham began with the entire village of NunCotham in its possessions, including all the men of the village and the church there. By the time Pope Alexander III confirmed its possessions, NunCotham had accumulated more than two dozen bovates of land, more than twenty-five other acres of land, marshland, a salt pan, a fish pond, a toft, free use of a ferry, pasture for 200 sheep, and the possession of one and a half churches.[55] By the end of the century, NunAppleton had at least three churches and extensive lands, including pastureland for over 700 sheep, 30 beasts, 30 swine, and 30 goats.[56]

On the other hand, the few priories in the North that were for women alone seem to have had the same type of property as their counterparts in the South. For instance, like one of the manor houses in the South, Keldholme Priory had its site, some land on the north, a small plot for vegetables, the right to gather wood for building and burning, pasture in a woods, bark from certain trees, and other pasture for sheep, pigs, and cows.[57] Wallingswells was founded in a park near some springs, with some land already under cultivation, revenue from the land held by five men, an underwood to enclose, a little pastureland, pannage for ninety pigs, a right of way for carts, and use of a river flowing from the spring.[58] Nuns with a few hired servants could manage such well-established forms of revenue.

The correlation between the endowment and the membership of the monasteries appears to have been greater than between the endowment and the order of the monasteries. "Cistercian" Keldholme's property was more like that of the single-sex Benedictine house of Wallingswells than like that of its sister "Cistercian" priories of NunCotham, NunAppleton, or Stixwould, all three of which included both sexes. Although in its early days the Cistercian order had frowned on the acceptance of feudal dues, its attitude had no effect on either the Gilbertine or the "Cistercian" priories for women (and indeed little effect even on the Cistercian abbeys for men). No correspondence can be found between a priory's order and its property, but certain types of possessions needed certain kinds of labor. Whether the endowment preceded the internal arrangement or vice versa, the priories that received the widest variety of properties were the most diversified communities, including nuns, canons, and lay brothers.

In part, the inclusion of men in these monasteries was essential because the lay founders of the North did not typically endow their nuns with established forms of revenue, and forty-four of the forty-six new monasteries for women had lay founders.[59] None of these founders were from the royal family, and only two were magnates at the top of feudal society. Barons of the highest rank began Stixwould and Keldholme priories, the first two "Cistercian" houses,[60] but all other monasteries had lay founders of less renown. A few were begun by members of the new elite whom King Henry I had favored as a counter to the influence of the barons. Foremost among these *novi homines* was Eustace fitz John, founder of Malton Priory for Gilbertine canons and cofounder with his wife Agnes of Watton, the only Gilbertine priory for both sexes in Yorkshire.[61]

Most of the founders were a rank below both the great barons and the key figures of Henry I's "Northern Strategy." These were men and women with local prestige, often Norman in background, on the fringes of power politics, trying to cement their influence through judicious marriages and careful alliances. One such extended family, all related in some way to Osbern de Arches, founded four monasteries between 1147 and 1153: the Gilbertine priory of Bullington; the "Cistercian" priory NunAppleton for nuns, canons, and lay brothers; and two Benedictine priories: Nunkeeling, probably for nuns and lay brothers, and Nun-Monkton, for nuns alone.

Although only rarely are women named as foundresses, the de Arches women were the links in this familial network. Agnes de Arches, foundress of Nunkeeling, was the sister of William de Arches, the cofounder of NunMonkton. Agnes was also the mother of Alice de St. Quintin, cofoundress of NunAppleton and mother-in-law of the founder of Bullington. In addition, Alice de St. Quintin's husband gave the church of Coveham which stood on her dowry land, "for constructing and founding there a monastery of convent nuns . . . of the congregation, profession, and order of the holy nuns of Appleton." This daughter house for Nun-Appleton never materialized, the church instead passing to the priory of Royton.[62]

Norman families like these were the vassals and officials of the great.[63] Often wealthy enough to own demesne land and have vassals under them, these lay people could give *culturae* and land in severalty, like the founders of Catley, Gokewell, Greenfield, Heynings, and NunCotham. A few had important positions of their own: the founder of Marton, Betram de Bulmer, was a sheriff of York. But Normans of this stature, one rank below the barons and the new elite, were not wealthy enough to give substantial grants, and their foundations reflected their economic position. The priories they created had limited estates and demanded extensive labor in order to produce revenue. Some founders were people of even less social standing—like the inhabitants of the town of Torksey who combined their resources to endow Fosse Priory.[64]

The laity who supported women were not as prominent as the founders of monasteries for men. In a recent study of Cistercian monasteries for men in Yorkshire, Bennett Hill concluded that between 1130 and 1155 their founders were "barons of the highest rank, tenants-in-chief of the crown . . . [who] often inherited or gained the title and dignity of earl." These men founded monasteries as part of their attempt "to increase their personal political authority and private power." In a region that tried to remain autonomous, resisting royal rule from the South, monasteries assumed political importance; Hill argues that "the monasteries, by the very fact of their dependence on the nobles and by the fact of their close connection with the Holy See, implicitly supported the barons in their opposition to royal authority." Economic motives also were factors. Instead of sacrificing financially to found their monasteries, in Hill's view the laymen actually rid themselves of knight's service they would otherwise have owed on unprofitable land. By requiring payments from the monasteries for some of their "donations" and by improving their own sheepherding through shared pasturing with the skillful Cistercian shepherds, founders of the Cistercian monasteries for men actually gained financially.[65]

If Hill's conclusions about the founders of Cistercian monasteries for men are accurate, male and female monasticism expanded for different reasons. The founders of monasteries for women were lay people, but there the resemblance ends. They were not barons, but people one level

DE ARCHES FAMILY AND FEMALE MONASTICISM

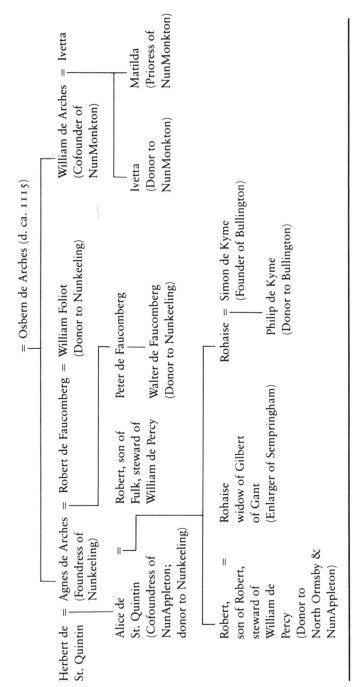

= Osbern de Arches (d. ca. 1115)

Herbert de St. Quintin = Agnes de Arches (Foundress of Nunkeeling) = Robert de Faucomberg = William Foliot (Donor to Nunkeeling)

William de Arches (Cofounder of NunMonkton) = Ivetta

Alice de St. Quintin (Cofoundress of NunAppleton; donor to Nunkeeling) =

Robert, son of Fulk, steward of William de Percy

Peter de Faucomberg

Walter de Faucomberg (Donor to Nunkeeling)

Ivetta (Donor to NunMonkton)

Matilda (Prioress of NunMonkton)

Robert, son of Robert, steward of William de Percy (Donor to North Ormsby & NunAppleton) =

Rohaise widow of Gilbert of Gant (Enlarger of Sempringham)

Rohaise = Simon de Kyme (Founder of Bullington)

Philip de Kyme (Donor to Bullington)

Note: This chart is based primarily on material in Farrer, *Yorkshire*, esp. p. 420. Included are donors and founders of monasteries for women and people necessary to explain relationships. This chart does not list all members of the families.

below the leaders of the realm, people less engaged in the civil struggles than the great lords.[66] They did not represent one side in the war between king and barons, nor did the superior lords they served have just one political persuasion.[67] Even the same economic motives did not apply, for the founders and donors to nuns usually seem to have given gifts free of any stipulations or requirements.[68] Nor is there evidence that the founders were ridding themselves of undesirable land in order to be free of the services they owed their superiors.[69] Even though many of the monasteries remained poor, the nuns needed the help of religious men not because their founders were profiting at their expense but because their founders were not people of great means.

The founders of monasteries for women did not even require that the monasteries provide a living for their kin. Alvingham, a Gilbertine priory founded when several people combined their resources, is the only monastery that a founder or foundress is known to have joined.[70] Other than Alvingham, only three priories are known to have received even kinswomen of the founders. Matilda, daughter of Ivetta and William de Arches, became prioress of NunMonkton, the only woman in that family known to have become a nun. Also, the founder's daughter joined Marrick, and the founder's granddaughter entered Wykeham.[71] In contrast to the men Hill identified, it is hard to find any evidence that these founders of female monasticism benefited in any practical way.[72]

The more varied and less powerful group of people who supported nuns do not appear to have been as economically and politically motivated as the great barons who supported Cistercian monasteries for men. Yet the political strategies of the great Northern barons had an effect on female monasticism. In the years of civil strife and gradually expanding Norman hegemony, the region was relatively free of royal domination. In these unusual circumstances, with little royal interference, lay people were free to improvise, to devise forms of monasticism particularly suited to the moors and wasteland of the North. With few prototypes for female monasticism in the area, without the influence of aristocratic models, they were able to import new religious orders from the Continent and to create their own institutional forms. Their willingness to improvise and to experiment with institutional arrangements realistic for the setting insured the success of female monasticism in the North.

THE NUNS

Another explanation for the form of monastic life preferred in the North may be the social background of the nuns themselves. When a woman joined a monastery, often her family gave a donation to the house. Customary but not mandatory, these grants insured that the new member would not be a financial burden on the community, and they guaranteed that the family would be remembered in the community's prayers. Although at a later time such donations were criticized as simoniacal payments, this was not the case in the mid-twelfth century, and many records of these donations have been preserved. An example is the gift given during the reign of King Henry II when Heloise, daughter of Supir of Bayeux, became a nun at the Gilbertine priory of Sixhills. Heloise's father, with the assent of his wife, son, and other heirs, gave Sixhills one bovate of land in East Wykeham with a toft and all its appurtenances, free and quiet from all service, custom, and exaction.[73]

When all the preserved records of this sort are compiled, a rough estimate can be made about the economic background of the nuns. Conclusions must be tentative, however, for the grants are not infallible indicators of a family's financial status. If the grant was unusually generous, it may lead to an inflated view of the family's economic position.[74] Or if the grant was parsimonious, or only a portion of the family's total investment in the priory, the nun's wealth could be underrated.[75] Since large grants are the ones most likely to have been documented, women from poorer families who entered may not be recorded at all. Furthermore, the demarcation of what was given is often insufficient to determine the value of the grant. For instance, an "acre of land" might be prime grain-producing gardens or uncleared waste; a "tithe" of a mill cannot be translated into its monetary equivalent.

Even with all these caveats, the evidence indicates that the grants accompanying the nuns could cover their living expenses. For instance, some entrance gifts to Gilbertine priories were in land of fairly precise sizes. The smallest was 10 acres; next in size was 12 arable acres with 2 acres of meadow and pasture for 12 cows and a bull. Three of the gifts were of a bovate with some appurtenance, such as a toft. Another grant was 20 acres of arable demesne land with pasture for 100 sheep. One family gave 1½ bovates, another gave 2 bovates, and a third provided 11 acres of arable land with a *cultura*. When two daughters became nuns, their family gave the monastery a church.[76] Entrance gifts to Nun-Cotham Priory were similar; it accepted three women, each of whom brought an annual rent of two shillings.[77] When one woman joined Stixwould Priory, she brought with her a virgate of land.[78] These grants were sufficient to support a peasant, and therefore they would have maintained a woman living an ascetic life.

With adequate means, but not great wealth, the nuns—like the founders themselves—were not from the most eminent families. Perhaps the absence of women with social and political prominence helps explain the control religious men assumed in so many of the monasteries. If women of the highest social standing had joined, women accustomed to ruling large households, probably they—and not the male religious—would have assumed the leadership roles. But instead, the women who became nuns came from families whose position did not give them automatic claims to power.

Little is preserved about the women for whom the houses were founded. Even though the records for the North are far more numerous and detailed than those for the South, no references are made to holy women already leading a religious life. Apart from the seven women Gilbert inspired with his preaching, nothing is known about the religious practices of the women before they joined the priories. Were it not for the evidence from the South, one might assume that male leadership implied that the nuns were not spiritually gifted. But in the South, as we have seen, holy women noted for their asceticism and prayer accepted priors when they formally began priories.

Although the records give no hint of the women's earlier religious life, they do indicate that many women joined monasteries where they had relatives, or else they joined along with kin. In several documents, two sisters became nuns at the same time. In others, mothers and daughters lived together in the same priory. In the monasteries for both sexes, nuns joined with their natural fathers, brothers, and sons. For instance, at Sempringham, three nuns were sisters, their uncle was a member of the monastery, and their parents were affiliated, as part of the "fraternity."[79]

Once the women became nuns, they followed the typical Benedictine *horarium*, sometimes glossed with customaries of their order. Whether or not priors and lay brothers shared the monastery with them, the nuns' schedule was much the same, for they were primarily choir nuns, devoted to praying the office. The earliest information on daily life in the distinctive monasteries of this region—the ones for both sexes—comes from the beginning of the thirteenth century, and therefore may not be representative of mid-twelfth-century activities.[80] But sometime before the end of 1166, Aelred of Rievaulx, the Cistercian abbot and friend of Gilbert of

Sempringham, reported to his "dearest friend who is far removed from these parts," about events in one of the Gilbertine monasteries.

Aelred wrote that God was performing miracles anew at the Gilbertine priory of Watton. "In the midst of daily manual labor and the customary psalmody," the handmaids of Christ were devoted to "spiritual offices and heavenly theories. Many, as if saying farewell to the world and all things which are of the world, are often rapt in certain undescribable departures and seem to be among the choir of angels." In addition to participating in the heavenly offices, the nuns also spoke with good spirits "by whom now they are corrected, now educated, now strengthened for certain necessities."[81] The bulk of Aelred's letter recounted some difficulties concerning one nun, an episode treated in the next chapter. But the first part of Aelred's letter reveals an intense spirituality in one of these new monasteries of the North.

According to Aelred, mystical states, the perception of being both on earth and in heaven, encouraged the nuns to intercede for each other. A great exponent himself of spiritual friendship, Aelred reported that the Gilbertine nuns loved each other and were concerned with their friends' salvation. When one nun died, the other nuns never ceased praying for her until they were certain either of her punishment or glory. Aelred then recounted a vision that one of the nuns had had in response to her incessant prayers about the fate of her friend, another nun who had recently died. On the anniversary of her friend's death, the Gilbertine nun saw a ray of sun illuminate the step before the altar during mass. In that ray of light, her friend was visible, shining with exceeding splendor, proof of her salvation.[82]

In another context as well, Aelred reported on the spiritual fervor within the priories. In a sermon on the differences between corporeal, spiritual, and intellectual visions, Aelred used as an illustration a story about another Gilbertine nun. Able to exclude from her heart all love of the world, desires of the flesh, concern for the body, and anxiety about exterior things, this nun began to burn with longing for heaven. Sometimes when she knelt for prayer, she was overcome with a certain wondrous sweetness that extinguished her other thoughts and affections. While in this state, she seemed to be snatched from the world; and in an ineffable and incomprehensible light, she saw Christ, seemingly in a corporeal form but actually in a spiritual vision. After she spent more than an hour in this departure from her body [excessus], the other nuns struck her so that she returned to her senses.[83]

In reporting this vision, Aelred included information about interrelationships between the nuns: the mystical experiences of one became the aim of the others. When they tried to imitate the first nun, they too began to receive this grace, some even unwillingly. One nun, a virgin and woman "of great distinction," objected. She attempted to dissuade her sisters on the grounds that the "knowing" was not spiritual but the result of illness or illusionary phantoms. Criticizing the others for paying more attention to these visions than to virtues, the skeptic asked God to make it plain to her if the visions were from him. Although she wanted the gift of discernment, she insisted that she did not want mystical experiences herself: she did not want her soul to be seized from her body and lifted from her mind, nor did she want to be separated from all the things she loved.

Finally, in Lent, while contemplating the passion of the Lord, the skeptic was "snatched up." In a spiritual vision, she saw Jesus hanging on the cross—bound with nails, pierced by the lance, profusely bleeding from his five wounds—and looking at her with tender eyes. Returning to herself, she broke into tears. According to Aelred, this experience convinced her that she had simply been less worthy than the others, and hence she had earlier been denied the same light they had enjoyed.[84]

Aelred's portrayal of Gilbertine nuns shows a spiritual vitality that otherwise goes unmentioned in the records. Nuns were in rapture for more than an hour; the gifted nun inspired the others; and the skeptic was converted. Without question, there was a strong spiritual dimension to the rapidity of the monastic expansion in the North. Without this religious fervor, without this intense desire for prayer, the expansion in the North could never have happened, no matter how practical the institutional arrangements devised.

PART THREE

Regulation (1165–1215)

CHAPTER 6

Enthusiasm Curtailed

Around 1165, some lay brothers of the Gilbertine order were said to have reported to Rome "certain evil things" about the houses under the rule of Gilbert of Sempringham, "namely that canons and brothers and nuns live together."[1] Pope Alexander III was sufficiently convinced of the seriousness of these accusations to order an investigation. In doing so, he was raising questions about the very institutional innovations that had made the Gilbertine order so successful and displaying the first hint of dissatisfaction with the monasteries for both sexes that had proliferated in the North in the preceding generation.

Another sign of changing attitudes was the decreasing number of new monasteries founded for both women and men. Between 1165 and 1200 in the North, only a few monasteries for women were begun, and none of them included men. In the South, monasteries for both sexes had never been as typical, but there patterns altered as well. In contrast to the earlier years, religious men rarely created new priories for women, nor did they bring holy women into their hermitages and monasteries. In the last three decades of the century, in the North and in the South, new priories for women were normally single-sex houses, and the founders were usually lay people.

In part, the shift reflected an altered situation. In the last third of the century, women seeking a religious life were not as needful as their predecessors, for by then, over a hundred priories for women existed in England. The feverish pace of the expansion in midcentury had created so many priories that women no longer required as much aid from religious men. With the void filled, growth slowed of its own accord. As the momentum lessened, a counterforce for stabilization became stronger. The wisdom of the novel arrangements that had proliferated in the period of experimentation was challenged. A desire to preserve and standardize the forms that had evolved became more pronounced. The tendency toward greater regulation first became noticeable between 1165 and 1170, in conflicts concerning the Gilbertine order.

THE NUN OF WATTON: CA. 1165

Shortly before Pope Alexander III ordered an investigation of the Gilbertines, an episode that may have underlain his inquiry disrupted one of the Gilbertine houses, Watton Priory in Yorkshire. An adolescent nun of Watton became pregnant after a secret tryst with a male religious of that priory. Known only from a letter which Aelred of Rievaulx wrote sometime before the end of 1166, the pregnancy had occurred earlier in that decade. In his letter, Aelred meant to show that God's miraculous intervention had delivered Watton from a potentially devastating scandal, so theological and moral presuppositions colored his telling of the episode. Still, Aelred was so convinced that God Himself had saved the adolescent nun that he was willing to reconstruct in detail the history of the events there.[2]

In the process of offering this unparalleled view of a Gilbertine priory operating in a crisis, Aelred revealed his own fear of close associations between male and female celibates. Convinced that only a miracle spared the monastery, Aelred had little confidence that such lapses could be prevented in the future. Hence, the story of the nun of Watton has an importance for the history of female monasticism beyond the confines of the tale, for it reveals that a monastic leader like Aelred, who admired Gilbert and publicly lauded the spirituality of the Gilbertine nuns, in reality distrusted the monasteries for women and men at the height of their expansion.

For modern readers of Aelred's letter, the punishment the Gilbertine nuns inflicted on the pregnant girl and her lover is shocking. When the nuns of Watton uncovered the love affair, they locked the pregnant girl in chains in a cell where they kept her until the brothers of the monastery captured her lover, who had fled. Then some of the nuns, pretending to want secret information from the lover, asked the brothers who were holding him "to let them have the young man for a short time. . . . He was taken by them, thrown down, and held." Brought in "as if for a spectacle," the pregnant nun was given an instrument and "compelled, unwilling, to cut off his manly parts (*virus*) with her own hands. Then one of the women standing there, snatching the parts of which he had been relieved, thrust them into the mouth of the sinful woman just as they were, befouled with blood."[3]

Aelred himself was distressed that the nuns exacted such a harsh penalty. However, since the sin of individuals implicated the whole community, Aelred could still praise the nuns for their zeal in avenging "the injury to their virginity." Reflecting on the morality of their bloody deed, Aelred reasoned that "by mutilating him and attacking her with shame and insult they avenged the injury to Christ." The breaking of God's laws affected the entire group, and in exacting a penalty, the nuns were, in Aelred's view, behaving like the people of God in Scripture. However, while Aelred commended the nuns for acting, he did not approve the form their action took. "I praise not the deed but the zeal; I do not approve the shedding of blood but I extoll the zealousness of the holy virgins against evil."[4]

In relating the affair at Watton, Aelred's purpose was not to exonerate the nuns for their treatment of the couple. Rather, Aelred wanted to recount the miraculous outcome. So he quickly moved from a critique of the nuns' actions to a step-by-step recital of the surprising next phase. One morning, about the time the pregnant girl was due to give birth, her guards entered the cell where she was chained. To their shock, she no longer appeared to be pregnant, nor was there any evidence that she had given birth. Accusing her of killing and hiding the baby, they searched the cell, to no avail.

When questioned, the girl related that two nights earlier she had dreamt that she saw the deceased archbishop Henry Murdac, the man who had originally asked Watton to receive her into the monastery. In this dream Henry Murdac chastised the girl for her troubles and told her to recite certain psalms. On the following night, she again dreamed about Murdac, who this time was accompanied by two women. Telling her that she would not be able to understand what was being done since she was not cleansed by confession, Henry Murdac and the two women took away an infant. When the girl awoke, she felt like a heavy weight had been removed from her body.[5]

Amazed at her appearance and her story, the girl's guards checked for signs of pregnancy or afterbirth. They felt her stomach; it was indeed slim. They squeezed her breasts; no milk appeared. Searching the cell, they uncovered no evidence that she had given birth. The story spread as her guards called in others, and still others. All found the same thing: "all was well, all was clean."

According to Aelred, the nuns did not presume to judge what had happened until they consulted Gilbert of Sempringham. In the meantime, they kept the girl in her prison cell, chained to a large trunk and door-bolt. One night one of the chains came undone; the girl said she had had a vision of two ministers of divine mercy coming to her. Later one of the fetters fell. Gilbert, who had been informed of the events, was not certain whether the girl should be released.

It was at this point, after the seeming miracles had taken place, that Gilbert called in Aelred. Entering the girl's cell with his companions, Aelred held the remaining fetter in his own hands. Recommending that the girl be left as she was, Aelred told the Gilbertines to put their hope in God, who could free her if it was His will. A few days after Aelred had returned to Rievaulx, he received a letter from Gilbert reporting that the remaining fetter had also fallen. Telling Gilbert not to bind one whom God had absolved, Aelred was satisfied that God had miraculously resolved the potentially devastating situation.[6]

In the way he recounted the events that had led up to the tryst, Aelred never explicitly criticized Gilbert or his institution. Indeed, Aelred emphasized that the girl, given to Watton when she was only about four years of age, had never been suited for monastic life. Her teachers had tried to correct her with words and with beatings, but she had preferred her own fantasies to religious discipline. Although she wore the habit and appeared to be an honest member of the community, the nuns supported her "due to fear instead of love." As Aelred understood the background, years of discord had preceded the affair, one explanation for the violence of the nuns' response.[7]

But it was precisely because such situations could exist that any contact between celibate men and women was dangerous, as Aelred also made clear in his account of the beginnings of the affair. "It happened that brothers of the monastery, to whom the care of exterior was entrusted, entered the monastery of the women to do some kind of job." Somehow the young girl was able to approach the brothers and curiously watch their work and faces. "There was among them an adolescent who was more attractive in appearance and more blooming in youth than the others." Noticing each other, the girl and boy exchanged a nod, then a sigh, then a sweet word of love; they agreed on a place and time where they could more freely talk and enjoy each other. The boy arranged to signal their meetings at night by tossing a rock onto the wall or roof of the building where the girl was accustomed to rest.[8] The first steps were rapid and unreflective, evidence for Aelred of the speed with which sinful thoughts could become actions.

Once the attraction had been formed, in Aelred's view the new institutional arrangement was powerless to prevent the affair. Breaking his narrative to address the girl rhetorically, Aelred reflected that neither fear nor love of her order, her sponsor, or Christ Himself had checked her sexual desire once it was inflamed. Addressing Gilbert in the same rhetorical aside, Aelred asked, "Where then, father Gilbert, was your most vigilant sense in the keeping of discipline? Where were those many well-thought-out mechanisms (*exquisita machinamenta*) for keeping out the opportunity for failings?" Gilbert had not trusted reason and loyalty alone to discipline his religious, but "where then that care so prudent, so cautious, so shrewd? Where that watch so faithful around all doors, windows, out of the way places so that evil spirits seem not to be able to enter?"[9]

Instead of challenging Gilbert to watch more diligently or to institute more regulations, Aelred comforted him: "One girl, father, foils all your diligence, because 'unless the Lord watches over the city, he who watches it keeps alert in vain.' You did, blessed man, you did whatever a man could do, since that was useful. But just as no one can correct whom God despises, even so no one is able to serve him whom God will not have him serve."[10] If such a sympathetic response was meant to excuse Gilbert and his order, it also offered no hope of preventing such liaisons in the future. If a mere glance could lead to sexual desires, if well-thought-out mechanisms could not prevent abuse, close contact between the sexes was fraught with danger.

As Aelred told the story, the girl, whom neither loyalties, reason, nor Gilbert's rules could restrain, "went out a virgin of Christ; after a short while, she returned, an adulteress." Aelred's harshest judgment was reserved for the boy. The girl "thought only of love," whereas the boy meditated on debauchery. "She goes out, just like a lulled dove, not having any judgment, soon caught by the hawk with his claws, ruined." Naive at first, "her mind already corrupted, her flesh is corrupted. Knowing the wicked pleasures from experience compelled her to repeat them." For Aelred, the girl was a victim, the boy her ruin, the monastery the setting for the tragedy.[11]

In the uncovering of the affair, chance played a larger role than any institutionalized guidelines. The secret meetings continued until the young man fled, "leaving the monastery for the secular world" once he knew the girl had conceived. Only then did "the sisters," already suspicious because of repeated strange sounds at night, interrogate the girl. Even then no official investigation took place, but certain nuns, whom Aelred called the wiser mothers (*matronae sapientiores*), questioned the girl. She confessed, "past being able to conceal it. Then stupor overtook all who heard the word," but Gilbert still was not consulted.

Learning that the girl was pregnant, the nuns in anger began to beat her, falling on her with their fists and tearing the veil from her head. When some of them wanted to knock her senseless or burn her at the stake, the older women (*matronae*) finally checked the fervor of the younger ones by insisting that only the discipline allowed under the rule be imposed. The girl was whipped and imprisoned in a cell where she was chained and fed only bread and water. The nuns reproached her daily; "meanwhile her swelling stomach revealed the conception." But still none of the women informed Gilbert, nor did they tell the men of the monastery.

Terrified of the consequence this affair could have for all of them if it became public, the nuns themselves debated what to do. Should they expel the girl and risk infamy for them all? Although their reputation would be safer if they kept her concealed in solitary confinement, would that threaten her life and that of the child? And would their tending her secretly in a cell make them vulnerable to a charge of conspiracy? This sense of panic, when every course of action invited ruin for their monastery, underlay their later castration of the lover. But even after all these events, Gilbert and the men at Watton apparently remained unaware of the dilemma facing them all.

The men were brought in only because the girl made a confession. Nurturing a hope that the nuns might resolve the crisis in another way—by dismissing her to her lover's care—the girl revealed that he had arranged to meet her again at a certain time and place if she too fled the monastery. "Then the master of the congregation, certain things having been admitted from the brothers, uncovered the matter." Finally finding out about the events, Gilbert set a trap for the lover. One of the Gilbertine brothers disguised himself to look like the girl by dressing in a habit and veil, and he sat where the pair had arranged to meet. When the lover, now in secular clothes, came running to the veiled figure, other hidden brothers lying in wait seized him, beat him, and took him captive.[12] Even after his successful ploy had captured the lover, Gilbert did not remain in control for, as we have seen, the nuns acquired the boy from the brothers and forced the girl to castrate him.

Aelred's letter about these events, sent to a friend "far removed from these parts," may not have been known in England, for no mention of it occurs in other documents. Yet the episode itself had serious repercussions on the largest, most successful new organization for celibate women and men. The Gilbertines obviously did not think they could keep the matter secret, or they would not have consulted Aelred and had him come to Watton Priory with several companions. But even if they thought they could prevent a scandal, in part because of the miraculous outcome, the Gilbertine leaders would have consulted to devise rules to prevent any repetitions of such trysts. Certainly the leaders at Watton would have reconsidered both the existing legislation and how well it was kept.

The Gilbertines were not able to dismiss this affair as a unique occurrence, unlikely to happen again. Aelred was not the only one to remind them of the dangers of close association of the sexes. In addition, also in the 1160s, Rome ordered an investigation into the relationship between the sexes in their monasteries. Whether a cause or a symptom, the affair at Watton marks the beginning of the period when the sexes were again segregated.

GILBERTINES ON THE DEFENSIVE (1165–1169)

Although there is no evidence that the problems at Watton had become public, just when Gilbert was recovering from the crisis there, or even before it had been resolved, he learned about some charges his lay brothers had made at Rome.[13] Gilbert probably received his first written account of the complaints in 1165, in a letter from his old friend Archbishop Thomas Becket, who was in exile in France. Whatever triggered the lay brothers' journey to the pope, the events at Watton Priory would have come rapidly to Gilbert's mind when he received Becket's letter. With no details of the charges but a tone of great concern, Becket wrote, "You know" how "we have loved, favored, and protected" you and your order "above all others." The regard was clearly mutual, for the Gilbertines had aided Becket's escape to France and they were accused of sending him funds there. "Because we have loved you so greatly," Becket continued, "how greatly we are disturbed and grieved when we have learned such things to have arisen from you and your order which offend not only the eyes of men but even God Himself." Now everywhere, even "at the ears of the lord pope," a "certain great scandal" had become known. "To correct this scandal," Becket commanded Gilbert to receive some letters that the pope had sent, read them to his order, and accept their recommendations.[14]

Rumors must have been circulating widely, for before Gilbert had received any direct communication from the pope, two other men wrote him with advice on how to respond. Gilbert's friend William Turbe, a Benedictine monk and bishop of Norwich, shared Becket's perspective. William encouraged Gilbert to accept the pope's letter even though it contained harsh words, for, like the bee that makes honey from many types of flowers, the bitter as well as the sweet, Gilbert could increase his wisdom if he utilized even critical statements.[15]

King Henry II disagreed. Commanding Gilbert to persevere in what he had begun so well, King Henry told Gilbert to keep diligently all the institutes of his order just as the holy see had already authorized them. No one, not even Pope Alexander, should convince him to do otherwise.[16] By early 1166, the stage was set for another scene in the drama between the king, the pope, Archbishop Thomas in exile, and the English episcopacy. This time, the Gilbertines were on center stage and the script was scandal in the Gilbertine order.

After all this preliminary advice from the leaders of church and state in England, Gilbert claimed he never did receive the much heralded papal letters. The ringleaders of the complaining lay brothers, however, purported to have copies that they liberally quoted everywhere. As charges and rebuttals flew back and forth, letters in Gilbert's defense were sent to Pope Alexander. The five that have been preserved were from King Henry II and four ecclesiastical leaders. Two were bishops who were prominent allies of Henry in his struggle to curtail papal interference in English church affairs: Roger of Pont l'Evêque, archbishop of York, a Norman and ardent opponent of Archbishop Thomas; and the powerful Cluniac bishop of Winchester, Henry of Blois, a cousin of Henry II. In addition to these two bishops and the king himself, men who would probably have automatically supported Gilbert because of their opposition to papal control, two others wrote in Gilbert's defense: his friend William Turbe, bishop of Norwich, and an unnamed prior of Bridlington.[17]

After receiving these letters in support of Gilbert, Pope Alexander authorized English church leaders to resolve the affair themselves. Episcopal inquiries were held in both the archbishoprics of Canterbury and York. The charges directed against the Gilbertines are usually surmised from the reports of these episcopal inquiries and from Gilbert's own autobiographical recollection. However, the five letters sent to the pope just as the turmoil began reveal better what contemporaries thought the "scandal" was. Far more than the episcopal hearings, these letters focused on relationships between the Gilbertine women and men. Based either on the rumors or their own knowledge of the papal letter, the five men who wrote the pope assumed sexual license was the scandal he meant to correct.

Every letter informed the pope that he was mistaken if he thought the sexes were allowed to associate freely in the Gilbertine monasteries. As Roger, archbishop of York, wrote, "we have heard" that your holiness has been told "certain evil things about those houses which are under the rule of Master Gilbert of Sempringham, namely that canons and brothers and nuns live together, but far otherwise is the case. For they live apart, eat apart, and from each other are segregated so that no canon or brother is allowed admission to the nuns."[18]

Henry of Blois echoed Roger's sentiments. Although he said he had not personally inspected Gilbert's dwellings of canons and nuns, he reported on their holy reputation and Gilbert's own virtue. Informing the pope that Gilbert was a man honored for using his patrimony to train souls of both sexes in the yoke of Christ, Henry called Gilbert a guardian of virginity, a cultivator of continence, and a shepherd who placed his lord's sheep in "separate and distinct dwellings." In terms that stressed the complete segregation of the sexes, he continued, "The whole realm of England approves and admires the enclosed virgins and the canons ministering sacraments to them. The canons perform separately and are not allowed to be admitted to the women unless for extreme urgent necessity and then with witnesses from both sexes."[19]

Praising the sanctity of his close friend Gilbert, Bishop William Turbe of Norwich swore that he had heard no word of infamy concerning the canons whose innocence was being denounced before the pope. William assured the pope that, because he lived nearby and frequently visited the Gilbertines, he could not be ignorant of any scandal involving the canons. If the affair at Watton was between a nun and a lay brother, William Turbe may have been choosing his words judiciously. Repeating the defense offered in the other letters, William explained that the canons were denied access to the nuns. The nuns and canons each had their own cloister and chapel where they slept, meditated, and prayed. Both the prior of Bridlington and King Henry II reiterated the same claim: the literate brothers had their own churches and dwelt far enough outside the wall of the women to prevent any problems from arising. The persistent denials reveal the assumed charge: that the Gilbertine canons and nuns lived too closely together and prayed together.[20]

A letter from Cardinal-legate Hugh, written either around the same time or a few years later, further confirms that the pope feared the Gilbertine women and men were too intimate. Praising Sempringham as a place where the conversation was more in heaven than among men, Hugh explained, "Just as I had heard for certain, [the nuns] hide their faces and live secluded from all men." Reminding the pope of the Gilbertines' good reputation, Hugh asked him to be merciful toward the order despite the disturbances caused by Ogger the Smith, one of the lay brothers.[21]

Although the basic defense offered to the pope was an assurance that the sexes were segregated, other lines of argument were included as well. "Rome does not reverse its decrees," the prior of Bridlington pronounced, using a legal perspective to sway the lawyer pope. Bishop William Turbe of Norwich warned the pope, "Do not presume to change" what you and your predecessors have formally accepted.[22] According to these supporters, any disruption of Gilbert's arrangement was potentially ruinous. Roger, archbishop of York, was emphatic: "If the canons and brothers were separated far from the nuns, as we take to be ordered by your suggestion, they would not be able to remain in that house." According to Roger, "the supporters who have conceded their possessions to the canons and nuns with pious intentions would by no means support them but would take back" what they had freely given before if the pope further segregated the sexes.[23] What Archbishop Roger warned, King Henry II threatened: "Clearly let it be known that we and our barons would take back our possessions" if the pope interfered with institutes he had already approved.[24]

Instead of changing the Gilbertine *Institutes*, the pope should discipline the disruptive lay brothers: Cardinal-legate Hugh offered this advice in his report to the pope, and Henry of Blois and King Henry II reiterated it. Both Henrys blamed all the trouble on certain insolent lay brothers, who after almost forty years of service desired to leave. In Henry of Blois's opinion, the pope should correct the rebels instead of harming the pastor of the flock. King Henry II called the lay brothers thieves, men who had carried off the possessions of their monasteries. He claimed they had offered him three hundred marks of silver as a bribe, an unbelievably astronomical sum unless the lay brothers actually were thieves or acted in collusion with wealthy backers. Recommending that the lay brothers should either be ejected from the order or punished with death, King Henry warned the pope not to listen to rustics who before their conversion were mere serfs, bound to the soil. In King Henry's opinion, the lay brothers sought two ends, neither of which the pope should endorse: a change in the already approved *Institutes* and the elimination of the canons from the Gilbertine monasteries.[25]

Probably in 1167, and certainly by 1169, when the episcopal hearings were held in the provinces of York and Canterbury in accord with the papal mandate, the focus had successfully been shifted to the lay brothers' dissatisfaction.[26] The investigations were held under bishops who had already defended Gilbert—Bishop William Turbe of Norwich in the South and Archbishop Roger of York in the North. The bishops asked very specific questions. Had Gilbert ever made the lay brothers vow a second profession to the abbey of Savigny against their first profession of Sempringham? Had any of the lay brothers been imprisoned or excommunicated? Had Gilbert refused to accept certain lay brothers back into the order in accordance with the pope's instructions? The issue of the relationship between the canons and nuns had fallen into the background, perhaps a sign of the sympathy of the investigators to Gilbert's cause.

Basing their assessment on the verdict reached at these inquiries, two modern scholars—David Knowles and Raymonde Foreville—gave credence to only one of the lay brothers' complaints: that they had suffered under an extremely strict rule. Gilbert himself later admitted as much when he modified the regulations on food and clothing for the lay orders. The investigators themselves conceded only that Gilbert might have at one time sought a vow to the abbey of Savigny, but any such profession was no longer in effect. Whatever the validity of the other charges, the question about the relationships between the sexes had receded into the background.[27]

As Gilbert recounted the events some years later, he was most disturbed by the ingratitude of the lay brothers who led the dissension. Two were lay brothers whom he had commissioned before the rest; a third Gilbert had received when he was "almost a beggar, seeking a living by the art of weaving." Ogger the Smith was the fourth ringleader. When Ogger was still an inexperienced boy, Gilbert had aided his entire family. Receiving Ogger along with his three unskilled brothers, Gilbert had trained Ogger and one brother as smiths and the other two as carpenters. Gilbert had also accepted Ogger's poor, "almost decrepit" father and "his aged mother along with his two sisters, beggars who had been ill for a long time." Complaining that Ogger and the other lay brothers had taken property from the monastery, ridden around on stolen palfreys, followed their own will, made a mockery of chastity and honesty, defamed the order, and even roused Pope Alexander against him, Gilbert lamented that the pope, "believing the words of Ogger," had given Gilbert a most "severe mandate and cruel sentence, which later was revoked." Gilbert himself insisted, "As God is my witness, I spoke the truth and have not lied."[28]

Gilbert's lament helps explain the lay brothers' discontent. Among the first to join Gilbert at Sempringham, with him for more than a decade before the canons were added, these lay brothers had lost influence. Ogger and the other rebellious lay brothers might have resented any attempt of Gilbert's to submit his priories to Savigny, for this would have lessened their own responsibilities in the community. They certainly resisted Gilbert's other innovation, the introduction of canons. Ogger told Bishop William Turbe of Norwich that he wanted an arrangement in which all four groups—canons, nuns, lay sisters, and lay brothers—were placed equally and commonly under one rule. Calling this an older arrangement, one which might indeed have been in effect during the first few years of Gilbert's plan, Ogger and the others apparently did not demand the total elimination of the canons, as Henry II had thought. Rather, they wanted a return to earlier practices.[29]

Even though the episcopal inquiry, Gilbert's autobiography, and recent scholarly literature have focused on the lay brothers' dissatisfaction, the one legislated result of the investigation was increased segregation of the canons and nuns. Pope Alexander wanted the canons and nuns to celebrate mass in their own separate churches. Only two or three canons were to be designated successively to say mass in the women's church. To further remove suspicion, Bishop William of Norwich added that the lay brothers also should be restricted to the canons' oratory.[30] Whatever sparked the lay brothers' complaints, the result was a curtailment of their joint liturgies with the nuns and further separation of the Gilbertine women and men.

Knowing Aelred's account of the affair at Watton Priory, one might be surprised by the report of the inquiry by Roger, archbishop of York, the diocese where Watton was located. Roger declared, "concerning those houses which [Gilbert] has in our diocese, we dare to assert with certainty that they are regulated most honestly and religiously."[31] How could the affair at Watton have remained undetected? Possibly Roger was choosing his words carefully, for even in a well-regulated house, an affair could take place. One almost imagines a decision, justified by the miracle at Watton, in favor of Gilbert and the king in opposition to still more papal interference in English affairs.

Accepting the report of the inquiries, Pope Alexander sent three surviving letters. In one he assured King Henry II, in another all the church leaders of England, that he loved and protected the Gilbertines. In a letter of reconciliation to Gilbert, Alexander restored to him and his successors the right to govern and legislate for his order in accordance with the Gilbertine statutes, which the pope again approved. Sometime within the next fifteen years, the rigorous separation of the sexes mandated at that time was somewhat relaxed. The Gilbertines were again allowed to worship in a common church, although henceforth a large partition divided it in a way that prevented the sexes from seeing each other.[32]

Although the Gilbertines were officially declared innocent and Pope Alexander again praised their institution, the damage of years of suspicion could not be erased. The relationships between the sexes in the Gilbertine houses, and by extension in other monasteries of the North, had become a debated topic, with Rome's censure widely known. The innocent enthusiasm of the middle part of the century was replaced with caution and regulation. Although they are not the only explanations for the shift in attitude, the controversies that shook the Gilbertine order marked the moment when new monasteries for both male and female religious ceased to be popular. After 1170, growth and experimentation came to a halt.

DECREASED PARTICIPATION OF MALE RELIGIOUS IN FEMALE MONASTICISM (1165–1200)

After 1165 in the North, the expansion of female monasticism virtually ceased. For almost a quarter of a century, no new monasteries for women were founded in the entire region. In the middle third of the century, women received forty-six new priories; in the last third, they acquired only four more, all at the end of the century. Not only did the number of new foundations drop precipitously. Their institutional form changed as well. In contrast with the earlier monasteries, all four of the new priories were Benedictine houses for women alone. Moreover, only one of them, Foukeholme Priory, sometimes called Thimbleby, in Yorkshire, was in a shire where the earlier expansion had been concentrated. The other three, Armathwaite and Seton priories in Cumberland and Lambley

Priory in Northumberland, introduced female monasticism to remote areas of the region that had barely been penetrated in the years of rapid growth. Clearly a change had taken place.[33]

Another sign of the shifting mood in the North was the conversion of one of the priories for both women and men into a single-sex house for women alone. During King Stephen's reign, the sheriff of York had begun Marton Priory for Augustinian canons and nuns. Both sexes were still present in 1180–81 when King Henry II gave "the canons and nuns" of Marton land worth forty shillings. However, in 1158 King Henry had given some nuns a nearby site, the land and place of Moxby. Sometime in the last third of the century—beginning around 1167 in the opinion of Knowles but only partly completed by 1180 according to King Henry II's donation—the nuns remaining at Marton Priory were moved a mile and a half to the south, to Moxby Priory. Instead of serving celibate women and men, Marton became a priory for Augustinian canons alone.[34] The enthusiasm for including both sexes in one monastery was lessening in the North.[35]

At first glance, the South seems to show more continuity between the middle and final third of the century. Expansion continued, with about twenty additional monasteries for women founded before 1200. However, in contrast to the earlier years, religious men initiated, oversaw, or joined only a tiny fraction of these new houses. The spirit of cooperation between religious women and men that had underlain many of the earlier foundations had weakened. Even though new monasteries were founded in the South, the trend there, as in the North, was away from experimental models back to traditional single-sex houses.[36]

In the last third of the century, monks founded only one new religious house for women, and it was as much a hospital as a monastery. Around 1194, the men of St. Albans Abbey began St. Mary de Pre in a church that its abbot, Warin, had recently built to honor the relics of St. Amphibalus. Unlike the hermitesses whom his predecessor Abbot Geoffrey had aided a generation earlier at Markyate and Sopwell, the women Abbot Warin introduced at St. Mary de Pre were leprous women who had been living with men at a nearby hospital. Abbot Warin separated the leprous women from the men, had them veiled, and restricted them "by the limits of a rule lest wandering around they would become entangled in secular errors."

St. Albans retained supervision of St. Mary de Pre. To oversee the women and serve their church, Abbot Warin appointed a chaplain and a clerk. These two men were fed with provisions from St. Albans, which also set aside tithes and other payments for their support. St. Albans diverted for the women's use the *procurationes*, allotments of food and drink, which it had received in honor of its deceased abbots. Until the corrodies were sufficient to feed all thirteen women, St. Albans sent them bread from its own oven, and also promised bread from the nuns of Sopwell Priory. Tending to all the women's material needs, St. Albans provided clothing, cartloads of wood, some tithes, some land, and even food for two horses. However, even though St. Albans remained closely tied to St. Mary de Pre, it treated the new house not as a daughter priory, but as a dependent hospital, founded to segregate leprous women from men.[37]

Further evidence of the changing attitudes toward close associations between male and female religious was the difficulties some hermitesses in the South encountered when they looked for supporters during the last part of the century. According to the fourteenth-century Register of Crabhouse Priory, "a maiden whose heart the Holy Spirit moved to seek a desert place where she might serve God without disturbance of any earthly thing" located an appropriate site, "all wild, and far around on every side was no human habitation." After "the aforesaid maiden found that place to her liking," she "assembled along with her other maidens, and there caused a chapel to be reared," events recalling the background of Sopwell, Markyate, and other priories earlier in the century. The foundation of Crabhouse Priory is usually dated to this gathering of women around the chapel, in about 1181.[38]

"But the devil, who never ceases from pulling down all good works, put it into the hearts of those who were his ministers to rob the aforesaid maidens." Instead of finding sympathetic donors, the women were driven by these otherwise unknown men to settle elsewhere. Choosing a place near a river, the women were later forced to flee again because of a flood. "Wherefore they went away and did not again return, and how and where they lived is not known, except only of the one who made herself a recluse in the cemetery of Mary Magdalene of Wigenhall." Conflicting claims over this site arose because the monks of Castle Acre Priory already had rights in "the hermitage of Wigenhall which Joanne held." In the last decades of the twelfth century, when the women of Crabhouse faced a most precarious future, their survival was hampered both by property disputes with the monks of Castle Acre and by complicated transactions with the canons of Ranham Priory. Not until the early thirteenth century did the women of Crabhouse gain full possession of their priory. The plight of these women, driven from their first settlement, involved in protracted negotiations with the canons of Ranham and the monks of Castle Acre, was a far cry from the support earlier hermitesses had readily received.[39]

Still another example of the change was the establishment of Buckland Priory in 1180, the first Hospitaller priory for women in England, for this house was created to separate female and male Hospitallers and regularize their relationship. At Buckland, the Hospitallers were given a priory that in 1166 had been created for Augustinian canons. By 1180 the Augustinians at Buckland faced legal sanctions because of the murder of their steward, a relative of the founder. As part of his vow to reform monasteries in penance for his role in Thomas Becket's death, King Henry II decided to transfer Buckland to the Hospitallers so that they could provide a place in England for their "sisters."

The transfer took place gradually over a number of years. First the prior of the Augustinian canons was deposed. The other canons stayed at Buckland until the founder gave his consent to the transfer; then the remaining men—seven canons and a lay brother—were placed in other canonries in England. Only then did Garner of Naples, prior of the Hospitallers in England, receive possession of Buckland, with its numerous churches and dependent chapels. Around 1180, or shortly thereafter, Garner introduced there at least eight "sisters" of the Hospitallers. Henceforth at Buckland a preceptory of Knights Hospitaller with its own church existed alongside a priory for the sisters with their own church. A prioress governed the women, but their priory was dependent on the preceptory for men. Since Buckland relied for its support primarily on churches and chapels in its possession, the male religious functioned somewhat like the Gilbertine canons, serving the churches and supervising the women.[40]

Since King Henry II had so adamantly supported the Gilbertine arrangement, one might imagine that he wanted to encourage the Hospitallers, who officially did not include sisters at that time, to assume responsibility for women. But this was definitely not Henry's intention. When Prior Garner and King Henry agreed to found Buckland Priory, they were not supporting an increased association between the sexes in the Hospitaller order. Instead they were regularizing relationships that had heretofore existed informally at seven Hospitaller preceptories in England, where "sisters" had been living singly or in pairs. Formalizing the status of these sisters, Prior Garner moved them from these seven locations in order to supervise them at one.[41] In accepting Buckland Priory, Garner agreed that henceforth the sisters would be "in no other place in England . . . except in the house of Buckland."[42] By eliminating the problematic Augustinian canons and then regularizing the Hospitaller sisters, King Henry II had initiated a twofold reform at Buckland Priory.

The religious women and men of Harrold Priory were also separated in the last quarter of the century. In 1177 the Abbey of Arrouaise attempted to divest itself of responsibility for its daughter house at Harrold by assigning the priory and its two churches to Missenden Abbey, an English house of the Arrouaise order. Since the time of its foundation at the suggestion of Hilbert Pelice, Harrold Priory had remained under Arrouaise Abbey, and that abbey had installed its priors "one after another, for a long time, until after the death of prior Guy, brother of the foresaid abbot G[ervase], without contradiction." As the blood ties weakened, with the death of Gervase's brother Guy and probably of his sisters at Harrold as well, Arrouaise Abbey decided to minimize relations with Harrold.

The women and men of Harrold objected, obtained letters from Pope Alexander III authorizing an investigation, and appealed to Bishop Hugh of Lincoln, who assigned the case to the priors of Kenilworth and Warwick. According to the decision reached in 1188, Harrold became an independent priory under its own prioress. The abbots of Arrouaise and Missenden "freed [the nuns] and their house with all its appurtenances from all subjection" in return for a payment of one half mark yearly to Missenden. After 1188 the records of Harrold contain no mention of canons or priors. Nuns and the prioress alone were claimants in a well-documented dispute at the century's end over rights in a church. Another formal link between celibate women and men had been dissolved.[43]

Bishops also showed less willingness to become involved with religious women. Only one bishop in the last third of the century founded a monastery for women, and that was short-lived: established by Archbishop Richard of Canterbury between 1174 and 1184, Ramstede Priory survived only a few decades. In 1200–1204 Archbishop Hubert, with "the advice of prudent and religious men and with the consent of those nuns," transferred Ramstede Priory with all its buildings and appurtenances to the prior and canons of St. Gregory, Canterbury. According to Archbishop Hubert, the nuns of Ramstede "were living in that place with less honesty and less religiousness, in fact they were keeping there an observance so irregular and beyond the custom of their order that not a little scandal was arising from the place."[44] No further information is provided about the problems at Ramstede, but with its transfer to canons, Ramstede became one of only two monasteries for women dissolved for irregularities during the entire century.

Only one Gilbertine priory for both sexes was founded in the later part of the century, the second such monastery in the South. Shouldham Priory illustrates that barons of sufficient rank, motivated by familial loyalties, could still support the arrangement the previous generation had favored despite the decreasing popularity of such institutional forms. Sometime after 1193, Geoffrey fitz Piers, earl of Essex and chief justiciar of England, granted his manor of Shouldham with all its registered property, located in some twenty places, including five churches, to "the nuns and their clerical and lay brothers."[45]

In founding Shouldham Priory, Earl Geoffrey specified that it was to be the burial site of his first wife, Beatrice de Say, who had died in childbirth. Although Beatrice had temporarily been buried at the Gilbertine priory of Chicksands, the monks of Walden Abbey had hoped to acquire her body and her family's support. Earl Geoffrey's decision disappointed the monks of Walden, and so, in their cartulary, the monks entered a critical comment about the earl's foundation of Shouldham. "So this man, with the conceit of others (*caeteris vana*) admiring and following the new, namely that order recently invented by Gilbert of Sempringham, founded . . . Shouldham. And there, just as that new and unheard of for ages form of religion demanded, he gathered canons with nuns, brothers and sisters."[46] The monks' comment was a clear sign of the growing distrust of religious houses for both sexes. In their view, Gilbert's arrangement was new and therefore as unwise as the empty conceit of those who recommended it.

Indeed, the Gilbertines themselves appear to have been reluctant to found new houses for both sexes. Shouldham Priory was the only Gilbertine monastery for both sexes begun in the last third of the century, either in the North or the South. Instead, several new monasteries were created for men alone. In the South, canons were provided with Marlborough and Mattersey priories, and a hospital for leprous Gilbertine men was begun at Clattercote. Even in the North only priories for men were founded: Newstead and Bridge End in Lincolnshire; St. Andrew's, York; and Ravenstonedale, a cell for the canons of Watton. Before 1165 the only Gilbertine house for men had been Malton Priory, so, again, a new trend is discernible in favor of single-sex monasteries.[47]

Even the French-based Order of Fontevrault seems to have succumbed to the same pressures. Around 1165 the order installed male religious at Grovebury Priory; these men apparently were charged with overseeing business affairs for the entire Order of Fontevrault in England.[48] If in reality these men had authority over the prioresses of the Fontevrauldine priories, a major change had occurred in the organization of that order in England. But even in beginning priories for men alone, the Gilbertine and Fontevrault orders reveal the altered mood.

Virtually nothing is known about the other sixteen new priories for women in the South. Although earls began two of these houses, the rest were poorly endowed creations of lay people with only local prominence. Countess Lucy became a nun at her husband's foundation, Castle Hedingham; and Bristol's foundress Eve became its first prioress. Very little survives about the women for whom these houses were begun. Around 1195 two women, Joan and Agnes, built Campsey Ash for themselves and other religious women on an estate their brother, Theobald de Valoines, gave them. Hermitesses may also have been at Limebrook and Tarrant before they became priories, but the records are inconclusive. Religious men are not mentioned in the documents of any of these houses.[49]

The only evidence of a continuing spirit of innovation was in the religious affiliation of these priories in the South, for a smaller percentage of them claimed to be Benedictine. The women of Bristol, Limebrook, Campsey Ash, and perhaps Bungay and Brewood White Ladies identified with the Augustinians. Although the Cistercian order did not recognize them in the late-twelfth century, the nuns in at least five new priories—Wintney, Tarrant, Catesby, Cook Hill, and Sewardsley—apparently considered themselves to be Cistercians. But even though they claimed an identity with these religious orders, the nuns and sisters of these new priories did not have the close relationships with religious men that their sisters enjoyed in the "Cistercian" and Augustinian houses for women begun earlier in the century. The only exception was at Catesby, where canons apparently lived along with the nuns, in imitation of the Northern model from the midcentury.[50]

Thus even though expansion continued in the South, it conformed to the pattern in the North. Everywhere founders abandoned the new institutional forms for religious women and men and returned to more traditional, single-sex arrangements. A change of this magnitude cannot have had a simple cause. Since fewer hermitesses set out on their own, women did not require the same help from monks and canons. The pressing needs of religious women had been met, and so existing houses were sufficient. Certainly the crises in the Gilbertine order would have dampened the ardor for close associations between male and female celibates.

Although King Henry supported the Gilbertines against the papacy, that order became increasingly regularized and institutionalized as well, the subject of the next chapter. As King Henry II tightened royal control, he may have discouraged experimentation. Many factors were involved, but the result was clear: the trend in favor of close relationships between female and male religious had been reversed.

CHAPTER 7

The Gilbertine Vision

At Christmas 1188, Gilbert of Sempringham seemed to be near death. After he received extreme unction at his island canonry of Newstead, his companions furtively whisked him along back roads the forty miles to Sempringham Priory, for they feared that if he died elsewhere, some other church might become his burial site. Gilbert recuperated briefly at Sempringham, where he received his priors "and many other of his disciples" for final words and blessings. Slipping into a stupor on February 3, 1189, Gilbert awoke only to murmur the verse: "He has dispersed; he has given to the poor; and he has gone back." Around Matins Gilbert died.[1]

Since Gilbert was more than a hundred years old when he died, his order had long anticipated his passing, and plans had been made for a smooth transition in leadership. There was no chance that the order would disappear. Even after the affair at Watton and the revolt of the lay brothers, the Gilbertines still were the single largest organization of female religious in England. At Gilbert's death fifteen hundred Gilbertines lived in nine monasteries for both sexes and four for men alone.[2]

Two substantial Gilbertine documents from the early thirteenth century reveal the order's self-understanding in the period after the death of its charismatic leader. Before 1202, one of the Gilbertine canons—possibly Ralph, sacrist of the church of Sempringham—composed a *vita* of Gilbert to aid his canonization. This *vita* survives in the somewhat expanded version of 1205, revised to include the additional material presented to Pope Innocent III on behalf of Gilbert's canonization earlier that year. The only surviving edition of the *Institutes of the Gilbertine Order* also comes from the early thirteenth century.[3]

These two documents show how the Gilbertines justified their order in a period of decreased enthusiasm for monasteries for both sexes. Instead of abandoning their decision to include women and men in one religious order, the Gilbertine leaders proposed three main lines of defense: their founder was a saint; the communities of celibate men and women were a foretaste of the millennial kingdom; and their legislation was a sufficient bulwark against potential misconduct. By the early thirteenth century, what had begun as Gilbert's personal response to seven women had become a fully developed, self-conscious form of Christian life.

THE CULT OF GILBERT THE SAINT

After Gilbert's death, the Gilbertines' most immediate goal was his canonization. In their view, nothing could aid them more than official recognition that Gilbert was holy in his earthly life and still interceding on their behalf in the next. When Hubert Walter, archbishop of Canterbury, began to promote Gilbert's canonization, Pope Innocent III informed him that two tests would be applied: "the virtue of habit and the virtue of signs, namely merit and miracles . . . ; neither merit without miracles nor miracles without merit are sufficient."[4]

To convince Rome that these criteria had been met, a host of English dignitaries besieged the pope with letters witnessing to Gilbert's holy life and miraculous cures. "Many men as well as women, many religious as well as seculars" attested to the merits of his life, his largesse, and his construction of numerous monasteries. Those writing on Gilbert's behalf included the abbots or priors of Barlings, Croxton, Kirkham, Kirkstall, Kirkstead, Revesby, St. Albans, and Swineshead, and the bishops of London, Ely, Coventry, Norwich, Rochester, and Bangor. King John himself and Geoffrey fitz Piers, earl of Essex and founder of Shouldham, added their support as well. In contrast to the letters sent to Pope Alexander III in the 1160s, which defended the Gilbertine inclusion of women and men, those sent to Pope Innocent III promoting his canonization avoided the subject: they referred to Gilbert's "nine monasteries for nuns" and the four for canons as if they all were single-sex houses.[5]

Although non-Gilbertines promoted Gilbert's cause, Gilbertine canons were the most active proponents of his cult. One of them composed Gilbert's *vita*, and two canons traveled to Rome to present the material and attest in person to the miracles: "at his tomb the blind see, the lame walk, the mute speak, the paralyzed are restored, fevers drops, swellings disappear, the deaf hear, and demoniacs are freed."[6]

To determine if these claims warranted canonization, Pope Innocent III authorized a hearing at Sempringham in September 1201, which was conducted by Archbishop Hubert Walter of Canterbury, Bishop Eustace of Ely, and the abbot of Peterborough. After learning the results of the three days of hearings he had commissioned at Sempringham, Pope Innocent III was convinced. He pronounced Gilbert's life to be "immaculate and holy, for he was admirable in abstinence, distinguished in chastity, devout and vigilant in prayers, [and] discreetly solicitous in providing care for his flock." Innocent praised Gilbert for combining the active and the contemplative life; even though Gilbert was a model leader, he was "devoted to contemplation in those hours which he was able to free, so that he alternated contemplation and an active position in the world."[7]

The miracle stories preserved in the *vita* reveal the awe in which Gilbert's contemporaries held him. Particularly informative are the miracles that the *vita* attributed to him during his lifetime. Gilbert was not credited with the full repertoire of spiritual gifts common in lives of saintly medieval figures: he was not clairvoyant; he was not—like Christina of Markyate—famed for his visions or his abilities in astral projection; and in only a few miracles was he shown courageously overcoming hostile natural forces. Instead, most of Gilbert's miracles reveal his effect on his followers. Because they perceived him to be holy, his disciples expected Gilbert to work miraculous cures, which they then witnessed.

The miracles in the *vita* portray Gilbert busily governing his order while his supporters—Gilbertines and non-Gilbertines alike—were equally busy saving his discarded personal items. A canon had access to Gilbert's old footwear, which he put on to cure his swollen feet; his feet got better. One of the Gilbertine's baronial supporters, the wife of Simon de Beauchamp, saved some bread Gilbert had blessed; it remained uncorrupted for years and worked many cures. A childless couple was finally able to conceive after Gilbert slept in their bed.[8]

Many of the miracles reveal Gilbert's strong personality. Even in his old age, Gilbert could fill his followers with dread, and his accusations could torment the guilty. On one occasion, when there had been a fire, Gilbert wanted whoever had started the fire to confess; the guilty nun suffered bodily torments until she revealed her carelessness. After Gilbert lost his sight, his disciples believed he could still "see" the impact he had on them; for instance, Gilbert could "see" when his words moved the nuns to tears.[9]

In some of the episodes his followers considered miraculous, Gilbert may actually have been teasing them. Once when Gilbert had a fever, he asked his sympathetic chaplain Albinus if he was willing to assume the fever in Gilbert's stead; when Albinus got a fever just as Gilbert recovered, he thought Gilbert had miraculously transferred the fever to him.[10] These stories reveal the kind of leader Gilbert had been, a man willing to use humor or threats to sway his communities, a person equally likely to inspire awe or provoke remorse.

An independent source written just a few years before the *vita* provides another account of Gilbert the leader rather unlike those the anonymous canon selected. In his collection of stories about churchmen of his day, Gerald of Wales tells an incident involving Gilbert. When Gilbert was an old man, one of the young nuns confessed to him in secret that she lusted for him. "Gilbert was shocked beyond belief by what he heard and put off giving his advice until the following day." The next morning, after preaching to the nuns in their chapter meeting about the virtue of chastity, Gilbert revealed that "even though he was old and withered and weak, one of their nuns . . . cast lustful eyes on him." Gilbert then disrobed entirely and stood there naked before them, "hairy, thin, and covered with scabs." Probably pointing at the crucifix, Gilbert cried, "Behold, this is the man who ought to have been desired by a woman consecrated to God, by a spouse of Christ!" Indicating himself, he moaned, "Behold the mean little body for which the poor wretch of a nun considered it worthwhile to lose her body and soul in hell." Gerald concluded, "By this remedy the woman was cured forever of her concupiscence."[11]

The veracity of this story is uncertain. Gerald wrote his *Jewel of the Church* within ten years of Gilbert's death. Its most recent translator, John Hagen, points out that Gilbert and Gerald were both "very close to the bishops of Lincoln and to Henry II." Because Gerald lived in Lincoln shortly after Gilbert's death, Hagen concludes that Gerald might have had the incident from "firsthand hearsay." Whether or not the story is reliable history, it indicates again Gilbert's contemporaries' concern about the dangers of associating both genders in one monastic community. They thought even Gilbert himself was shocked at the thoughts his followers could have, and that he might resort to dramatic acts to cool their ardor.[12]

In addition to the miracles attributed to Gilbert when he was alive, the inquiry conducted in September 1201 uncovered thirty miracles for named individuals that had occurred in the dozen years since Gilbert's death. Although Gilbert's posthumous miracles reveal less about his character, they show his ongoing influence. In part the Gilbertines survived Gilbert's death with no discernible crisis because he was believed still to be active among them. Women were the primary recipients of Gilbert's posthumous aid, and lay people reported more miracles than Gilbertines. The miracles to which laity attested outnumbered those that religious reported two to one. Accounts of cures came from people of all walks of life, including a maid, a pauper, a priest, and the wife of a

knight. Gilbertine nuns, canons, and lay brothers vouched for many
miracles; only lay sisters were absent from the list of the healed.

Gilbert's aid was invoked for withered legs, gout, tumors, eye trouble,
leprosy, sore heads, and mental problems. Gilbert's tomb at Sempringham, placed so that both women and men had access to it from their
respective sides of the partitioned church, was the usual site for the cures.
Sometimes the supplicants at Gilbert's tomb dreamed they saw Gilbert
before they were cured. Often they spent at least one night there, sometimes a whole week. The Gilbertine nuns in other monasteries, unable to
visit the tomb at Sempringham easily, relied on another remedy: they
drank the water in which his corpse had been washed. Contact relics,
like Gilbert's girdle, were utilized as well. Convinced that Gilbert's intercession had healed them, these women and men and the witnesses to
their cures kept Gilbert's presence alive long after he had died.[13]

In Pope Innocent III's instruction, miracles alone could not establish
a person's sanctity. In addition to reporting the miracles, the *vita* itself
was a long panegyric, presenting every episode in Gilbert's life in a favor-
able light. A particularly telling example of the *vita*'s reinterpretation of
events in Gilbert's life was its handling of a dream Gilbert had had while
still a young man. When he was running the school he had organized at
Sempringham before he joined the episcopal court at Lincoln, Gilbert
boarded with a family in the parish. One night Gilbert dreamt about the
daughter of the family. In his dream, Gilbert placed his hand on the girl's
breast and could not take his hand away. Fearing that the dream "por-
tended a future crime of fornication," Gilbert moved to a dwelling he
constructed in the cemetery of the church. In case some might think
that the dream meant that Gilbert had sexual desires inappropriate in a
founder of monasteries for women, the *vita* interpreted the dream. Relating that this girl was later one of the first seven women for whom Gilbert
built Sempringham, the *vita* reasoned that her bosom was "the secrecy
and peace of the church," "a place of good conscience and perpetual
peace" which Gilbert provided for her and from which his hand, his
unshakable care, could not be removed. Hence the dream prefigured
"glorious merit."[14]

The *vita* emphasized above all Gilbert's dedication to the welfare of his
order. Gilbert had received the written profession of every new member,
and he had visited each Gilbertine monastery at least once a year. Constantly traveling to the different houses, not "to eat the bread of idle-
ness" but to labor, Gilbert had given counsel on business affairs and also
had helped with the writing of books, construction of buildings, and

other useful tasks. Serving as legislator, financial manager, and spiritual guide, Gilbert personally had been the locus of unity for his order.[15]

The *vita* presents the view Gilbert's followers had of him shortly after his death. None of the difficulties the order had faced had lessened their regard for their founder, and nothing had caused them to reconsider the wisdom of including both sexes in one monastery. However, the author of the *vita* shaped his account to highlight themes that would be appealing to an early thirteenth-century audience. Just as the letters in support of Gilbert's canonization neglected to emphasize the inclusion of both sexes in one monastery, the *vita* chose its material carefully. The *vita* indicates what made Gilbert laudable even in a period that distrusted the kind of organization he had designed. A model canon, successfully combining the active and contemplative life, Gilbert was so watchful over his community that he even remained active on its behalf after his death.

THE GILBERTINES' MILLENNIAL VISION

Even though Innocent III had only asked that Gilbert's life and miracles be examined at the hearings on his canonization, the author of the *vita* took on a larger task as well: the vindication of the Gilbertine order. Because Gilbert had both designed the Gilbertine order and lived as a Gilbertine most of his life, the way to assure his canonization was to establish the holiness of his order's way of life. Even when the *vita*'s version of the origin and growth of the order is not accurate history, it reveals the Gilbertines' defense in a period increasingly distrustful of close associations between female and male religious.

The *vita*'s technique is discernible in its use of a dream to explain the purpose of the Gilbertines. In NunAppleton, a Cistercian priory in Yorkshire about 150 miles from Sempringham, the prioress Agnes had a dream just before Matins on that February night in 1189 when Gilbert died at Sempringham. In her dream Agnes was admiring preparations for a funeral when she was told that the burial service was for Gilbert of Sempringham, who had just migrated from the world. Agnes then saw Gilbert himself as he suddenly rose up from where he had been lying. Taking into his hand a pastor's staff, Gilbert began chanting in a high, sweet voice a sequence with modulations Agnes had never before heard. Seeing Gilbert walking and singing, Agnes was sure that he was still alive, so she rebuked the informant in her dream who had told her the funeral was for Gilbert: "Do you think that I do not know Master Gilbert? I know him very well; and now he is not dead." Agnes's dream informant replied, "Are you ignorant about what happened to Blessed John the Evangelist? For just as he received the mother of God to himself, so [Gilbert] received those imitating her into his care. . . . Just as it happened to him, so it will happen for this one." Then Agnes dreamed that Gilbert led into a beautiful church a vast throng of people, such a huge crowd that Agnes felt claustrophobic and awoke with a start, the sweet smells of the ceremony still in her nostrils. The bell for Matins rang; Agnes told her sisters of Gilbert's death. Sometime later they received an announcement that confirmed the accuracy of the date and the hour of her dream.[16]

In recounting Agnes's dream, the *vita* gave its readers one possible explanation for the Gilbertine mission: like John the Evangelist who cared for the Virgin Mary, Gilbert aided the handmaids of Christ. But the *vita* did not develop this interpretation. Rather, it chose a more eschatological justification, one that placed the Gilbertines in an intermediate time, in the millennial period before the final fulfillment of the kingdom. Much like his contemporary Joachim of Fiore, whose predictions fueled the Spiritualist Franciscans' eschatological expectations, the author of the *vita* thought the Gilbertine order signaled the beginning of a new age.

The apocalyptic overtones of the *vita* are especially clear in its account of the foundation of Sempringham Priory. In place of Gilbert's terse account of his gathering of the seven women at Sempringham, the *vita* claimed Gilbert had imitated the apostles, to whom Jesus said, "Look around you, look at the fields; already they are white, ready for harvest! . . . I sent you to reap a harvest you had not worked for." Similarly, the *vita* related, "Certain secular girls in the village of Sempringham, whose minds had received the seed of the word of God which [Gilbert] had often ministered to them, now, having been cultivated with dew and heat, were white for the harvest." Not only had Gilbert followed Jesus' command to his disciples to reap the harvest prepared for them; he had also sowed and watered the field.[17]

Selecting biblical passages rarely used for female monasticism, the *vita* described Gilbert as preparing for the kingdom. When Gilbert conferred his wealth on women instead of men, he was following the advice in Luke 16:9 where Jesus reportedly said, "Use money, tainted as it is, to win you friends, and thus make sure that when it fails you, they will welcome you into the tents of eternity." The *vita* reasoned:

When he did not find men [*viri*] who wanted to live so strictly for God, he considered it worthy to confer all his wealth for the use of such who were truly poor in spirit and who might purchase for himself and others the kingdom of heaven. Therefore by means of unrighteous mammon, he made for himself friends (*amici*) who might receive him into the eternal tabernacle. But he did not make men his friends first, but women; for he called together for rejoicing female friends (*amicae*) found by the coins who later produced many male friends (*amici*) by their chastity.

Women were the "poor in spirit," for "[Gilbert] repeatedly said, and divine counsel admonished, that more freely should be benefited those who are naturally weaker and more compassionate, and thus more fully could reward be hoped for."[18]

With such reasoning, the *vita* gave a theological justification for what Gilbert's account described as just a historical evolution. The *vita* not only found scriptural imperatives for what Gilbert had presented as his personal response to women he knew; in describing Gilbert's inclusion of lay brothers, the *vita* also departed from Gilbert's historical narrative and suggested instead a scriptural explanation. Like the servant in the parable about the kingdom in Matt. 22:10–14, Gilbert on the king's command went into the city and found "paupers and cripples, the blind and the lame" and compelled them to come in.[19]

The *vita* did not say that the lay brothers wanted to imitate the Cistercian *conversi*. According to the *vita*, the lay brothers were displaced men, desperate enough to accept strict regulation. It emphasized that some had been paupers, supported for years with alms in Gilbert's parish. Some it identified as fugitive villeins and as people on the margins of society, the poor and the beggars. The revolt of the lay brothers undoubtedly had tarnished the relations between the Gilbertine men, for the canon who authored the *vita* omitted all references to the Cistercian influence on the lay brotherhood, and he did not mention the positive motives of the lay brothers. Perhaps the *vita* accurately describes those who became lay brothers in the early thirteenth century.

The *vita* first referred to the Cistercians when Gilbert decided to "deliver up the care of his houses to the guardianship of the Cistercian monks." According to the *vita*, the growing numbers in his communities made Gilbert want "to put off the honor and burden" and lay it upon others whom he judged "stronger and more able."[20] At this point, the *vita* most markedly deviated from Gilbert's own account." Although Gilbert had described his mission at Cîteaux as a failure, the *vita* pronounced it a success. "The Lord did not want the congregation of Sempringham to be deprived of its own pastor, who was better for its future than ten others."[21]

In addition, the *vita* supplemented Gilbert's account with a story that implied he had followed the advice of Bernard, abbot of Clairvaux, and Malachy, archbishop of Ireland, when he added canons to his order. The *vita* claimed that Gilbert stayed on at Cîteaux, where he became friends with Malachy and Bernard, who then helped him devise the institutes of his order. For Gilbert to have met both Malachy and Bernard, he would have had to stay at Cîteaux for more than a year. Such an extended visit is most unlikely since Gilbert made no reference to it in his account and reported instead only about a rejection at Cîteaux.[22] What is particularly striking is the way the *vita* omitted Gilbert's report that the Cistercians inspired the lay sisters and lay brothers and introduced instead this story of Cistercian input on the addition of the canons.[23]

Although each group was in fact added seriatim, the *vita* focused on the theological significance of the finished institutional form. Women and men, monks and clerics, and literates and illiterates were all included in one order. Gilbert had combined the types of people that the world normally kept apart, and in so doing, he was "the vicar and imitator of Peter." As Peter had learned in his vision of a "four-sided piece of linen lowered from heaven, filled with every kind of animal," Gilbert had discovered that he should accept those honored in the world and those rejected by it.[24]

The *vita* rhapsodized on the apocalyptic meaning of Gilbert's plan with images from Isaiah 11. The new concord Gilbert had created between usually discordant groups was like the wolf living with the lamb, the panther with the kid, the calf and the lion led by the small boy. "There the fox is not cunning, and the raven scorns the offered cadaver." Love having overcome hatred, all lived as one, united without murmurings. "There young men and virgin girls, the old with the young, will praise the name of the Lord, because all ages, every condition, and both sexes exalt there not their own but the name of the Lord alone."

For the author of the *vita*, only God could be responsible for placing such unlikely groups in one monastery, under one master, with one set of institutes. Although the *vita* had introduced the story that the Cistercians had encouraged the final fourfold arrangement, it could still argue that such an order had never existed before. Gilbert could not have discovered the arrangement anywhere else or learned it from men, for it was a new creation. As the apostle Paul claimed to have done in Galatians 1, Gilbert must have received his plan directly from God, through the teaching of Christ and the unction of the Holy Spirit.[25]

Such millennial enthusiasm was absent in the mid-twelfth-century records, but it was needed in the more hostile climate of the early thirteenth century. Like the apostles Peter and Paul, Gilbert had assumed a unique mission, one that many people could find shocking. The Gilbertine order was the result of Gilbert's *apostolica vita*, but for the author of the *vita* the Gilbertines had more significance than even Gilbert had imagined. A foretaste of the coming kingdom, the Gilbertine communities were an apocalyptic sign. The order that Gilbert had devised to meet particular circumstances had come to see itself as the herald of a new age.

GILBERTINE GOVERNANCE

The Gilbertine *Institutes* structured what the *vita* envisioned.[26] An amalgamation of regulations from many decades, the surviving manuscript of the *Institutes* from the early thirteenth century merges the primitive mandates of Gilbert with later legislation. Some regulations were added after Gilbert's death, such as the instructions for the celebration of his feast. Some rules, like those limiting the number of horses the master general could use on his rounds, logically seem later than others specifying the main duties of the master general. For the most part, however, the different chronological strata in the *Institutes* are impossible to separate. After Gilbert's own narrative in the preface,[27] old legislation and new legislation have been thoroughly interwoven. A revision of the *Institutes* must have immediately preceded, and perhaps been the occasion for, this sole surviving transcription.

The early thirteenth-century manuscript of the *Institutes* is organized in a dozen chapters, containing almost two hundred sections of regulations. Topics covered included everything from how many haircuts and hair washings were allowed each year to how a canon should act if his nose began to bleed while he was celebrating mass.[28] Although it is possible that the *Institutes* were not always strictly obeyed, they present what the Gilbertines thought their eschatological community should be like. And they were more than just an ideal. Unlike the ninth-century never-constructed ideal monastery depicted in the *Plan of St. Gall*, the *Institutes* were the laws of an actual community. Its general chapter passed and continually revised this legislation, which was mandated and enforced.

Because the Gilbertines made so many ideological claims, one might expect to find in their organization a radically transformed society, one in which traditional roles were altered in light of the millennial kingdom. But whereas gender and class roles were reconsidered, they do not appear to have been redefined. Instead of challenging church law or cultural expectations about each group, the Gilbertines attempted to permit each class, sex, and order to perform the tasks for which it was "ideally" suited: tasks that in some "less fortunate" arrangements an inappropriate person might have to assume. Because this entire marvelous unity of disparate groups was under the master general of the order, also called the prior of all, the first set of rules in the *Institutes* concerned this pivotal position.

When Gilbert created and was the first to assume the office of master general of his order, he was supporting an atypical form of leadership. Robert of Arbrissel did not maintain similar control over his Order of Fontevrault, nor did Norbert of Xanten over the Premonstratensians. Not only did Gilbert deviate from the course his peers in new religious orders chose; his position over a whole order was virtually unprecedented. Gilbert could not base his power on the abbatial rights granted in the *Benedictine Rule,* for Gilbert was neither an abbot nor a monk. Indeed, for years Gilbert had remained a secular priest; only late in his life did he become a Gilbertine canon, to insure that future master generals would be Gilbertines. Because Gilbert was not the head of Sempringham Priory, his authority over the other Gilbertine monasteries was not like the abbot of Cluny's rights over Cluniac monasteries. Nor did he assert the claims of a parent abbot as in the Cistercian system. In the mid-twelfth century, the only similar leaders were the master generals of the military orders.

Historical circumstances and Gilbert's own charisma had catapulted him into an unrivaled position in his order, so it was not necessary for his role to be institutionalized. Yet, just as the *vita* presented Gilbert as the preserver of the unity of the whole, the *Institutes* entrusted this role of master general to his successors. According to the *Institutes*, the master general was judge, manager, and disciplinarian. Since he was not affiliated with any one monastery, the master general could travel freely and constantly. He was the judge to whom all controversial or difficult decisions were referred.

To enable him to have complete access to all information, the master general was allowed to speak privately with the sisters, the only man granted this permission. The master general could enter the women's enclosure to hear any confessions that the prioresses had reserved for his special attention, especially first confessions and those considered grave. On those occasions, companions accompanied him, but they remained at a discreet distance, out of earshot. The master general had final authority in legal and economic matters, for charters were binding only with his seal, and nothing with a value of more than three marks could be sold, transferred, or purchased without his approval. Since he received the profession of all new members of the order, he visibly personified the order's unity.[29]

Assisting the master general was a group called scrutinizers (*scrutatores/scrutatrices*) or traveling inspectors (*circatores/circatrices*). Three male scrutinizers—two canons and a lay brother—visited each Gilbertine house at least once a year. The female scrutinizers—two literate nuns and an illiterate woman (probably a lay sister)—visited all the monasteries with women once a year, or more often if there was manifest necessity. Charged with aiding the master general in the maintaining of discipline and "the proper practice of religion," the scrutinizers heard complaints, made judgments, and reported directly to the master general and the general chapter. Since they could converse freely with any Gilbertines of their own gender, the scrutinizers extended the master general's ability to keep informed of the minutest details. Because they were his aides, the master general chose and installed them, with the consent of the general chapter.[30]

Another group further enhanced the master general's authority: the scrutinizers of the cloister (*scrutatrices claustri*). In each monastery for women, the master general and the female general scrutinizers appointed three sisters, or "as many as are sufficient." Required to report everything that would enable their superiors "to correct errors of the house and improve good things," these sisters were guaranteed protection from interference or reprimands by the prioresses. The scrutinizers of the cloister could make their confessions and receive their penances directly from the master himself, "lest the power of the prioress suppress their freedom in the correction of these things."[31] No similar group existed among the men in the monasteries, presumably because the master general himself had freer access to the men. Probably the affair of the nun at Watton had an effect, for the scrutinizers of each cloister would insure that the nuns never again could keep a matter of such magnitude concealed from the master general.

In numerous ways, the *Institutes* augmented the position of master general and curtailed local autonomy. The phalanx of scrutinizers under the master general limited the power of the prioress, and that office was further constrained by an unusual system of rotation. Each monastery had three prioresses, each of whom exercised in turn the office of prioress. When one of the three prioresses was unable to fulfill her duties, a subprioress temporarily replaced her, insuring that the authority of the other two prioresses did not increase. Although the nuns of each monastery elected their prioresses, even that autonomy could be challenged. If the nuns had not elected a new prioress within fifteen days after the death of the previous one, then the master general appointed his own choice. Rarely, if ever, was a prioress in any other order so limited in her access to power. With so many restrictions, a prioress could never gain enough influence to challenge the master general.[32]

Although the prior of the local monastery did not have to share his office as did the prioresses, his authority was limited in other ways. Placed and deposed at the will of the master general, the prior of each monastery referred to him all large financial decisions and controversial judgments. Although the prior could address the entire monastery in his weekly sermon at the Sunday mass, his authority was basically over the men alone.[33] He did not even hear the confessions of the women. Typically the women confessed their failings to the prioress, either in the chapter of faults or more privately in the parlor, and she adjudicated penances. If any of the women had committed sins needing sacramental absolution, these were confessed not to the prior but to either the master general or the general confessor, a priest whose identity was concealed and who traveled to all the communities. Nor did the prior hear all the confessions of the men, for they saved their more serious confessions for the general scrutinizers, the master general, or the general confessor.[34]

The annual general chapter was the only check on the master general envisioned in the *Institutes*, and it functioned more as an extension of his power than as a sounding board for local leaders. Annually the general chapter met at Sempringham Priory, where it judged all matters crucial to the operation of the order and revised legislation in the *Institutes*. Although the annual chapter could also depose the master, the only possible grounds were incontinence or serious infirmity. Any resistance of the general chapter to the master general was unlikely, for his appointees were in control there. The majority of those who attended the general chapter were officials he selected—the six general scrutinizers, the general confessor, and the prior and cellarer of each monastery. The only locally elected officials who attended the general chapter were the two prioresses sent from each house, and they too held office only with his approval.[35]

On the death of a master general, a special meeting was held at Sempringham. The representation was basically the same as at the annual general chapter, with the addition of a third nun, a third canon, and a lay sister. The balance of men to women was roughly equal, offset slightly by the additional canons from the all male monasteries. But there was no question that the canons were primarily in charge of selecting the master general. The only lay brother present was a general scrutinizer, and even after elaborate procedures to permit the nuns to attend, their voice was heeded only in the preliminary stages. The process began when the entire group, called the *universitates* in the *Institutes*, elected four canons. These four canons in turn chose nine more—five priors and four other canons. With the assent of the "greater and wiser" part of the collective, these thirteen canons were entrusted with the selection of the master general, who might or might not be one of them.[36]

According to the *vita*, the Gilbertines' strength had lain in Gilbert, the creator and guardian of their order. No other model of leadership was proposed on the death of their revered founder. Certainly the *Institutes* did not transfer power to the nuns. When the Gilbertines were first organized in the mid-twelfth century, many priories of women had had religious men as their custodians, guardians, and priors. At the beginning of the thirteenth century, the Gilbertines still considered this arrangement so desirable that they legislated even greater authority for male religious, especially for the master general. The Gilbertines knew both genders could flourish in one monastery, but they retained the belief that strong male leadership was essential. Their eschatological community was not egalitarian: they preferred a constitutional monarchy to a democracy.

DAILY LIFE ACCORDING TO THE *INSTITUTES*

When in the 1160s the lay brother Ogger had complained about inequality in the Gilbertine order, his perception was accurate. According to the *Institutes*, the Gilbertines sought harmony between the canons, nuns, lay sisters, and lay brothers, but they did not seek to eliminate distinctions of sex and class. The millennial kingdom imaged in the *Institutes* was like many thirteenth-century depictions of heaven, where virgins, martyrs, clergy, monks, and lay people formed separate groups. The Gilbertines sought to bring together in one "marvelous unity" those whom society divided into male and female; clerics, monastics, and laity; servants and the served; rulers and the ruled; and even literates and illiterates. But each group in this harmonious whole was to remain distinct.

Basic to this unity was the proper functioning of each group, so the *Institutes* were primarily comprised of sections of legislation for the nuns, canons, lay brothers, and lay sisters. The Gilbertine nuns were Benedictines, and like other nuns, their day was organized around the monastic offices. Following the musical reform that the Cistercians had spearheaded, the nuns said the hours in plain chant. Because nuns and canons were forbidden to say the office in the same choir, the women met alone in the simply furnished priory church. A nun who had already proven her ability in reading at meals or the collation led the other women. A basic distinction between the nuns and the lay sisters was the nuns' ability to recite the office; before making her profession, a Gilbertine nun had to know the psalter and the requisite hymns and canticles.[37]

The daily chapter meeting of the nuns was led by one of their prioresses, who expounded the rule or gave a sermon. Here they also confessed their faults and accepted penances. Only serious sins needing sacramental absolution were reserved for the visit of the general confessor or the master of the order. For their meals, the nuns ate in their own refectory, where they listened silently to edifying readings. At the designated times for labor, the nuns worked in their cloister, with the face of one to the back of another. Their tasks included sewing, reading, embellishing manuscripts, or copying works specified by the master.[38] Thus, in the view of the *Institutes*, Gilbertine nuns were not expected to deviate from the practices of other nuns; instead, what was to distinguish them was their ability to devote themselves to the monastic offices and manual labor with none of the disturbances that might demand the attention of nuns in single-sex houses that lacked the services of resident canons and lay brothers.

Although they were modeled on the Cistercian *conversi*, the lay sisters and brothers were not actually Benedictines. While the nuns were Benedictines and the canons were Augustinians, the lay sisters were servants who lived lives as disciplined and ascetic as the other members of the community. Of the traditional monastic virtues, obedience was the one in which a lay sister was to excel. Admitted only if she was at least twenty years old and if she had proven during a year's novitiate to be "obedient, humble, and devout," a lay sister was to obey the nuns "without any murmuring or contradiction, . . . so that by God and her superiors she deserved to be promised remuneration and grace." Responsible for preparing all the food for the community and for cleaning the women's section of the monastery, the lay sisters also served any female guests who visited the monastery.[39]

When their schedule permitted, the lay sisters attended the monastic offices in the nuns' church; at other times they recited on their own the Our Father, creed, Miserere, and certain verses and responses. On Sundays and fourteen feast days during the year, they were excused from manual labor to join the nuns at mass, where eight times a year they received communion. Even though they were not expected to spend long periods in prayer, some lay sisters apparently did, for legislation warned the lay sisters not to be excessive in their devotion, not to enter the church before the designated time for offices, and not to remain too long. In addition to attending the nuns' liturgies, the lay sisters received spiritual direction from either the prioress or other designated nuns. Although the *Institutes* encouraged the lay sisters to develop their spiritual life, it emphasized that their primary task was to free the nuns more fully for prayer and reading and to insulate them from guests. Twice weekly they held their own chapter meeting; a prioress and a few other nuns supervised these meetings, another sign of the lay sisters' subordinate role in the monastery.[40]

Most of the lay brothers were involved in agricultural labors. Some of them lived on granges under the supervision of the granger, a lay brother himself, who decided what to plant and when to harvest. But many brothers served at the monastery itself, as cobblers, smiths, bakers, weavers, tanners, and tailors. Some helped with the guest hospice for men. Like the lay sisters, the lay brothers followed the monastic *horarium*, either attending the offices in the canons' oratory or saying on their own the Our Father, creed, Miserere, and certain responses. On Sundays and the feast days that the order celebrated, the lay brothers attended mass and heard the prior's address in chapter. Once a week they held their chapter meeting, under the supervision of a few canons.[41]

The canons' lives combined service and prayer. Several of the seven to thirteen canons per house held offices. Most important was the prior, whom the master general appointed. The prior presided over the canons' daily chapter, where he heard their confession of faults, adjudicated their penances, and instructed them about their two rules, the Gilbertine and Augustinian. During the week, the prior shared priestly duties with other canons, but on Sundays and feast days, he officiated at mass in the common church. There only the men could see him, but all could hear his words.

The cellarer had responsibility for the property of the monastery; he kept all the accounts, paid the servants, supervised the granges, and distributed clothes. A subcellarer handled the housekeeping for the canons' section of the monastery; the subcellarer also supervised two major chores: the baking of bread and reception of guests in the hospice for men. Canons not assigned other tasks labored much like the nuns; in their cloister, the canons sat face to back, reading or copying works designated by the master. All the canons were literate; their own novice master taught them how to read and to perform the liturgical services. Even though Gilbert had originally chosen canons because they were literate and ordained, according to the *Institutes*, not all canons received priestly ordination.[42]

In the plan set forth in the *Institutes*, most of the time the four groups functioned independently. But since responsibility for the monastery was entrusted to both sexes, at times it was necessary for the women and men to have some communication. Touching was absolutely forbidden. Private correspondence was outlawed. Nor were the women and men allowed eye contact; as Aelred of Rievaulx had emphasized in his report about the nun of Watton, a simple look could give rise to lust. The *Institutes* tried to insure that any necessary communication would be by sound alone.[43]

At liturgical events, the worshippers could hear each other, but they could not see each other. On those feast days when the entire community processed into the church, curtains hung in the cloister blocked the opposite sex from view. On Sundays, the women entered their own side of the partitioned church, which had its own altar. On the other side of the wall, the prior, or a visiting dignitary, preached and celebrated mass at the canons' altar. The kiss of peace was a "stone of peace" passed to the female sacristan through a revolving window beside the nuns' altar. Hosts, the eucharist chalice, and the water of benediction were transferred in the same way, to be distributed by the women themselves. If the medieval mass had become primarily a visual drama, as liturgical historians have argued, the price the Gilbertine women had to pay for the inclusion of men in their monasteries was high indeed.[44]

When the Gilbertine women and men had to communicate with each other, they used "windows," but these were windows through which no one could see. Close relatives could visit twice a year at a small window, a finger length long and a thumb in breadth, a slot for conversation but not vision. Confessions were made at the same type of window. Otherwise windows were turning windows, designed for the exchange of provisions, money, or eucharist hosts in a way that prevented either side from seeing the other. With sight deemphasized, the Gilbertines may have been more attuned to the sense of hearing. Perhaps a side effect was a greater sensitivity to Gospel readings, the psalms of the office, sermons, and the words of the mass.[45]

Because they were not allowed to see each other, the Gilbertines invisibly performed services for each other. The nuns did not see the canons who served as their priests, business managers, and legal advocates. The canons who officiated at mass could not see the women; even the prior was forbidden access to the women's section of the monastery. The precentrix, who was in charge of all the books in the monastery, passed manuscripts that the canons requested through a turning window. Almost a symbol of this type of communication, the female sacristan could be heard but not seen when she rang the bells that called everyone to the offices.[46]

Only at two liminal points—when a Gilbertine joined and departed from the community—was the prohibition against eye contact relaxed. The nuns, lay sisters, and lay brothers all made their profession and received their habits at the nuns' altar in the presence of the master of the order. When a canon was received, the ceremony began on the canons' side of the church; there he laid his written profession on the canons' altar and renounced all claim to his property. After he was clothed as a canon, the canons as a group then presented him to the nuns who were assembled in their chapter house. Denied any communication with nuns before his profession, a canon could hold conversation with certain nuns at the time of his reception if the prior approved.[47]

Death was the other disrupter of the usual scheme. When a nun was critically ill, the sacristan rang the bell to summon a canon. Accompanied by three other canons and a lay brother as witnesses, the canon then entered the women's section to give extreme unction and the viaticum. In life known to the other sex only by voice, after death the deceased was placed in church in a location where he or she could be viewed by all.[48]

To carry on the daily business of the monastery, the Gilbertine men and women passed goods, money, and records back and forth through the turning window that separated them. While the canons conducted all business matters, the nuns had a say before any wool, butter, cheese, or property was disposed of or before any money was spent. The care of the property was entrusted to four men—the prior, cellarer, and two lay brothers—but they verified their decisions with the nuns. At least monthly the cellarer provided the nuns with a detailed list of expenditures and a report on all sales, purchases, and property transactions. Except for thirty shillings that the prior reserved for small purchases, all money, all gold and silver (including the liturgical vessels), and all precious cloth was kept in the nuns' treasury and locked with three locks, the keys of which three different nuns held.[49]

Other financial arrangements would have been simpler. For instance, the canons could have had total control. Or traditional monastic economic systems could have been adopted, like the Benedictine obedientiary arrangement where certain individuals were given complete responsibility for specific tasks. Revenue could have been divided in advance between the groups, a plan adopted in part when the nuns were given free disposal of a tithe of the income from all the lambs that the monastery owned.[50] But in general, the Gilbertines preferred a check and balance system, making cooperation mandatory.

In the preparation of clothes, the Gilbertines showed that unseen partners could cooperate in a shared task. Lay brothers sheared the sheep they shepherded in the fields. Lay sisters wove the wool into cloth and cut the material for the garments. The nuns helped sew the clothes, one of the few occasions when nuns were allowed to work side by side, instead of face to back, in the cloister. Finally, the canons sold the excess clothing or gave the garments as gifts. Another example of acting together was the monthly clothes washing: in this case, the nuns and lay sisters washed their clothes and the canons'; the lay brothers cleaned their own. Both sexes participated in the making of shoes, for the lay sisters made the thread the lay brothers needed to sew the leather.[51]

Food preparation was also a joint endeavor. Lay sisters prepared the food for the whole monastery under the direction of a nun, the appointed kitchener/cook for the week. Each day the men announced to the lay sisters how much food they and their male guests needed. The nuns' cellarer, in charge of the monastery's storehouse, distributed the required ingredients for the lay sisters to use: bread, fish, eggs, milk, cheese, butter, beans, salt, and flour. Many of these items had been acquired from the lay brothers, who prepared the flour; brought eggs, honey, fruit, and vegetables to the kitchen; tended to the geese, chickens, and bees; and insured an adequate daily supply of fuel and water. The lay sisters made ale from malt the lay brothers had prepared. After the meals, the men returned leftover food to the women who distributed it to the poor or fed it to the animals.[52]

In the arrangement outlined in the *Institutes*, the Gilbertine nuns, canons, lay sisters, and lay brothers could work together while exemplifying the "best qualities" of their sex, age, and class. As the *Institutes* reveal, the Gilbertines passed numerous laws to help make their vision a reality. Yet because each of the four groups represented a fundamental division within society, identity with one's own group was psychologically compelling. With each group having its own character and goals and following its own schedule, the "marvelous unity" could disintegrate. Even before the early-thirteenth-century edition of the *Institutes*, the lay brothers had rebelled; and in his preface to the *Institutes*, Gilbert condemned anyone who encouraged discord between the groups.[53] Even though the Gilbertines were neither levelers nor aggrandizers, they recognized that a successful confederation of such disparate types of people was in itself apocalyptic, a foretaste of an unearthly harmony.

CHAPTER 8

Abbeys and Anchorholds

Although the twelfth-century transformation of religious life was discernible primarily in the new monasteries, some of the preconquest royal abbeys were also affected. At least one abbey—Amesbury—became a monastery for both sexes when in the 1170s it joined the Order of Fontevrault. There also are late, rather ambiguous, references to canons who held prebends at Winchester and Wherwell abbeys. Since both of these monasteries were rebuilt after they were burnt in the middle part of the century, during the civil wars between Stephen and Matilda, possibly male religious joined them then.[1]

The criticism of the relationships between religious women and men that plagued the new monasteries later in the century was directed at some of the older abbeys as well. For instance, in the mid-1150s, Abbess Alice of Barking received a letter from Archbishop Theobald of Canterbury warning her to end her intimate relationship with the administrator of her church, her officer Hugh.[2] Whether other preconquest abbeys were similarly affected is hard to assess, for only Barking and Amesbury abbeys have sufficient remaining records to permit a charting of twelfth-century developments.[3]

Change is more evident in that other form of holy life surveyed in the early pages of this study: religious life outside the monastery walls. In the latter part of the century, women who lived like hermitesses, informally alongside hermits, no longer appear in the records. Rather, the norm seems to have become the woman permanently enclosed in a small house or cell, the anchoress or recluse in the narrow sense of the word.

The seeming disappearance of hermitesses may reveal an actual development in ways of life, or it may reflect simply the type of documentation that survives, for most of what is known about these women comes from the literature of advice they received from religious men. Although these tracts may indicate more the ideal than the reality, they reveal a new self-consciousness about the purposes of the recluse's life. Emphasizing the uniqueness of the anchoress's vocation, this literature proposes for them a distinctive spirituality. The raison d'être for the solitary life had evolved since the days of Eve of Wilton, as had the attitudes toward close friendships between female and male religious solitaries. By the beginning of the thirteenth century, anchoresses were warned against the very types of relationships that had sustained their counterparts two generations earlier.

AMESBURY AND BARKING REVISITED

In 1177, supposedly as penance for Becket's murder, King Henry II dispersed the Benedictine nuns still living at Amesbury Abbey and introduced in their stead twenty-four nuns sent from Fontevrault. Henceforth, the royal abbey of Amesbury was a monastery for women and men in the Order of Fontevrault. According to the chronicle of Henry's reign attributed to Benedict of Peterborough, a scandal at Amesbury necessitated the transfer. Although historians have accepted Benedict's account, his seemingly straightforward narrative may misrepresent the troubles at Amesbury.

According to Benedict's chronicle, in January 1177 King Henry II with papal approval ordered the bishops of Exeter and Worcester to investigate problems at Amesbury. During their inquiry there, these bishops learned that "after [the abbess] had received the religious habit, she was proven to have given birth to three infants." Benedict reported that the bishops then dispersed the nuns "whose shameful lives scandal had disgraced." The only women allowed to remain were those who renounced the evil of their errors and who agreed "to hold the Order of Fontevrault." Benedict added some information about the abbess: "Lest the aforesaid abbess perish from her degrading reputation and poverty," the king arranged for her to be given ten marks of silver a year and permission to go wherever she wanted. King Henry then asked Fontevrault "for a convent of nuns to whom he desired to entrust that abbey," and Fontevrault duly sent twenty-four nuns.[4]

The claim of Benedict's chronicle that three infants were born to the abbess of Amesbury is so anomalous that the charge in itself raises questions. No other nun in the entire century was accused of having even one child.[5] Given the harsh treatment of the nun of Watton a decade earlier, it is almost unimaginable that King Henry would have been so merciful—indeed generous—to the profligate abbess as to supply her with a pension of ten marks of silver a year and permission to wander wherever she wished. A settlement of this sort would more likely be given to an abbess unfairly displaced than to a licentious one.

The chronicle's account is made even more suspect by a bull from Pope Alexander III dating probably from September 1176, certainly from before the investigation that the bishops of Exeter and Worcester conducted. In this letter, Pope Alexander asked the abbess and sisters of Fontevrault to cooperate with a plan of King Henry's to increase the endowment of Amesbury Abbey and establish there the Order of Fontevrault. To bring this about, Henry planned to instruct the archbishop of Canterbury and the bishops of London, Exeter, and Worcester to go to Amesbury. The pope gave no hint that there was any question of immorality at Amesbury. Rather, he told the abbess of Fontevrault that the archbishop and bishops were going to inform the nuns of Amesbury of the projected transfer and give them the option of staying under the new rule or joining other monasteries.[6]

An episode a decade earlier at Amesbury gives another context for King Henry's actions at the abbey. Around 1160, in a dispute over the advowson to the church of Froyle, the abbess of Amesbury actually deprived King Henry and Archbishop Theobald's nominee of possession of the church. Angry that the abbess had imposed her will "by violence and armed force, a thing which does not become any woman, nun, or religious," Archbishop Theobald warned the abbess not to use the church of Froyle's tithes. If she used the tithes, the archbishop threatened that the queen might correct her "by condign punishment," which he would not prevent. "We shall ratify it, since on the authority of the canons, when law is treated with such contempt military force must be called in for repression of malice."[7] Although the abbess of Amesbury was not the only twelfth-century abbess involved in a bitter fight in defense of the abbey's property,[8] her battle was particularly fierce.

If, as the letter of Pope Alexander asserts, King Henry had already decided to transfer Amesbury to the Order of Fontevrault before any "scandal" was uncovered, the king may have been carrying the war with the abbess of Amesbury one stage further. Subject to Fontevrault, an order favored by the royal family, the new prioress of Amesbury could never carry out her own will as had the independent abbess of Amesbury in the 1160s. One can imagine the scene when the bishops appeared at Amesbury to announce Henry's plan. Would an abbess accustomed to a tradition of vigorous defense of her monastery's rights quietly bow to Henry's wish to dissolve her house? Quite likely King Henry broadcast the sensational scandal to discredit the abbess and gain sympathy for his plan to introduce congenial nuns from Fontevrault.

Barking Abbey also was challenged by Archbishop Theobald in the middle years of the century. In the 1140s and 1150s, when Osbert of Clare addressed some laudatory letters to nuns of Barking, there was not yet any hint of discord.[9] In the mid-1150s, Osbert even sent Abbess Alice a traditional panegyric to virginity, which gave no sign of problems at Barking.[10] But between 1153 and 1160 Abbess Alice of Barking received another letter quite unlike the treatise on chastity Osbert dedicated to her. In harsh language, Archbishop Theobald informed Alice, "We cannot any longer shut our eyes to the manifold and grave excesses arising from your negligence—to give it for the time being no worse name— since your offences have reached the ears of the Pope and are provoking the indignation of the holy Roman Church against our innocent self."[11]

Although Abbess Alice was disputing heatedly with a priest over some tithes,[12] Theobald was not referring to this controversy, for he continued, "We have often warned you to abstain from your notorious familiarity and cohabitation with Hugh your officer, who is an offence and a scandal to all religion since according to the Lord's commandment even a foot or eye must be cast away for such a cause." Theobald warned that grievous consequences would result unless she changed her life "for the better" and studied "by prompt correction to reform the reputation of [her] house." In conclusion, Theobald ordered Abbess Alice, "Remove the said Hugh from the intimacy of your house, within the seventh day from the receipt of these present, and . . . suffer him no longer to administer your church."[13]

The precise nature of Abbess Alice's scandalous misconduct is not specified. Clearly sexual misconduct is implied, and is possible. But Abbess Alice's intimacy with Hugh may have been a close relationship of the type that flourished elsewhere in the middle part of the century. Perhaps Hugh was helping the abbess defend her abbey's rights in the conflict over tithes, an alliance that might fuel the wrath of Archbishop Theobald against the headstrong abbess. Whatever the nature of Abbess Alice's offense, there is no evidence that she changed her ways; soon thereafter the abbacy of Barking became vacant and remained vacant, held by the king from 1166 to 1173.[14]

Although the nuns of Barking were not displaced like those at Amesbury, the king brought them in line when he appointed abbesses there of his own choosing. First, reportedly in another penitential act for his role in the murder of Thomas Becket, Henry appointed Becket's sister Mary as abbess. Then in the later 1170s, Henry made his own natural daughter abbess.[15]

In this situation, the nuns of Barking turned increasingly to literature, one of the outlets that remained opened to them. Like the nuns of Wilton, who were known for their versifying in the late eleventh century, the nuns of Barking became famous for their hagiography. Whereas Goscelin had translated Anglo-Saxon lives into Latin, which the conquerors could read, late twelfth-century nuns at Barking translated Latin saints' lives into their own vernacular French, indications that many of the nuns were members of the new Norman aristocracy.

One nun "en Berkinges en l'abeie" is known because between 1163 and 1189 she prepared a French edition of the life of Edward the Confessor. She could not have written her version before 1163 because it relies primarily on the life of Edward that Aelred of Rievaulx finished in that year, the date of the translation of Edward's remains to Westminster Abbey. In her edition, the nun apologized for her insular French. She even refused to name herself, saying that she was not yet worthy to write her name in a book where the saintly king's name was written. Although the nun expanded Aelred's text with selections from other lives and with exhortations of her own, she provided little information about life at Barking. But the very existence of her life of St. Edward proves that a nun of Barking was able to complete a translation of considerable difficulty.[16]

In the last quarter of the century, another life—that of St. Catherine of Alexandria—was translated into French by a nun of Barking Abbey. This nun identified herself as Clemence, and she may or may not also have been the translator of the life of St. Edward.[17] In some elaborations on her Latin source, the *Longer Vulgata*, Clemence revealed her sensitivity to dilemmas human love might entail.[18] The conflict between passion and duty, the relative weight of human and spiritual love, the question of whether love was ennobling or debilitating: these issues Clemence treated in her version of Catherine's life. Such topics were familiar to Clemence's generation, accustomed to the courtly literature that had flourished under Eleanor of Aquitaine. Clemence skillfully blended these new themes with traditional encomiums to virginity in her version of the life of St. Catherine.

Despite the controversial rule of Abbess Alice in the middle part of the century, Barking Abbey remained a congenial place for aristocratic women. Clemence's life of St. Catherine was an ideal piece for women of education and high social standing, for Catherine herself was supposedly an educated woman able to defend her ideas skillfully before a royal and learned audience. Thus, at the end of the twelfth century, Barking was one preconquest abbey which still met the needs of ladies of rank.

Other ancient royal abbeys also appealed to the Norman rulers. Sometime before 1160 King Stephen's daughter Mary left her newly founded Higham Priory to become abbess of Romsey.[19] Late in the twelfth century, Mary, the half sister of King Henry II, was abbess of Shaftesbury.[20] These preconquest abbeys had a greater influx of prominent women than the new monasteries.[21] Although kinswomen of the founders joined a few baronial foundations, only Godstow Abbey enjoyed comparable prestige with the ancient foundations; and even Godstow's prominence was in part the result of the favor it received from King Henry II, its patron. But prestige had a price. The corollary of status seems to have been greater subjection to royal control.

RECLUSES (1150–1200)

In the last half of the twelfth century, the only known eremitic women were strictly enclosed recluses. Although nomenclature is never a sure sign of a particular way of life, if any women continued to live informally as hermitesses, they have escaped notice in the records. Early in this century, Rotha Mary Clay compiled a list of all the medieval English hermits, recluses, anchorites, and anchoresses she found in the *Curia Regis Rolls*, registers of episcopal courts, and other medieval documents. Thirteen of the women Clay named were from the late twelfth and early thirteenth century, and all of these were called either anchoresses or "enclosed ones" (*inclusae*).[22] Other sources from the late twelfth century not included in Clay's list also use exclusively the terms "anchoress" or "enclosed one." Ann Warren's findings concur with this conclusion.[23]

The elimination of the less-structured eremitism common earlier in the century was in part a result of the increased number of monasteries that could now meet the needs of religious women. But also the distrust that had grown of such informal arrangements led to the curtailment of a way of life that depended on close contact between female and male religious. Hermitesses had ceased to live alongside their hermit friends.

Some nuns might retire temporarily to small houses for periods of retreat and more solitary prayer; the Gilbertines had several hermitages that seem to have served this purpose.[24] But eremitism was no longer a stage in a process leading to cenobitism. Women of all social classes continued to be attracted to the eremitic life. Indeed, Warren concludes that throughout this period, more women became anchorites than men.[25]

The eremitism they chose, however, had become a defined and distinct form of religious life.

The recluse's vocation is vividly presented in the enclosure ceremony recorded near Canterbury in the mid- to late-twelfth century. "Go into your rooms, my people, shut your doors behind you. Hide yourselves a little while until the wrath has passed." With these words from Isaiah 26 echoing in her ears, a recluse entered the cell where she would remain for the rest of her life. According to this ritual for the enclosure of a recluse, apocalyptic imagery shaped her expectations, much as eschatology colored the Gilbertine's self-understanding. But the words of Isaiah that dominated for the recluse were not prophecies of harmonious concord. Recalling Isaiah's predictions of a day of wrath, the recluse hid away in the "delightful vineyard" where God's care was promised: "I, Yahweh, am its keeper; every moment I water it for fear its leaves should fall; night and day I watch over it."[26]

A skillful alternation of joy and sadness, balancing affirmation of God's presence with warnings of His judgments, the ritual of enclosure took place during a mass, over which a bishop normally officiated. The recluse lay prostrate during the office of readings in the western part of the church, "where it is customary for women to stay." There she heard the passage from Isaiah already quoted in part: in hiding she was to await the great day when the Lord would slay the evil monster and tend his faithful vineyard. After the recluse was sprinkled with holy water and censed with the thurible, she stood to receive two lit candles, "so that she might be fervent in love of God and neighbor." Remaining standing for the gospel reading, the story of Mary and Martha in Luke 10, the recluse was to recognize herself in the role of Mary, sitting at the Lord's feet and choosing "the better part" that could "not be taken from her."[27]

After the gospel reading, the recluse made her petition. While the choir chanted, "Come creator spirit," the recluse was accompanied to the steps of the altar where she genuflected three times saying, "Receive me Lord, according to your promise so that I may live. Do not confound me from my expectation." After placing her two candles in a candelabra, the recluse then returned to her place, where she waited, sitting silently or lying prostrate, while a homily was given on the readings. Requesting that the faithful pray for the recluse, the bishop or a priest celebrated the mass of the Holy Spirit.[28]

At the completion of the mass, the choir intoned the funeral antiphon, "May angels lead you into paradise," and the rites for the dying were begun, "lest perhaps prevented by death she lack this holy service." If the purpose for the last rites was in part precautionary, they set the tone for the recluse's enclosure. With holy water and incense, the celebrant prepared the recluse's cell, called a "sepulcher" in the liturgy. She then entered her "sepulcher" singing the antiphon, "Here I will stay forever; this is the home I have chosen."[29] Sprinkling a little dust over the recluse, the celebrant chanted the antiphon "From the earth you formed me," while the choir continued Psalm 139: "Yahweh, you examine me and know me. . . . Where could I go to escape your spirit?" Once the recluse was in her cell, the service concluded with prayers traditionally said over the body of the deceased in the bier. The doors of her house were closed, and the recluse was left alone inside.[30]

Utilizing prayers from burial services, the enclosure ceremony had the usual funereal tension between sorrow at the person's death and joy at their reception into paradise. Yet although the recluse was declared to be no longer part of this world, in fact she remained alive in her cell. To actualize the goals of her vocation as verbalized in the liturgy, she had the dual task of insuring that her cell was both a safe haven and "a resting place for Yahweh." While continuing to receive food, clothing, the eucharist, and visitors, she had to keep the world at bay. And having chosen the "better part" with Mary, she needed to find ways to enjoy "sitting at the feet of Jesus."

Between 1160 and 1165, Aelred of Rievaulx wrote a guide for recluses to help his sister, a recluse, carry out these ideals. Aelred divided his rule into instructions for the exterior and interior life, paralleling the liturgy's dual emphases on death to the world and life in the presence of God. In his rules for the exterior self, Aelred shared many of the assumptions Goscelin had revealed in his letter to Eve eighty years earlier. Like other religious women, the recluse should follow the typical monastic *horarium*, with set times to rise, pray, recite the office, read, eat, work, and sleep. But the developments of the mid-twelfth century were reflected in Aelred's repeated emphasis on the need for solitude and on the danger of close relationships, especially friendships with religious men.[31]

Aelred was scornful of recluses who too actively engaged in business matters, worried about income from their flocks of sheep, held classes for children in the porch outside their window, and were surrounded by beggars seeking gifts.[32] But above all, Aelred warned his sister not to imitate the recluses who were preoccupied with men; who listened to gossip about "the face, appearance and mannerisms of now this priest, now that monk or clerk"; who followed the "common custom now to send a young monk or priest a belt, a gaily embroidered purse, or some such thing." Calling the visits of the opposite sex to a recluse's cell a misfortune "only too common today among both men and women," Aelred decried the shamefulness "of some who, grown old in uncleanliness, will not even forego the company of undesirable persons. Dreadful as it is to say, they share the same bed with them, embrace them and kiss them, and yet declare they have no fear for their chastity because their body has grown cold and their members are powerless to commit sin." In contrast, Aelred warned his sister to speak only infrequently even with a bishop, abbot, or prior, and then in the presence of a witness. Even better, "happy the recluse who is unwilling to see or speak with a man."[33]

Aelred's diatribe may indicate that some twelfth-century recluses practiced that ancient form of testing one's chastity called "syneisactism." In some other periods and places, celibate women and men lived and slept together to prove their conquest of temptation.[34] However, to assume such practices on the basis of a criticism like Aelred's, with no other substantiation in the records, would be unwarranted. What is certain is that Aelred did not trust the close relationships that had characterized the generation of expansion.[35]

For her "spiritual father," the recluse should accept an elderly priest from a neighboring monastery or church who would monitor all her contacts with young men or persons of doubtful character. Never should she exchange messages or gifts with any man, whether the purpose was to show kindness, arouse fervor, or seek a spiritual friendship. Frequent conversations, even with a holy man, could endanger her reputation and threaten her peace of mind; with the man's voice or face engraved on her memory, her meditations might be disturbed. Even a simple exchange of gifts could foster illicit affections. Aelred warned her against the recluse who was "quite satisfied if she preserves bodily chastity, if she is not drawn forth pregnant from her cell, if no infant betrays its birth by its wailing."[36]

In contrast to the practices of earlier hermitesses, Aelred insisted on the recluse's strict solitude. He even discouraged visits from nuns and other women. To insure that the recluse would remain isolated, Aelred advised his sister to find an elderly woman of proven virtue. This woman would take responsibility for admitting or refusing guests. To furnish all the recluse's necessities, this woman could be aided by a strong girl servant.[37]

In this stress on isolation, Aelred actually reversed the attitude toward friendship he typically expressed in his other writings. Aelred's injunc-

tions reflect his understanding of the special vocation of the recluse:
"Before all else the recluse must jealously preserve her peace of heart and
tranquility of spirit, so she shall have ever dwelling in her soul the Lord
of whom it is written: 'His dwelling has been established in peace'." The
recluse was to "sit alone then, in silence, listening to Christ and speaking
with him." "For then she is with Christ, and he would not care to be with
her in a crowd."[38]

Separated from the world, the recluse felt the same range of emotions
and passions as other people, but hers were to be focused on God alone.
Although some form of human love was necessary, Aelred did not recommend the spiritual friendships of her predecessors. Praying and weeping for all people, showing them a love characterized by beneficence and
innocence, the recluse could "embrace the whole world" with her love
and "in that one act at once consider and congratulate the good, contem-
plate and mourn over the wicked." Aelred advised, "The performance of
such good works as these help you to live out your profession instead of
upsetting you; . . . they are a safeguard, not an obstacle to tranquillity of
mind."[39]

As a replacement for the love of friends, Aelred emphasized that the
recluse could experience an intense love of God. In a threefold meditation on the past, present, and future, Aelred proposed reflections which
would enable her "to stir up the love of God . . . , feed it and keep it
burning."[40] Virtually any thought that intensified the recluse's love of
God was desirable. For instance, during Lent, she should "apply herself
more frequently to prayer, throw herself more often at Jesus' feet, and by
the frequent repetition of his sweet name draw forth tears of compunc-
tion and banish all distraction from her heart." "Let her consider this
season to be her wedding day as she yearns with all her ardor for Christ's
embrace."[41]

In meditations on the past, the recluse was encouraged to imagine
herself as people in the historical life of Christ. As Mary Magdalene, she
could anoint Christ: "Break then the alabaster of your heart and whatever devotion you have, whatever love, whatever desire, whatever affection, pour it all out upon your Bridegroom's head, while you adore the
man in God and God in the man."[42] In her chapel, adorned only with a
crucifix and pictures of the two models of virginity, Mary and the disciple John, the recluse could recreate the scene of the crucifixion. Christ's
"outspread arms will invite you to embrace him, his naked breasts will
feed you with the milk of sweetness to console you."[43]

In reconstructions of the Passion Week, Aelred evoked intense emotional attachment to Christ. Aelred told his sister to picture herself as being at the crucifixion and watching as the soldier opened Jesus' side. "From the rock streams have flowed for you, wounds have been made in his limbs, holes in the wall of his body, in which, like a dove, you may hide while you kiss them one by one. Your lips, stained with his blood, will become like a scarlet ribbon and your word sweet." If anything surpassed the emotion of this moment, it was the passionate response Aelred reconstructed when Mary Magdalene met the risen Christ in the garden, sought to touch him, and joyfully clasped his feet. "Linger here as long as you can, virgin. Do not let these delights of yours be interrupted by sleep or disturbed by any tumult from without."[44]

In addition to recalling the earthly life of Christ, the recluse could feel great love when she anticipated the future beatific vision, where Christ's "face, so longed for, upon which the angels yearn to gaze, will be seen."[45] Examining her present life for similar affective experiences, Aelred reminded his sister of all the signs of Christ's love. "How often he came to your side to bring you loving consolation when you were dried up by fear, . . . how often he shed upon you the light of spiritual understanding when you were singing psalms or reading, how often he carried you away with a certain unspeakable longing for himself when you were at prayer."[46]

Aelred also suggested that his sister meditate on her virginity as a way to enflame her love for Christ. "Bear in mind always what a precious treasure you bear in how fragile a vessel. . . . What could be more precious than the treasure with which heaven is bought, which delights your angel, which Christ himself longs for, which entices him to love and bestow gifts? What is it he gives? I will make bold to say: himself and all that he has." Comparing her virginity to gold stored in earthenware vessels, Aelred warned his sister to guard her "priceless treasure of virginity." "Thus the spikenard of your virginity breathes out its fragrance even in heaven and leads the king to desire your beauty."[47]

Despite all his prescriptions to help the recluse be dead to the world, Aelred was primarily interested in meditations that would evoke Christ's presence. Aelred stressed virginity in an attempt to fill the recluse with love for her bridegroom Christ so that He would be a satisfactory substitute for the human friends her predecessors had enjoyed. His theology of virginity was certainly more developed than that in Christina of Markyate's *vita*. And so was his distrust of the flexible way of life Christina and the hermitesses of an earlier generation had enjoyed. Whether such heterosexual friendships continued to exist, Aelred heatedly warned against them. A suspicion of close relationships between celibates was not only evident in the decreased number of monasteries for both sexes and in the increased regulations within the Gilbertine order. Aelred's attitude confirms that the strict enclosure mandated in the service for a recluse had become the ideal for eremitic women in the latter part of the century.

ADVICE TO RECLUSES IN THE EARLY THIRTEENTH CENTURY

Early in the thirteenth century, a small group of young women recluses received the *Ancrene Riwle*. A friend of theirs, a well-educated cleric, had composed this tract for them on their request. Partly because some versions of this text were written in Middle English and French, scholars have analyzed in detail the text of the *Ancrene Riwle*, prepared careful editions of the surviving manuscripts, published translations, and considered its content and context in numerous scholarly articles. After much speculation on the identity of the author and the female recipients, historians now agree that neither can be identified with certainty. The earliest manuscript, however, can be reliably traced to the southwest midlands of England and identified as a copy made between 1224 and 1230 of the urtext, or original, written a decade or two earlier. The author may have served as the master of the community he addressed.[48]

The advice given recluses in this tract at the beginning of the thirteenth century does not represent a great change from what Aelred of Rievaulx offered his sister. Like Aelred's *Rule*, the *Ancrene Riwle* assumed that the recluse had chosen to devote her life to the love of Christ, the epitome of all human affections. "Four chief kinds of love are known in this world: the love between good friends, between man and woman, between mother and child, between body and soul. The love which Jesus Christ has for His beloved goes beyond these four and surpasses them all." Using the familiar language of the Song of Songs, the *Ancrene Riwle* assured the recluse that she was waiting in solitude for the embrace of Christ. "Our Lord does not kiss with [the kiss of the mouth] any soul that loves anything but Him or those things which help it to possess Him for His sake."[49]

Love imagery is so pronounced in this work that a recent study has called the *Ancrene Riwle* an example of "erotic spirituality."[50] However, although the love between the recluse and Christ was presented in highly emotional terms, there was less focus on the longing of the bridegroom Christ for his bride's virginity than in Aelred's letter to his sister several decades earlier, a work with which the author of the *Ancrene Riwle* was familiar.[51] The bridegroom-bride imagery that Aelred favored became only one of many metaphors for the recluse's relationship with her spouse Christ. Instead of emphasizing Christ's longing for a virgin bride, the *Ancrene Riwle* stressed his faithfulness, devotion, sacrifice, and entreaties.[52] Often the *Ancrene Riwle* had a homely spouse in mind, not a seductive lover. Departing from the lyrical language of the Song of Songs, the *Ancrene Riwle* compared the recluse to a lonely wife: "If a man had made a long journey and someone came and told him that his dear wife was grieving for him so much that without him she had no pleasure in anything, but had grown thin and pale with thoughts of love for him, would this not please him better than to be told that she was enjoying herself, amusing herself, flirting with other men and living a life of pleasure? In the same way Our Lord, who is the spouse of the soul and sees all that she is doing even though He sits on high, is very glad if she longs for Him."[53]

Some of the advice in the *Ancrene Riwle* encouraged the anchoress to redirect to Christ the emotions she might have felt for a man: "Touch Him with as much love as you sometimes feel for a man." But probably the most erotic passage in the work is a reference to receiving Christ in the eucharist, in imagery as evocative for a priest as for a female recluse: "When the priest communicates, forget the world, be completely out of the body, and with burning love embrace your Beloved who has come down from heaven to your heart's bower, and hold Him fast until He has granted you all that you ask."[54] While the *Ancrene Riwle* presented Christ as the recluse's spouse, he was also the perfect friend who laid down his life for another. Or the savior whose sacrificial death let humans live forever. Or the mother who was willing to give her own blood to save her child.[55]

Although the *Ancrene Riwle* encouraged the recluse to enjoy a love relationship with Christ, the largest portion of the tract was dedicated to penance.[56] Death to the world was the dominant image; and the highest goal presented was to suffer with Christ.[57] Ways to increase the recluse's sorrow for sins were recommended: meditations on Christ's sufferings, reflections on the seven deadly sins, and considerations of the temptations that assail each of the five senses. The *Ancrene Riwle* proposed morbid reflections for times of great temptations: "For example," think "what you would do . . . if you heard that someone very dear to you had been suddenly drowned, or slain, or murdered, or that your sisters had been burned in their house. Such thoughts as these will often root out carnal temptations."[58]

The flesh needed to be chastised. The soul was "united to the flesh, which is mere mud and dirty earth," because "God did not want it to leap into pride, . . . and therefore God tied a heavy clod of earth to the soul, like a man hobbling a cow or any other animal that is liable to stray." Hence, the *Ancrene Riwle* recommended ascetic acts that would discipline the body: "Of two men who are both ill, which is the wiser, the one who goes without all the food and drink that he likes, and drinks bitter infusions of herbs in order to recover his health, or the other, who follows all his inclinations and pursues his desires in spite of his illness, and soon loses his life?" The tract's key advice was, "Let no one expect to go up to heaven in comfort."[59]

Committed to a life of penance, devoted to Christ alone, the recluse of the *Ancrene Riwle* certainly had no room for close personal relationships with men. Some early-thirteenth-century recluses may have tried to maintain heterosexual friendships or simply hold conversations with men, but the author of the *Ancrene Riwle* deplored these practices: "Some anchoresses are so learned or can talk with such wisdom" that they not only are "ready with a reply" when a priest talks to them but sometimes set up as scholars, teaching those who have come to teach them. In contrast, the *Ancrene Riwle* recommended, "Give your advice only to women. . . . Through giving . . . rebukes, an anchoress has sometimes brought about, between herself and her priest, either a harmful love or a great enmity."[60]

The fear of heterosexual celibate friendships in the *Ancrene Riwle* reflects the moment when relationships previously necessary for a recluse's survival had come to be seen primarily as opportunities for sin. Advising the recluse never to look at a man, the *Ancrene Riwle* defended its position: " 'But do you think,' someone will say, 'that I shall leap upon him because I look at him?' God knows, my dear sister, more surprising things have happened." Moreover, the recluse herself would be held accountable if any sinful conduct resulted: "If the man is tempted in such a way that he commits mortal sin through you in any way, *even though it is not with you, but with desire for you, or if he tries to yield with another person to the temptation awakened in him through your doing,* be quite sure of the judgment: you must pay" (emphasis mine). Blaming Bathsheba for "unclothing herself before David's eyes" and Dinah for getting raped, the *Ancrene Riwle* even advised the recluse to be cautious in making her confessions, not telling her "temptations of the flesh" to a "young priest."[61]

Despite these warnings, the *Ancrene Riwle* did not mean for recluses to live totally alone. They were just to be isolated from men. Serving women were still necessary, to insulate the recluses from visitors and to care for their material needs. The recluses who received the *Ancrene Riwle* lived with other recluses, three of them in one version, twenty in another. The women were to encourage each other: "[Let] your dear faces ... be always turned towards each other with loving looks and with an expression of sweetness, ... joined together in unity of heart and will."[62] Required for spiritual and material well-being, such relationships with women would not distract the recluses from their primary focus on Christ.

Further evidence that the *Ancrene Riwle* reflects a period when the friendships of earlier years were increasingly distrusted comes from some related contemporary literature called the "Katherine Group."[63] Included in this collection is a thirteenth-century version of the life of St. Margaret of Antioch directed specifically to women: widows, wedded women, and maidens. In this version of the life of St. Margaret, there is a dramatic episode not found in any other known version of her life. In this added segment, the demonic dragon that St. Margaret has conquered explains how it has often ensnarled good people trying to lead clean lives. The dragon informs Margaret: "I let [cause] some whiles a clean man won [dwell] nigh a clean woman. . . . I let em talk and tattle of good and truely love em [one another], without evil willing . . . so that either of other as of his own be trusty, and truly to know [each other] and the securer be to sit together and game by em one [themselves alone]." The dragon delights to see the loving looks and words these friends exchange, for "then thump I into em loving thoughts," the first stage of leading them into the pools and swamp of sin. Although such friends can still resist the devil, the struggle is difficult indeed.[64] In the speech of St. Margaret's dragon, the attitude of the early-thirteenth-century literature for recluses is particularly explicit: heterosexual friendships are so dangerous they must be avoided.

This fear of close relationships between celibates appears not only in reworkings of saints' lives but also in chronicles of earlier events. When the thirteenth-century historian of St. Albans Abbey incorporated stories about Christina of Markyate and the hermit Roger, he either could not believe or would not accept that Christina had lived adjacent to Roger's cell and had joined him nightly for prayers. So the chronicle suppressed the account of their intimacy. According to the *Gesta Abbatum Monasterii Sancti Albani*, the version most widely known until Talbot's edition of Christina's life in the 1950s, Christina lived in a small building near Roger, and in her four years there Roger never consented to see her face.[65]

Henceforth recluses were warned against the types of relationships that had permitted their predecessors to flourish in the early twelfth century. No longer were hermitesses free to shape their own form of life and forge their own alliances, for they were to be strictly enclosed. The anchoritic way of life remained viable for women, but only if they accepted more restrictive norms. The tension women like Christina of Markyate had experienced between their desire to remain virgin and their need for heterosexual friendships was resolved: virginity was protected and the friendships abandoned. Thus the recluses' emotions and reflections could be focused exclusively on Christ.

CONCLUSION

Female monasticism lost much of its appeal, influence, and prosperity in the later middle ages. As Power, the historian of the decline, observed, "It must be remembered . . . that there were more nuns at the beginning than at the end of the period 1270–1536; the convents tended to diminish in size."[1] But the future was not apparent in the early thirteenth century; only the wisdom of hindsight reveals that growth had come to an end.

For early-thirteenth-century women, the success of their religious movement was more discernible than its incipient decline. As Knowles concluded, in a verdict equally valid for male and female monasticism, "The monastic order in England approached the new era that was to open after the death of John no longer as the paramount influence in the cultural and spiritual life of the nation, but more happily situated than had seemed possible a few years before."[2]

Nuns and sisters of the early thirteenth century had no reason to expect that their monasteries would cease to exist. Throughout the twelfth century, women had made numerous accommodations in order to lead religious lives, and repeatedly their ingenuity had been rewarded. In the beginning of the monastic revival, innovative women had set out on their own or with a few companions, often with no specific rule or predetermined schedule. Some sought a stricter asceticism than was possible in the preconquest houses. Others were unable to enter one of the few, aristocratic abbeys. To lead the holy lives they desired, these women were resourceful and creative.

Especially in their relationships with celibate men, these women were adaptive. They accepted shelter from hermits, manor houses from bishops, new priories from monks and canons. Male religious became their friends, transferred monasteries to them, joined their priories, and served as their chaplains and guardians. Women cooperated with canons and lay brothers in the creation of new forms of monastic life.

The most visible signs of innovation were the approximately thirty new monasteries for women and men; in these communities, women often comprised two-thirds, and men one-third, the total membership. The men acted for various reasons, but regardless of the men's motives, the women needed male help, and they accepted it. Despite often poor documentation, the records reveal numerous, virtually unprecedented alliances between nuns, lay sisters, canons, monks, and lay brothers.

Women accepted these new arrangements even though men assumed the leadership positions. In these new communities, canons and monks exercised more control over religious women than was typical in the history of female monasticism. Perhaps these women were willing to relinquish the model of the strong, independent abbess because few of them were of high social status. Accepting the realities of their social and economic position, women cooperated with men even though the other side of male aid was male supervision, extensive regulation, and often strict enclosure as well. These nuns and sisters were willing to pay a very high institutional price for their alliances with male religious.

In the last third of the twelfth century, a distrust of monasteries for both sexes prevented their further multiplication. Hence, even the successful Gilbertine order never expanded beyond the limits reached in its first generation. Despite the atmosphere of suspicion, however, the women and their male supporters found ways to thrive. The Gilbertine *Institutes* reveal the amount of regulation women were willing to accept in order to preserve their radical model of both sexes and all conditions of people in one community. Gilbertine women and men not only adopted rules that would permit them to survive; they also took the offensive, asserting the wisdom of their institutional form. With images of the millennial kingdom, the Gilbertines propounded an ideological justification for their distinctive way of life.

Although modern sensitivities may be more attuned to the heroic, early phase of experimentation, the rigid structures that the Gilbertines and other congregations had accepted by the early thirteenth century were better suited for the period to come. Pope Innocent III wanted religious life to be well-regulated and supervised; his will became law in 1215 at the Fourth Lateran Council. Henceforth, all new foundations were to adopt one of the already existing religious rules. Moreover, monasteries that had been independent were to associate, with provincial chapters every three years and regular visitations. Congregations, like the Gilbertines, that already had such systems in operation were allowed to continue with the institutional form they themselves had developed.

To suggest when and why the twelfth-century creations later proved nonviable is beyond the scope of this work. Although only a few scholars have concentrated on mid-thirteenth century England, their work does not suggest any untoward onslaught of problems. Throughout the thirteenth century, the Gilbertines retained their right to self-government and to episcopal exemption; popes repeatedly reconfirmed their *Institutes*.[3] Nor did the "Cistercian" priories immediately encounter hardships. In a recent study of "Stixwould in the Market-Place," Coburn Graves portrayed a priory with a "dynamic economy" continuing from its foundation until the Black Death. Graves concluded, "Put simply, the characterization of english nunneries drawn by Eileen Power as houses beset with hardship, managerial incompetence, and indebtedness does not apply to Stixwould, at least not in the first two centuries of her history."[4]

Vocations to monastic life continued to remain high. Power identified overcrowding as a major cause of the financial troubles that monasteries for women eventually experienced. Between 1250 and 1320, popes and bishops issued injunctions against receiving too many women to Marrick, Swine, Wilberfoss, NunAppleton, Hampole, Arden, Thicket, Nunkeeling, Nunburnholme, Esholt, Arthington, and Sinningthwaite.[5] Although the influx of so many women taxed the material resources of the monasteries, women's eagerness to join indicates the ongoing appeal of religious life.

The alliances that had been forged between religious women and men continued to be practical in the thirteenth century. Indeed, the system of entrusting oversight to a male *custos* was so advantageous that in the later middle ages bishops often imposed male guardians over houses of nuns when the women had financial or moral problems. Acknowledging that the imposition of a custodian was often the most effective way for nuns to resolve their difficulties, Power noted that the women themselves sometimes asked to have a *custos* appointed.[6]

Despite the advantages women gained from such male support, it became increasingly rare for men to join monasteries of women. By the later middle ages, even the "Cistercian" monasteries for women that had included a *custos* became all-female houses.[7] Power reflected, "It is difficult to understand why the practice of having a resident prior died out at the Cistercian houses and at Benedictine houses. . . . It is a curious anomaly that this remedy should have been applied less and less often during the very centuries when the nunneries were becoming increasingly poor, and stood daily in greater need of external assistance in the management of their temporal affairs."[8] Perhaps the practical benefits of close ties between female and male religious were no longer able to offset the feared liabilities of such relationships.

The explanation for Power's "curious anomaly," however, takes us far afield from the topic of this book. Since twelfth-century female monasticism grew in tandem with male monasticism, it is not surprising that their decline was concomitant as well. However effective the systems were that the women adopted in the peak period of expansion, they could not combat the change in attitude toward male and female monasticism in the later middle ages. Even though they were long-accustomed to improvising, religious women could not counter a general shift in values.

At the beginning of the thirteenth century, however, that decline was still far in the future. In 1215, religious women lived in a vast network of monasteries, so widespread that women of all social strata, in every part of England, could easily enter religious life. The moment of promise had come to fruition in 135 monasteries with diverse internal arrangements that were well-suited for the economy of their region. Such varied religious ways of life were possible because twelfth-century holy women had been flexible, practical, and pragmatic.

TABLE I.
*Monasteries in Existence in 1130**

Name of Monastery	Order	Approximate Date of Foundation
Preconquest royal foundations		
Barking Abbey	Benedictine	seventh century
Minster Abbey	Benedictine	seventh century
Shaftesbury Abbey	Benedictine	ninth century
Wilton Abbey	Benedictine	ninth century
Amesbury Abbey	Benedictine	tenth century
Romsey Abbey	Benedictine	tenth century
Wherwell Abbey	Benedictine	tenth century
Winchester Abbey	Benedictine	tenth century
Chatteris Abbey	Benedictine	eleventh century
New foundations by baronesses		
Elstow Abbey	Benedictine	1078
Redlingfield Priory	Benedictine	1120
New episcopal foundations		
Malling Abbey	Benedictine	1090
Canterbury Priory	Benedictine	1100
Stratford at Bow Priory	Benedictine	−1122
St. Margaret's Priory	Benedictine	−1129
** St. Clement's, York, Priory	Benedictine	1130
Brewood Black Ladies Priory	Benedictine	−1150
Possible other priories: founder and date of foundation uncertain		
Hinchingbrooke	Benedictine	
** Holystone	Benedictine?	
Lyminster	Benedictine	
** Newcastle upon Tyne	Benedictine	

* This table is based on information in Chapter 1.
** Located in the North.

TABLE 2.
The South (1130–1165):
Monasteries Founded with the Aid of Male Religious*

Name of Monastery	Probable Order	Approximate Date of Foundation
Daughter houses of male monasteries		
Kilburn Priory	Benedictine	1140
Markyate Priory	Benedictine	1145
Sopwell Priory	Benedictine	1145
Derby Priory	Benedictine	1149–59
Thetford Priory	Benedictine	1160
Stamford Priory	Benedictine	1160
Transfers from men to women		
Blithbury Priory	Benedictine	− 1148
Farewell Abbey	Benedictine	1140
Blackborough Priory	Benedictine	+ 1150
Haliwell Priory	Augustinian?	1133–50
Daughter house of a female monastery		
Langley Priory	Cistercian?	1150
Monasteries in federated orders		
Harrold Priory	Arrouaise	1136–38
Chicksands Priory	Gilbertine	1150
Westwood Priory	Fontevrault	1155
Nuneaton Priory	Fontevrault	1155

* This table is based on information in Chapter 3.

TABLE 3.

The South (1130–1165):
Monasteries Founded by Lay People*

Name of Monastery	Order	Approximate Date of Foundation
Founded and joined by a knight's widow		
Godstow Abbey	Benedictine	1133–39
Founded through cooperation layman and religious		
Clerkenwell Priory	Benedictine or Augustinian	– 1144
Founded by king or knights and joined by their kinswomen		
Wroxall Priory	Benedictine	– 1135
Higham Priory	Benedictine	1148–52
Littlemore Priory	Benedictine	– 1154
Founded for particular women:		
By king and his daughter		
Norwich Priory	Benedictine	1136–37
By barons		
Polesworth Abbey	Benedictine	restored in 1130
Chester Priory	Benedictine	1140
Northampton Abbey	Benedictine (Cluniac?)	1140
Bretford Cell	Benedictine	– 1154
By other laymen		
Pinley Priory	Benedictine	– 1135
Cambridge Priory	Benedictine	1133–38
Flamstead Priory	Benedictine	1150
Henwood Priory	Benedictine	1154–59
Kington St. Michael Priory	Benedictine	– 1155
Other lay foundations		
Wix Priory	Benedictine	1123–33
Goring Priory	Benedictine or Augustinian	during reign of Henry I or II
Cannington Priory	Benedictine	1138
Davington Priory	Benedictine	1153
Ickleton Priory	Benedictine	– 1154?
Polsloe Priory	Benedictine	– 1160
Swaffham Bulbeck Priory	Benedictine	1150–63
Ankerwyke Priory	Benedictine	1160
Wothorpe Priory	Benedictine	1160?
Rowney Priory	Benedictine	1164

* This table is based on information in Chapter 4.

TABLE 4.
The North (1130–1165)*

Name of Priory	Probable Order	Membership		
		Nuns	Prior/ Canons	Lay Brothers
Founded 1130–1147				
Sempringham	Gilbertine	x	x	x
Haverholme	Gilbertine	x	x	x
Gokewell	Cistercian	x		
Heynings	Cistercian	x		x?
Keldholme	Cistercian	x		
Kirklees	Cistercian	x		
Stixwould	Cistercian	x	x	x
Arden	Benedictine	x		x?
Handale	Benedictine	x		
Wallingswells	Benedictine	x		
Founded 1147–1154				
Alvingham	Gilbertine	x	x	x
Bullington	Gilbertine	x	x	x
Catley	Gilbertine	x	x	x
North Ormsby	Gilbertine	x	x	x
Sixhills	Gilbertine	x	x	x
Watton	Gilbertine	x	x	x
Lincoln Hospital	Gilbertine	lay srs.	x	x
Greenfield	Cistercian	x	x	x
Legbourne	Cistercian	x	x	
NunAppleton	Cistercian	x		x
NunCotham	Cistercian	x	x	x
Swine	Cistercian	x	x	x
Wykeham	Cistercian	x	x	
Arthington	Cluniac	x		x?
Broadholme	Premonstratensian	Srs.		x
Guyzance	Premonstratensian	Srs.		
**Marton	Augustinian	x	x	
Nunkeeling	Benedictine	x		x?

Table 4. continued

Name of Priory	Probable Order	Membership		
		Nuns	*Prior/ Canons*	*Lay Brothers*
NunMonkton	Benedictine	x		
Stainfield	Benedictine	x	x	
Wilberfoss	Benedictine	x		
Founded 1154–1165				
**Tunstall	Gilbertine	x	x	x
Ellerton?	Cistercian?	x		
Esholt?	Cistercian?	x		x?
Fosse?	Cistercian?	x		
Hampole	Cistercian	x	x?	x?
Hutton/Baysdale	Cistercian?	x		x
Rosedale	Cistercian	x		x?
Sinningthwaite	Cistercian	x		x
Orford	Premonstratensian	Srs.		
Grimsby	Augustinian	x		
Marrick	Benedictine	x	x?	x?
Moxby	Benedictine	x		
Neasham	Benedictine	x		
Nunburnholme	Benedictine	x		x?
Thicket	Benedictine	x		x?
Yedingham	Benedictine	x		x?

* This table is based on information in Chapter 5.
** Places where female religious no longer lived at the end of the twelfth century.

TABLE 5.
*The North (1165–1200)**

Name of Priory	Probable Order	Approximate Date of Foundation
Armathwaite	Benedictine	− 1200
Foukeholme	Benedictine	1200
Lambley	Benedictine	− 1190
Seton	Benedictine	1190

* This table is based on information in Chapter 6.

TABLE 6.
The South (1165–1200)*

Name of Priory	Probable Order	Approximate Date of Foundation
Founded in cooperation with religious men		
St. Mary de Pre	Benedictine/Hospital	1194
Crabhouse	Augustinian	1181
Buckland	Hospitaller	1180
Episcopal foundation		
Ramstede	Benedictine	1174–84
Founded by earls		
Shouldham	Gilbertine	+1193
Cook Hill	Cistercian	1180
Castle Hedingham	Benedictine	−1191
Other lay foundations		
Studley	Benedictine	1176
Cheshunt	Benedictine	−1183
Barrow Gurney	Benedictine	−1200
Broomhall	Benedictine	−1200
Rusper	Benedictine	−1200
Bristol	Augustinian	1173
Bungay	Augustinian	1183
Limebrook	Augustinian	1189
Campsey Ash	Augustinian	1195
Brewood White Ladies	Augustinian/ Cistercian	1199?
Catesby	Cistercian	1175
Sewardsley	Cistercian	1154–89
Tarrant	Cistercian	1186
Wintney	Cistercian	−1200

* This table is based on information in Chapter 6.

NOTES

INTRODUCTION

1. For these statistics, see *MRH* and tables 1 through 6.

2. After the twelfth century, seven new houses for Augustinian women were founded. The other later foundations were in religious orders begun after the twelfth century, primarily Franciscans and Bridgettines.

3. *MO*, primarily pp. 136–39.

4. For other studies of twelfth-century female monasticism, see de Fontette, *Les religieuses*; Baker, *Medieval Women*; and Nichols and Shank, *Distant Echoes*. A bibliography is provided by Constable, *Medieval Monasticism*.

5. In general, a twelfth-century manuscript with the seal still attached is a more trustworthy record than a copy of that manuscript in a later cartulary, and transcriptions summarizing the original document are less reliable than early manuscripts. Yet even twelfth-century charters have different states of reliability. Helpful chaplains could inflate the records of even small houses, either to augment the communities' possessions or to bring the written documents in line with the members' memories. For an example of a twelfth-century forgery, see Brooke, "Episcopal Charters for Wix Priory."

6. *Monasticon*, *MRH*, and *VCH*. Revised in the nineteenth century, the eight-volume *Monasticon* is essentially William Dugdale's seventeenth-century compilation of original charters and transcriptions. Since texts in the *Monasticon* are not always accurate, I have collated them whenever possible with the surviving manuscripts and transcriptions.

7. "Foundation" documents must be used with great care, however. Often "beginning" a priory was a gradual process, with a community of religious women living together for many years before they were formally recognized as a monastery of nuns or sisters. Sometimes a document that seems to be recording the foundation was actually written long after the event and includes later grants and explanations.

8. The Gilbertines are treated in Chapters 5 through 7; Christina of Markyate in Chapters 2 and 3; Eve of Wilton in Chapter 2. For one of the few female monastic authors, see Clemence of Barking in Chapter 8.

9. Thompson, "Why English Nunneries Had No History," esp. p. 144.

10. For the vexing problem of the Cistercian nuns, see especially Burton, "Yorkshire Nunneries"; Graves, "English Cistercian Nuns"; and Thompson, "Problem of the Cistercian Nuns."

11. See Chapters 3 through 5.

12. Varin, "Les causes de la dissidence." I have not seen this work, which is cited in Bateson, "Double Monasteries," p. 137.

13. Thompson, "Male Element in Nunneries," esp. p. 163. Compare the description in Berlière, *Les monastères doubles*.

14. Bateson, "Double Monasteries," esp. p. 197.

15. On the practice of testing chastity by living or sleeping together, see Gougaud, "*Mulierum consortia*," and Reynolds, "*Virgines subintroductae* in Celtic Christianity."

16. Even the most recent study of anchoresses treats them along with male anchorites rather than together with other religious women. See Warren, *Anchorites*.

17. Grundmann, *Religiöse Bewegungen*. For an extension of Grundmann's thesis into the twelfth century, see Thompson, "Problem of the Cistercian Nuns," and Gies and Gies, *Women in the Middle Ages*, pp. 87–96.

18. Hollingsworth, *Historical Demography*, p. 387. Although much of the monastic expansion was in the North, the population increase was primarily in the Southeast. Hallam claims that by 1300 nearly half of the people of England lived in the five counties between the Humber and the mouth of the Thames. Hallam, *Rural England*, p. 14.

CHAPTER 1

1. *VCH*, Essex, 2:116. A second Anglo-Saxon foundation, Minster Abbey, was later reinhabited; but at the time of the conquest, it was abandoned and in ruins. *MRH*, p. 261.

2. *MRH*, pp. 253–69; Meyer, "English Monastic Reform."

3. *Monasticon*, 4:327–28; *MO*, pp. 702–3. Computations are from *MO*, except for Wilton Abbey, which is inexplicably omitted from the list. According to *VHC*, Wiltshire, 3:233, Wilton's income was assessed in Domesday as £246. Minster Abbey was too delapidated even to appear in Domesday.

4. *VCH*, Wiltshire, 3:233; *VCH*, Hampshire, 2:126, 132. A priory definitely existed at Newcastle upon Tyne in the early twelfth century, but it is not clear when it was founded or by whom. *Monasticon*, 4:484; *MRH*, p. 262.

5. Lanfranc, *Letters*, pp. 166–67. Lanfranc reached a similar verdict for monks. In a letter written between 1071 and 1080 to Walcher, bishop of Durham, Lanfranc stated, "As to the priest that you said had been brought up in a monastery without being professed as a monk, I cannot recall giving you any advice on the case. But the legislation and letters of the holy Fathers do not permit those who wear the monastic habit for several days in public to return subsequently to secular life on any pretext. If the man will not obey you, use that Gospel precept which says 'Compel them to come in'." Ibid., pp. 140–43.

6. *Eadmer's History*, p. 127. In an earlier and shorter account of Anselm's decision, William of Malmesbury admitted that Matilda had been brought up among the nuns and had worn the veil, "the mark of consecrated profession." Hence, according to William, Anselm "could not be brought to consent" to the marriage until lawful witnesses swore that Matilda had "worn the veil because of her suitors, without profession." William of Malmesbury, *Gesta Regum Anglorum*, 2:493–94.

7. *Eadmer's History*, pp. 126–31. The Latin does not make it clear whether Matilda was customarily veiled or whether she was customarily seen among

veiled nuns: "eo quod publice visa fuerat earum inter quas vivebat more velata." Eadmer, *Historia Novorum in Anglia*, p. 121.

8. Anselm, *Opera*, 4:46–50, no. 169. The identity of this anonymous woman is debated. According to Schmitt, the most recent editor of Anselm's letters, no. 169 was addressed to Gunilda, the daughter of Harold, to whom Anselm also sent letter no. 168. However, Wilmart, the first editor of this letter, argued for two recipients in his "Une lettre inedite de S. Anselme." Although Wilmart's hypothesis—that there were two Matildas at Wilton both involved with Count Alans—is not convincing, his contention that the two letters were addressed to two different women seems likely. Internal evidence supports the theory of two recipients: letter no. 168 was written to a woman who had left the monastery without having made a profession, whereas letter no. 169 was addressed to a woman who had been professed. It is unlikely that the woman addressed in no. 168 returned to the monastery after receiving Anselm's letter, made a profession, and then left again when an abbacy failed to materialize. The best way to reconcile the known details is to suppose that no. 168 and no. 169 had different recipients, both royal. My treatment of these letters can stand whether there were two addressees or one.

9. Anselm, *Opera*, 4:48–50, no. 169.

10. Anselm, *Opera*, 4:43–46, no. 168.

11. Tatlock, "Muriel." For Eve: *LC*, esp. p. 41; and Hilary, *Versus et Ludi*, p. 2.

12. Knowles, Brooke, and Londan, *Heads of Religious Houses*, pp. 219, 223.

13. William gave his daughter Cecilia to Caen, where she later became abbess; another of his daughters, Adela, countess of Blois, joined Marcigny. Orderic Vitalis, *Ecclesiastical History*, 3:8–11; William of Malmesbury, *Gesta Regum Anglorum*, 2:455–56.

14. Lanfranc, *Letters*, pp. 174–75. On Aelfgyva, see Knowles, Brooke, and Londan, *Heads of Religious Houses*, p. 208.

15. The life and works of Goscelin were reconstructed by Wilmart, "Eve and Goscelin," 46:414–38, and 50:42–83. Compare the chronology in *LC*, pp. 1–22. For a detailed and perceptive study of Goscelin's lives of the holy abbesses, see Millinger, "Anglo-Saxon Nuns."

16. See esp. the letter to Maurice, bishop of London, that prefaced the life of Ethelburga: Esposito, "*Analecta Varia*," p. 87. Also see the letter, to this same Maurice, that prefaced the life of St. Wulfhilda; Esposito, "La vie de Saint Vulfhilde," p. 12.

17. *LC*, pp. 16–17.

18. Wilmart, "La légende de Ste. Edith," pp. 34–39. For Bezalel and the constructions of the temple of Jerusalem, cf. Exod. 35:30 ff.

19. Wilmart, "La légende de Ste. Edith," esp. pp. 36–37. In one of Edith's appearances right after the conquest, she asked the nuns to pray for their recently deceased abbess Aelfgyva so that all her sins would be forgiven. For a fuller treatment of these appearances of Edith, see Millinger, "Anglo-Saxon Nuns," pp. 120–23.

20. For the claim that the poems are original compositions by Goscelin, see Wilmart, "La légende de Ste. Edith," pp. 26–28. The poems are on pp. 46–47, 60, 68–70, 79–84, 89–98, 269–70, 277, 285, 293–94.

21. Horstmann, *St. Werburga*, pp. xix–xxvi. The unidentified manuscript source for this *vita* of Werburga is probably a thirteenth-century manuscript from Ramsey, now Bodley 285, fols. 159–61; this manuscript is identical with the printed versions except for minor variations, primarily in the spelling of names and in the dates given for certain events.

Genealogy is so fundamental a characteristic of Goscelin's royal saints' lives that Talbot remarked, "One of Goscelin's favourite beginnings . . . is to embark upon a long genealogy, and whenever we meet this, . . . we are more or less certain that we are reading Goscelin's work." *LC*, p. 16.

22. Horstmann, *St. Werburga*, pp. xxii–xxv.

23. Esposito, "La vie de Saint Vulfhilde," pp. 13–17. See also Millinger, "Anglo-Saxon Nuns," pp. 116–24.

24. Tatlock, "Muriel," p. 317.

25. Baudri de Bourgueil, *Les oeuvres poétiques*, pp. 256–57. The poem was from sometime before 1095.

26. Serlo, "Poemata," esp. pp. 235–37. Tatlock identified the Muriel whom Baudri de Bourgueil addressed with the Muriel whom Serlo wrote. (See Tatlock, "Muriel," pp. 317–19.)

27. Tatlock, "Muriel," p. 319. Cf. Tatlock's comment about Muriel on p. 321: "This charming and patrician lady, innocently flattered by ecclesiastics and confidentially corresponding with them, perhaps a trifle sentimental, a trifle worldly, certainly prominent socially. . . ."

28. Anselm, *Opera*, 4:67–68, 70–71, nos. 183, 185. For descriptions of the spirituality at Bec, see Vaughn, *Abbey of Bec*, pp. 9–41.

29. Anselm, *Opera*, 4:68–69, no. 184; 5:349–50, no. 405. For an argument that Anselm's injunctions to Mabilla indicate an increasing insistence on strict enclosure for nuns in the late eleventh century, see Schulenburg, "Strict Active Enclosure," p. 61.

30. Anselm, *Opera*, 4:144–45, nos. 236, 237. For the identification of Earl Waltheof as the recipient of the unwarranted veneration, see Brett, *English Church*, p. 83.

31. One sign of William's neglect is the infrequent appearance of abbeys for women in *RRAN*, vol. 1. On William's overall policy toward monasticism, see *MO*, pp. 110–27. The tradition that William founded the small, poor convent of Hinchingbrook is late and unreliable. *VCH*, Huntington, 1:389; cf. *MRH*, p. 259.

32. *MRH*, p. 263. See also *VCH*, Warwickshire, 2:62, where some confusion exists between Robert Marmion I and II.

33. *MRH*, p. 257; *VCH*, Sussex, 2:47.

34. *MRH*, p. 261; *VCH*, Kent, 2:149.

35. *MRH*, pp. 258, 253, where a misprint incorrectly dated the foundation c. 1178. See also *VCH*, Bedfordshire, 1:353 and *Monasticon*, 3:413, nos. 1–3.

36. *MRH*, pp. 260–61; *MO*, pp. 702–3.

37. The women may have already been living a life of prayer before Emma provided them with possession of the manor and parish church, for her gift was made "to St. Andrew and the nuns there serving God and diligently entreating St. Andrew day and night." *VCH*, Suffolk, 2:83; *Monasticon*, 4:26; *MRH*, p. 264.

38. It is possible, though unlikely, that the women of Holystone were Augustinians instead of the Benedictines. *MRH*, pp. 280–81.

39. *VCH*, Essex, 2:116; *RRAN*, vol. 2, nos. 630, 874, 883, 1160, 1634; *VCH*, Dorset, 2:74.

40. According to Barlow, *William I and the Norman Conquest*, p. 151, "There was no tradition in Normandy of monastic independence of the diocesan bishop." See also Vaughn, *Abbey of Bec*, pp. 1–21. Monks also aided nuns, for three of the wealthier monasteries for men were said to have supported nuns as well as the poor with their alms. However, no information survives about these women or the form of life they adopted. Bury St. Edmunds's list of dependents from 1085 included twenty-eight "nuns and paupers"; *MO*, p. 136, n. 2. At St. Albans Abbey, Abbot Paul (1077–93) attempted to regulate the clothing and schedule of "the crowd of nuns" in his almonry; Riley, *Gesta Abbatum*, 1:59. Somewhat later, at Evesham, under the rule of Robert of Jumièges (1104–22), five nuns were listed along with three "pauperes ad mondatum"; *VCH*, Worcester, 2:116; cf. *MO*, p. 136, n. 2.

41. Monacho Roffensi, "De Vita Gundulfi," p. 287. See also Saltman, *Theobald*, pp. 395–97, no. 173; *Monasticon*, 3:383–84; *VCH*, Kent, 2:146; Fairweather, "Abbey of St. Mary," pp. 175–76. Sometime between 1077 and 1089, before Gundulf founded Malling, Lanfranc sent him the letter with guidelines to determine which women were free to leave the monasteries to marry; Lanfranc, *Letters*, pp. 166–67 and n. 5 above.

42. Monacho Roffensi, "De Vita Gundulfi," p. 287; *Monasticon*, 3:384.

43. *VCH*, Kent, 2:142. Although a fourteenth-century chronicle lists Anselm as the founder of St. Sepulchre, Canterbury, other late evidence gives a lay founder. Whether or not Anselm was solely responsible for this new house, he played a crucial role in its establishment. See Thompson, "Why English Nunneries Had No History," p. 144.

44. *VCH*, Buckingham, 1:353; *Monasticon*, 4:269–70.

45. *VCH*, Middlesex, 1:156; *MRH*, p. 266. Maurice was the bishop Anselm sent to Barking Abbey to restore harmony there; he also was the recipient of Goscelin's lives of Ethelburga and Wulfhilda.

46. *VCH*, Stafford, 3:220; Mander, "Black Ladies of Brewood," pp. 177–220, esp. 178–79.

47. Farrer, *Yorkshire*, 1:278–81. By the time Thurstan founded St. Clement's, York, he was already the supporter of Christina of Markyate, discussed in Chapters 2 and 3. Moreover, Thurstan gave spiritual advice to Adela, countess of Blois, Cecily de Rumilly, and Gundreda de Mowdray. As well as being sympathetic to the religious needs of women, Thurstan also backed male monasticism, most notably at York and Fountains. See Nicholl, *Thurstan*, pp. 194–202.

48. Farrer, *Yorkshire*, 1:278–81, verified with Cotton Charter XI, 66, a manuscript circa 1130.

49. *VCH*, Yorkshire, 3:129; *Monasticon*, 4:325, no. 3.

50. *Monasticon*, 2:617; *VCH*, Cambridge, 2:220.

51. *MRH*, p. 261. There is some indication that the bishop placed Minster in Sheppey temporarily under the Augustinian Rule, another evidence of episcopal intervention.

52. Anselm, *Opera*, 4:190–91, no. 276. Abbess Athelitz (Alice) may have instead been the abbess of Romsey in the diocese of Winchester, the recipient of another of Anselm's letters.

CHAPTER 2

1. Warren, *Anchorites*, p. 8. See also her "Nun as Anchoress."

2. For Eve and Goscelin, see the introduction to *LC*, pp. 1–22, and Wilmart, "Eve and Goscelin."

3. *LC*, p. 28.

4. *LC*, pp. 28–29.

5. *LC*, pp. 28–29. Goscelin remained sufficiently in Eve's confidence for her to tell him a dream in which she received from him food for her spirit. Goscelin interpreted the dream as referring to the bread he gave Eve when he celebrated mass at Wilton.

6. Goscelin called Eve's companion "hec benedicta domina," either a reference to her name or her status as a nun of high birth. Wilmart, "Eve and Goscelin," 50:75, no. 1, and *LC*, p. 92.

7. *LC*, pp. 26–28. Asking anyone who might intercept the letter to pass it on to Eve, Goscelin stated that it was meant for Eve alone.

8. *LC*, pp. 30, 32. Goscelin praised several kinds of human love—including Abraham's for Isaac, Tobias's for Sarah, and Christ's for His mother; he also mentioned many admirable friendships: between David and Jonathan, Paul and his followers, Sabinus and Sabina, and John and the Virgin Mary. *LC*, pp. 32, 42, 43.

9. *LC*, pp. 26, 42.

10. *LC*, pp. 33, 37, 42. To emphasize the power of intercessory prayer, Goscelin reminded Eve that Monica's prayers had aided Augustine and Stephen's prayers had facilitated Saul's conversion.

11. *LC*, pp. 108–10, 113–17.

12. *LC*, p. 45.

13. *LC*, pp. 48–52, 67–68.

14. *LC*, pp. 50–55, 58–66. In addition to the female models he proposed, Goscelin also included male examples.

15. *LC*, pp. 70, 72, 75–79.

16. *LC*, pp. 79–81, 90. Among the examples of learned people whom Eve might imitate, Goscelin again listed women, including Paula, Eustochium, and Blesilla—the female friends of Jerome. Goscelin may have considered himself to be like Jerome; he not only imitated Jerome in sending a letter of instruction to his female friend but also referred frequently to Jerome.

17. Wilmart, "Eve and Goscelin," 46:414–31. Hilary's poem has been preserved in a twelfth- or thirteenth-century manuscript; see Hilary, *Versus et ludi*, pp. 1–8. On the eremitic movement in France of which Eve was a part, see Raison and Niderst, "Le mouvement érémitique."

18. Hilary, *Versus et ludi*, pp. 5–8.

19. Ibid. Since Hervey celebrated mass for Eve, Goscelin had needlessly wor-

ried when he recommended that Eve receive the viaticum daily.

20. Geoffrey, "Epistolae," col. 184.

21. *Christina*, pp. 126–27, 190–91. For some speculations about the identity of the monk and of the prelate Christina loved, see *Christina*, pp. 5–10. Because the last part of the manuscript of Christina's life is missing, we do not know if Christina was still alive when her biography was completed; the last datable episode in her biography occurred in 1142, thirteen years before her death. See *Christina*, pp. 14–15, for a brief chronology of her life. See also two excellent studies: Holdsworth, "Christina of Markyate," and McLaughlin, "Equality of Souls, Inequality of Sexes."

22. *Christina*, pp. 38–41, 86, 92.

23. Renna, "Virginity," esp. pp. 79–84. Renna's interpretation of virginity in the *vita* differs significantly from mine.

24. *Christina*, pp. 62–63.

25. *Christina*, pp. 40–47. Whether or not Ralph Flambard actually tried to rape Christina, she apparently considered his advances to be an attempted assault.

26. *Christina*, pp. 44–47. In the twelfth century, canon lawyers were still debating what constituted a legal marriage. Once Christina had publicly agreed to marry Burthred, she was officially betrothed, unless her earlier secret vow was considered to be binding. In the view of some canon lawyers, a public promise had more weight than an earlier secret vow, and a promise to marry (betrothal) obliged one actually to marry. See Brundage, "Concubinage and Marriage," esp. pp. 124–26.

27. *Christina*, pp. 66–69.

28. *Christina*, pp. 52–53.

29. *Christina*, pp. 36–41.

30. *Christina*, pp. 36–39, 54–59, 68–71, 78–81, 96–97.

31. *Christina*, pp. 80–97.

32. *Christina*, pp. 86–99; quote from p. 93. Even before Christina joined her, Alfwen may not have lived alone, for the biographer quotes Alfwen as using the pronouns "we" and "us." "Christina" was the name she adopted in place of her birth name, Theodora, perhaps when she joined Alfwen and assumed a religious habit or perhaps at the later public consecration of her virginity. The translation of Psalm 38 (Number 37 in the *Vulgate*) I have taken from *The Jerusalem Bible* (Garden City, N.Y., 1966); it is the source of all Biblical translations.

33. *Christina*, pp. 98–101. Christina's biographer did not explain why Christina moved from Alfwen's to Roger's, nor why Alfwen objected to the move.

34. *Christina*, pp. 41–45, 58–65.

35. *Christina*, pp. 64–71.

36. William of Malmesbury, *De Gestis Pontificum Anglorum*, pp. xv–xvii, 314.

37. For more on this, see *Christina*, pp. 10–13, and Holdsworth, "Christina of Markyate," pp. 202–4. For a consideration of the Norman and Anglo-Saxon groups in England shortly after the conquest, see Chibnall, *Anglo-Norman England*, pp. 208–17.

38. *Christina*, pp. 100–103.

39. *Christina*, pp. 100–105. Since Roger was only a deacon, he could not celebrate mass for Christina, as Hervey had for Eve, and as Abbot Geoffrey later would for Christina.

40. *Christina*, pp. 102–5.

41. *Christina*, pp. 106–11.

42. *Christina*, pp. 110–15. Seven years later, in 1130, Thurstan founded the priory for women at York (St. Clement's).

43. *Christina*, pp. 114–17.

44. *Christina*, pp. 116–19.

45. *Christina*, pp. 134–43.

46. *Christina*, pp. 126–29, 144–47. For the role of virginity in Christina's later life, see also the interpretation in Renna, "Virginity," pp. 84–88.

47. See *Christina*, pp. 124–27 for the invitations to other monasteries. No reference appears in the *vita* to the formal consecration of Markyate Priory in 1145, one indication that the surviving portion of the manuscript covers events only to 1142. According to pp. 80–81, Roger had chosen the site for his hermitage after three angels had led him there. The site legally, however, belonged to the canons of St. Paul's, London. Before Markyate Priory could be officially established, the canons had to give the property to Christina, a transaction recorded in a twelfth-century charter, with Bishop Alexander's seal still attached: Cotton Charter XI, 8; cf. Cotton Charter XI, 6, also from the twelfth century. Both charters were printed in *Monasticon*, 3:372, nos. 6 and 7, with no variations or omissions.

48. How many women lived with Christina at Markyate is not clear from the *vita*. Only three are mentioned specifically—including Christina's sister, Margaret—but apparently more were there. The *vita* does not provide much explicit information about these women and their relationship with Christina, perhaps because the author assumed the situation at Markyate was well-known to his readers and less noteworthy than Christina's memories and visions. See especially *Christina*, pp. 140–47, 182–93.

49. Pächt, Dodwell, and Wormald, *St. Albans Psalter*, pp. 136–46, esp. p. 137. The "unusual choice of Alexis subjects" illustrated in the psalter further reveals a preoccupation with virginity. See also Holdsworth, "Christina of Markyate," pp. 190–95.

50. *Christina*, pp. 134–83, esp. pp. 144–47, 168–69.

51. *Christina*, pp. 138–41, 148–49, 154–55, 178–83.

52. *Christina*, pp. 172–81.

53. John, Abbot of Ford, *Wulfric of Haselbury*, pp. 81–88. John of Ford wrote this life of Wulfric early in the 1180s. Since Matilda's death preceded Wulfric's in 1154, she must have been a recluse by 1136 at the latest.

54. Ibid.

55. John, Abbot of Ford, *Wulfric of Haselbury*, pp. 83–88. In addition to Gertrude, Matilda may have had a second disciple, a certain Christina, also of Wareham; see p. 93.

56. Reginald, *S. Godrici*, pp. 140–45, esp. p. 140. Reginald, a monk of Durham, wrote this *vita* before 1196. Burchwine died sometime before Godric, who died in 1170. See also Talbot, "Godric of Finchale."

57. Anselm, *Opera*, 5:359–62. A community of this size could be considered a small monastery instead of a group of hermits and hermitesses; on other such small communities, see Chapter 3.

58. William of Malmesbury, *Vita Wulfstani*, p. 67. Although William praised this relationship, he was well aware of the dangers of sexual temptations, for he also related an episode in Wulfstan's life in which a girl tried to seduce him. See pp. 6–7.

59. For friendships between celibates earlier in church history, see Clark, "John Chrysostom and the *Subintroductae*"; and Reynolds, "*Virgines Subintroductae* in Celtic Christianity." Gougaud, in "*Mulierum consortia*," argues that as late as the twelfth century, male and female ascetics lived together in order to prove their victory over the flesh. However, Gougaud does not have convincing evidence for twelfth-century England.

60. *Christina*, pp. 170–71. What the reference to Evianus means is unclear.

61. *Christina*, esp. pp. 48–49, 74–77, 108–11, 124–29, 186–87.

CHAPTER 3

1. *Christina*, pp. 14–15, 29–30. See also Riley, *Gesta Abbatum*, 1:101–4; according to Riley, the section of the *Gesta Abbatum* on Christina was not written by Matthew Paris but was an addition incorporated by Thomas Walsingham or by his anonymous predecessor; p. xiii. Compare the account in *VCH*, Bedford, 1:358–59. For a briefer treatment of some of the information in this chapter, see Elkins, "Nunneries."

2. The foundation charters for Markyate Priory as printed in *Monasticon*, 3:372, nos. 6, 7, and 8, are accurate transcriptions of Cotton Charters XI, 6, 8, and 36, twelfth-century manuscripts. Among the numerous witnesses listed in the charters from 1145 were archdeacons, heads of Benedictine monasteries, and Augustinian canons, including four Augustinian priors. Although monks and hermits had been her early friends, Christina had acquired Augustinian patrons as well. Two canons of Merton and Abbot Geoffrey were three of four men who witnessed both the transfer of land and the consecration of her church. Cf. *Christina*, p. 30, on the witnesses.

3. Riley, *Gesta Abbatum*, 1:80–82. This portion of the *Gesta Abbatum* was written by Matthew Paris. Cf. n. 1. In an attempt to correct supposed errors in Matthew Paris's version, *VCH*, Herford, 4:422–23 introduced unnecessary confusion between Sopwell and Markyate priories. It also made the unsupportable suggestion that Geoffrey's involvement in the foundation of Sopwell had the "object no doubt of accommodating the nuns who existed at St. Albans Abbey through the Saxon period down to about this date." Cf. Chapter 1, n. 40.

4. Riley, *Gesta Abbatum*, 1:80–82.

5. The account is preserved in the registry of charters and privileges of Westminster Abbey as transcribed in the time of Edward I. Currently Cotton MS, Faust. A III, it was reprinted with only minor, insignificant variations in *Monasticon*, 3:426, nos. 1, 2, 4. Nothing more is known about Godwyn, but a manuscript identifies the three women as maids (*camerae*) of Matilda, queen of King

Henry I; referred to in *Monasticon*, 3:424, n. a, this is now Cotton MS, Claud. A VIII, fol. 46. This identification of the women as maids appears to have been added to the chronicle many years after the events. Cf. the account in *VCH*, Middlesex, 1:178–79. See the rights the bishop granted Westminster Abbey in Gilbert Foliot, *Letters and Charters*, p. 491.

6. *Monasticon*, 3:426, no. 1. In a court case in 1207 the "master and guardian [*magister et custos*]" of the convent represented Kilburn since the prioress "was enclosed"; *CRR*, 44:23, for 1207. This master and guardian was Alexander from St. Paul's, London, the house of canons that retained rights at Markyate; hence the "suitable senior" did not need to be from Westminster Abbey.

7. Preserved in a fourteenth-century transcription, now Harl. MS. 743, fol. 271v, this MS has been printed in *Monasticon*, 4:477–78, no. 1 with some variants. From p. 477, col. 1, line 14 omit "de Linges"; to col. 2, line 6 add "et dilapidata" after "dissipata"; and to col. 2, line 9, add "canonicos" after "superstites." On p. 478, col. 1, line 5, after "molestiores," a line has been omitted that reads "et eo nobis acrius instabant quia de die in diem rem differebamus cumque." In line 15 substitute "discipulas proprias" for "discipulas suas." There are also several omissions from lines 24 to 25, which should read "quos singulos ex nomine longum esset in charta signare qui ob gratiam et reverentiam tantorum virorum sponte ac simul cum eis hinc inter[cessione] medios interiecerunt. Licet. . . ." The other variations are of no consequence. Cf. *VCH*, Norfolk, 2:354. It is unclear why canons were at the abbey's cell, but perhaps they were a remnant from the conflict described in *MO*, p. 132.

8. Harl. MS. 743, fols. 271v–272r. *VCH*, Suffolk, 2:85.

9. The information is in a confirmation charter of 1160 from Walter, bishop of Chester, printed in *Monasticon*, 4:302. At least by the late twelfth century, the nuns of King's Mead Derby had a *magister*. See Jeayes, *Derbyshire Charters*, p. 302; *VCH*, Derby, 2:43; *MRH*, p. 258.

10. The account preserved in one register of the abbey is printed in *Monasticon*, 4:260, no. 1. Cf. Peck, *Academia tertia Anglicana*, 5:1–13, 6:15–20; the account from Hugh Candidus is cited on 5:4. See also *VCH*, Northampton, 2:98. Abbot William of Waterville was deposed for mysterious reasons in 1175; he is also remembered as the planner of much of the still-existing cathedral of Peterborough.

11. *Monasticon*, 4:260–61, no. 2. Peck, *Academia tertia Anglicana*, 5:4–8, esp. 5:4. See also *Monasticon*, 4:261, nos. 3, 4; Cotton MS, Vesp. E XXII, fol. 39v.

12. Cotton MS, Vesp. E XXII, fols. 39v–40r; Peck, *Academia tertia Anglicana*, 5:13–14. This letter was written either around 1175, less than two decades after the foundation, or around 1230, to a later archbishop of the same name.

13. Grundmann, *Religiöse Bewegungen*, esp. Chapters 4 and 5. For more popular renditions of this theme, see Southern, *Western Society and the Church*, pp. 312–18, and Gies and Gies, *Women in the Middle Ages*, pp. 87–96. For interpretations particularly sensitive to women's history, see Schulenburg, "Sexism and the Celestial *Gynaeceum*," pp. 117–33; and Bolton, "Mulieres Sanctae," pp. 141–58.

14. *Monasticon*, 4:160, nos. 1–5, an accurate transcription of Harl. MS. 2044, fol. 123; see also fol. 124. See Mander, "Black Ladies of Brewood," pp. 201–3.

15. *Monasticon*, 4:206–7, nos. 1–5; I have verified nos. 1 and 2 with Dods. MS. 32, fols. 31r and 32v. *Monasticon* omitted two charters transcribed by Dodsworth in the seventeenth century. One of them, Dods. MS. 32, fol. 31v, is another confirmation by Roger de Scales and his wife Muriel to "the brothers" there, a parallel to *Monasticon*, nos. 1 and 4. But the other, Dods. MS. 32, fol. 32r, is the one from Roger's son Robert (who also is the donor in *Monasticon*, nos. 2 and 3) "to God, St. Mary, the virgin Catherine, all the saints, Hamon Wauter, and his mother Matilda [*Matilda mater sua*] and all serving God" there. This charter, therefore, indicates that blood ties facilitated the reception of women at Blackborough, for both Hamon Wauter and his mother were there. This Hamon Wauter may be the same Hamon named as a witness, along with Robert de Scales and his brother Roger, in Eng Hist MS. a 2, fol. 65, p. 19b. The proper chronological sequence for the charters probably is: first: *Monasticon*, nos. 1 and 4 and Dods. MS. 32, fol. 31v; second: *Monasticon*, no. 3 and Dods. MS. 32, fol. 32r; third: *Monasticon*, no. 2 and later. See also *VCH*, Norfolk, 2:359.

16. *Monasticon*, 4:111; *VCH*, Stafford, 3:222–23. This bishop Roger is the same one who had confirmed Saxe and Guthmund's possessions at Blithbury. More is known about this transfer at Farewell Abbey from another charter of 1140 in which Bishop Roger claimed he was acting "on the petition and request of the hermits Roger, Geoffrey, and Robert" and with the consent of the canons and brothers of the "mother church" of Lichfield. Bishop Roger also included in the gift some land assarted at Farewell by a canon and chaplain of Lichfield. (*Monasticon*, 4:111, no. 1.) Some things remain unclear. Although the three hermits must have been the men who received the women, were they also the canons and lay brothers who had assarted land at Farewell? And how was the canonry of Lichfield "a mother church"? One thing is certain: Farewell, originally for canons and lay brothers who had cleared land there, was given to nuns and other women devoted to God around 1140 through the intercession of hermits.

17. *Monasticon*, 4:221, no. 1. Around 1150, just a few years after women were recorded at Farewell, "the nuns of Langely who came from Farewell" were given "the site of the abbey," other land and the church of All Saints in Somerly by William Pantulf, the great grandson of the William Pantulf who fought in the conquest. Even though Earl William's confirmation charter clearly stated that Langley was "without subjection to any other religious house," by 1209 a dispute had broken out with Farewell that necessitated papal arbitration. A panel of five men was selected by the two houses; they determined that the only obligation Langley had to Farewell was that the prioress of Farewell had to be invited to be present at the election of new prioresses at Langley, even though she had to accept the decision of the nuns of Langley. If the prioress of Farewell did not come when asked, the nuns of Langley could elect their prioress without her. In addition, the judges determined that a certain nun of Farewell, Alice de Hely, who was living at Langley like the other nuns, had to return to Farewell in five

years unless another agreement was reached, a further curtailment of Farewell's influence.

In contrast to the male parent monasteries of female daughter houses, the only female parent lost control of its daughter house by the early thirteenth century. Final verdict of the judgment: "Priorissa vero de Farewell et conventus prae-libatis solempnibus fideliter sibi reservatis omni juri quod tempore compositionis factae in domo de Langele se dicebant habere in praesentia nostra, imperpetuum renunciaverunt." *Monasticon*, 4:112, no. 5, briefly recounted in *VCH*, Stafford, 3:223–24.

Although Farewell apparently was Benedictine, Pope Alexander III around 1185 considered its daughter house, Langley, to be Cistercian, which highlights the difficulty of assigning female houses in the twelfth century to particular orders. The nuns of Langley claimed the Cistercian exemption from certain tithes, a right upheld by Pope Alexander. *Monasticon*, 4:221–22, no. 2.

18. *Monasticon*, 4:393; *VCH*, Middlesex, 1:174–75. Canon Robert was supporting these women at Haliwell about the same time his monastery, St. Paul's, London, was granting Christina land at Markyate.

19. Foliot, *Letters and Charters*, p. 245.

20. For a fuller discussion of "double monasteries," see the introduction.

21. Fowler, "Records of Harrold Priory," pp. 7–9, 58–59. See also pp. 16–20 and 54–57 for other events at Harrold in the twelfth century. On p. 59, Fowler referred to Hilbert as a "kinsman of abbot Gervase," although Hilbert was actually related to Sampson; the correct relationships are on p. 9.

Begun by three canons in France around 1090, Arrouaise gained the status of an abbey and received its own rule in the 1120s under Gervase of Bologne, its third provost and first abbot. Its rule was primarily Augustinian, with a number of reforms: careful observance of the liturgy, almost complete silence, manual labor, and abstinence from meat and linen clothing.

22. Fowler, "Records of Harrold Priory," no. 2 (1136–38: "his sisters the nuns"); no. 7 (1138: "his sisters the nuns and those serving God with them"). See no. 70 on the biological sisters of Gervase. Since the women are called nuns, they probably were Benedictines, even though the canons with them were Augustinians.

A stipulation in the Constitutions of the Order of Arrouaise against receiving women was added to the rule after 1233. In the portion of the rule from the mid-twelfth century, there is a reference to sisters of the order, called *conversae*. See Milis, *L'ordre des chanoines réguliers d'Arrouaise*, pp. lix–lxii, 159, 216.

23. Fowler, "Records of Harrold Priory," no. 70.

24. Fowler, "Records of Harrold Priory," nos. 52, 54, 55 (1138/47: to brothers and sisters); no. 4 (1159–61: to "nuns and brothers . . . guarding them according to the institutes of . . . Arrouaise"); no. 9 (1158: to "prior and canons and sisters"). See also a remarkably well-documented legal suit in Cheney, "Harrold Priory."

25. Fowler, "Priory of Chicksand," pp. 101–28, esp. pp. 103–5, 113, 118–24.

26. Ibid., pp. 118–25. Countess Roaise was intensely loyal to her foundation and wanted her family to be supportive as well. Roaise's son Geoffrey, earl of Essex, added three churches and some chapels to the endowment of Chicksands

and confirmed Roaise's gift of the site of a grange that the "brethren and servants" of the nuns had established in his territory: 240 acres of arable land and
pasture for 500 sheep with their yearlings plus other pastureland. But when
Geoffrey died in 1166, his corpse was taken to Walden Abbey, his father's foundation. Trying to gain his body for Chicksands, Countess Roaise sent an armed
band. When her men failed to seize Geoffrey's corpse, they stripped the earl's
chapel at Walden of its furnishings and brought them to Roaise's chapel at Chicksands. *VCH*, Bedfordshire, 1:390–91, n. 20; Graham, *S. Gilbert of Sempringham*, pp. 37–39.

27. Stenton, *Danelaw*, pp. 241–55; *VCH*, Warwickshire, 2:66–67. See also
Chettle, "Order of Fontevraud."

28. *Monasticon*, vol. 6, pt. 2, pp. 1004–6; *VCH*, Worcester, 2:148–49.

29. Excellent recent literature on Fontevrault includes de Fontette, *Les religieuses*; Smith, "Robert of Arbrissel"; Gold, "Example of Fontevrault"; and
Gold, *Lady and the Virgin*, pp. 93–113, esp. p. 94, the source of my quotations
from Robert's biography.

30. See Gold, *Lady and the Virgin*, pp. 95–98, esp. p. 96; and Smith, "Robert
of Arbrissel," pp. 179–82.

31. Gold, *Lady and the Virgin*, esp. p. 110. For gift formulae, see Stenton,
Danelaw, pp. 241–55.

32. Occasionally the abbess of Fontevrault did intervene in English affairs.
Stenton, *Danelaw*, pp. 247–49. An illustration of the intricate network of male
and female officers is the grant of Eilieva, wife of Robert the cook, to Nuneaton
when she thought she was dying. Eilieva gave herself and many gifts (a mantle, a
cap, a gold ring, eight pigs, eleven beasts, nineteen sheep, and three houses) "to
God and the church of Fontevrault and the house of Eaton into the hands of
Hugh chaplain of the house, Lady Cecilia cellaress, Lady Eidiez preceptor, Lady
Julian prioress, and Lord Vitalis prior." The titles probably are those typically
given to monks and nuns and have no necessary reference to worldly standing.
Stenton, *Danelaw*, p. 247.

33. A large number of churches were granted to Nuneaton and Westwood
priories during the twelfth century. Nuneaton held about a dozen churches.
Churches were probably considered especially appropriate gifts since the priests
of the order could serve them. See esp. Stenton, *Danelaw*, pp. 238–39, 255.

CHAPTER 4

1. Clark, *Godstow*, prints the charters for Godstow as transcribed in a cartulary around 1450. For Latin charters, some of which have an earlier date, see
Monasticon, 4:362–65.

2. Clark, *Godstow*, esp. 129:26–27; 142:xvii–xxxvi. If Edith had this vision,
it would explain why she did not build Godstow near her home nor on her own
land. Another explanation for the location of Godstow might be that Edith was
too poor to provide a site for her house; even though she was the widow of a
knight, none of the surviving records include any gifts from Edith to her abbey.

3. *Monasticon*, 4:362, no. 1.

4. *Monasticon*, 4:362–63, nos. 1, 2. In Clark, *Godstow*, 129:28–30, "year-ly" has been added to some of these gifts, which in the Latin charters seem to have been one-time offerings. Edith's son later became abbot of Abingdon, suc-ceeding the abbot who made the donation; if Edith's son was already a monk at Abingdon, this might be why the abbot of Abingdon attended the consecration of Godstow.

5. *Monasticon*, 4:362–63, nos. 1, 2.

6. *Monasticon*, 4:362–64, nos. 1, 2, 3; Clark, *Godstow*, 129:27–31.

7. Precisely what was meant by "patronage" is not specified in the charter. Lay patrons typically had custody of the house (and its revenues) during a va-cancy—i.e., when there was no abbess; their permission was often needed to hold an election for a new abbess, and their approval of the woman elected was needed. See Wood, *English Monasteries*, pp. 11–14. Only rarely are patrons mentioned for these new lay foundations.

Later John of St. John passed this right of patronage on to his son-in-law Bernard of St. Walery. Before 1176 Bernard transferred "the site of the abbey of Godstow and all lordship and rights of the advocate" to King Henry II, so that Godstow would be "in the holdings of the crown of the realm, just like the abbey of St. Edmunds and other royal abbeys are constituted throughout the realm." *Monasticon*, 4:364, no. 6. The patron of Godstow from the 1170s, King Henry II was reputed to have a special fondness for Godstow Abbey because it was the burial place for his mistress Rosemund. See Clark, *Godstow*, 142:xxxvi; *Monas-ticon*, 4:364–65, nos. 6, 8; Hugo, *Mediaeval Nunneries*, pp. 4–10.

8. Clark, *Godstow*, 129:29, 216, 381; 130:655; 142:xv. There is no sugges-tion in the mid-twelfth-century documents that these entrance donations were inappropriate, although increasingly canonists began to judge that these pay-ments bordered on simony. See Lynch, *Simoniacal Entry*.

9. Clark, *Godstow*, 130:644–46.

10. Clark, *Godstow*, 129:39, 64, 74, 128, 341–42, 351–52; 130:641, 644–47, 651.

11. Clark, *Godstow*, esp. 130:651–65.

12. Almost half the recorded grants for women entering Godstow are for women who had kin either already in the abbey or joining along with them. For charters recording the entry of women—people named Isabel, Agatha, Rose, Cecilia, Odelena, Anne, Marjory, Maud, Agas, Amphelisia, and Mary—see Clark, *Godstow*, 129:29, 43, 49, 128, 154, 162, 178, 179, 180, 214–17, 381; 130:383, 570, 642. The value of gifts is hard to determine. Estimating the rela-tive worth of property described only by boundaries or size is, of course, impos-sible. Sometimes a man had already given a gift years before his kinswoman joined, and this earlier gift may have been considered part of the entrance dona-tion. In any case, there seemed to be no standard requirement for entrance, further evidence that these were not payments demanded of the nuns. In the middle part of the century gifts were usually of land free of any obligations, but by the century's end a rent or knight's service was frequently required of Godstow for the gift.

13. Hassall, *Clerkenwell*, is an excellent edition of the extensive cartulary pre-

served as Cotton Faust. B II. On the text tradition, see pp. ix, xv–xxi. For the genealogy of the founder, see Round, "Foundation."

14. Hassall, *Clerkenwell*, nos. 40–43. The original endowment was land next to "the fountain of clerks"; hence the name Clerkenwell.

15. Hassall, *Clerkenwell*, p. viii.

16. Chaplains were called either chaplains of Clerkenwell, of the nuns, or of St. Mary's. Hassall, *Clerkenwell*, nos. 19, 39, 47, 53, 65, 70, 76, 105, 131–36, 141, 161, 196, 229, and others.

17. Christina is named as prioress in a charter from between 1144 and 1161; Ermengarde is named between 1186 and 1199. Hassall, *Clerkenwell*, nos. 242, 296, 309, 310.

18. Hassall, *Clerkenwell*, nos. 144 and 146. When he made his donation, chaplain Richard said he would serve their church whether he was "in the habit of a secular or in the habit of a religious." This phrase probably indicates that while he could serve them as a secular priest, he might also do so as a religious priest, most likely as an Augustinian canon.

19. Hassall, *Clerkenwell*, no. 200.

20. Hassall, *Clerkenwell*, nos. 33, 39, 42, 94, 134, 145, 168, 189, 229, 258.

21. Hassall, *Clerkenwell*, no. 6.

22. Numerous charters record donations from Jordan de Breiset, his wife Muriel, their children, and their children's spouses: Lecia de Munteni, Henry Foliot, Reginald de Ginges, Emma de Munteni, Rose, Matilda de Munteni. See Hassall, *Clerkenwell*, esp. nos. 2–3, 10–11, 39, 50–51, 54–61, 73.

23. Hassall, *Clerkenwell*, nos. 6, 7, 9, 24, 25, 26, 34, 35, 37, 58, 72, 101, 105, 116, 125, 130, 131, 133, 136, 159, 258, 310. For a general description, see also *VCH*, Middlesex, 1:170–73.

24. On Godstow Abbey, see the first section of this chapter.

25. Saltman, *Theobald*, pp. 379–80. The explanation for the departure of Mary and her nuns from Stratford—"*propter ordinis difficultatem et morum dissonantiam*"—suggests that they wanted a less strict life and different customs from those observed at Stratford. Higham Priory possibly became a dependence of St. Sulpice, but evidence is inconclusive. See also *MRH*, p. 259.

Since Mary and her foreign companions left Stratford before 1152, they could not have been there long. The manor of Lillechurch which Mary had given to Stratford was only acquired by Queen Matilda herself between 1148 and 1152. (*RRAN*, vol. 3, nos. 221–24.)

Mary later became abbess of Romsey. Around 1160, when she was the sole surviving child of Stephen, she married a count but later returned to religious life. (Knowles, *Heads of Religious Houses*, p. 219; Saltman, *Theobald*, pp. 52–53; *VCH*, Hampshire, 2:126–27.)

26. *Monasticon*, 4:382.

27. *Monasticon*, 4:90–93; Ryland, *Records of Wroxall Abbey*, pp. 1–5. Donors to the house included Earl Robert of Leicester, founder of Nuneaton and supporter of Godstow. In 1163 Pope Alexander III confirmed the nuns' right to elect their own abbess.

28. In addition to Godstow and Wroxall, the only other monastery for women

said to be founded because of a vision was St. Mary de Pre; for this house, see Chapter 6.

29. The abbot of Abingdon at this time might have been Edith of Godstow's son. *VCH*, Oxford, 2:75–76. *Monasticon*, 4:492.

30. Although the Norman kings were often asked to confirm donations to priories for women, they rarely made gifts of their own. Apart from a few grants of Henry I to the preconquest houses of Chatteris and Romsey (and perhaps Elstow) and to the episcopal foundation of Malling, the charters preserved from his reign are primarily confirmations of others' gifts. King Stephen's grants were principally to Godstow, Romsey, and his own foundations. See records in *RRAN*, vol. 2, nos. 635, 1654?, 1828? (Elstow); 798, 1242, 1453 (Barking); 1501 (Chatteris); 630, 802, 811, 874, 883, 1160, 1634 (Romsey); 634, 635, 791, 943, 1081, 1271, 1398 (Malling); *RRAN*, vol. 3, nos. 573 (Malling); 37, 38 (Barking); 662 (Polesworth); 712–13 (Redlingfield); 818 (Shaftesbury); 138–39 (Cambridge); 203 (Clerkenwell); 614 (Northampton); 336–37 (Godstow); 722–24 (Romsey); and 842 (Stratford). For more on royal donations, see Brooke, "Princes and Kings."

31. *RRAN*, vol. 3, nos. 226–27, 615; the editors suggest that the text of the foundation may be inflated. According to *MRH*, p. 262, which follows a suggestion of Christopher Brooke's, the priory was moved to a new site in 1146–47. Whether or not this was the case, the involvement of King Stephen on behalf of the women remains the same. Cf. *VCH*, Norfolk, 2:351–52; *Monasticon*, 4:70–71; Rye, *Norfolk Antiquarian Miscellany*, 2:465–67, 500–501.

32. *MRH*, p. 263; some confusion between Robert Marmion I and II exists in the account in *VCH*, Warwickshire, 2:62. See also *Monasticon*, 2:367.

33. Harl. MS. 2101, fol. 18, printed as *Monasticon*, 4:313–14, no. 1. See also Husain, *Cheshire under the Norman Earls*, pp. 129–30. For a study of these barons in the period under Stephen, see Davis, *King Stephen*, esp. pp. 132–45.

34. Earl Simon had earlier confirmed a grant by one of his men to Arrouaise for the foundation of Harrold. *VCH*, Northampton, 2:114; *Monasticon*, 5:208, no. 1. *MRH*, p. 270.

35. *Monasticon*, 4:158; *MRH*, p. 256; on the identity of Geoffrey, see the *Dictionary of National Biography*.

36. *Monasticon*, 4:115; *VCH*, Warwickshire, 2:82. Pinley may have been Cistercian.

37. *Monasticon*, 4:212.

38. Robert Wayfer gave land to the nuns for their convent before 1155. *VCH*, Wiltshire, 3:259; *Monasticon*, 4:399.

39. The site where Flamstead was founded apparently was not the place where Alfwen had lived. *VCH*, Hertford, 2:423; *Monasticon*, 4:300.

40. *VCH*, Cambridgeshire, 2:218; *Monasticon*, 4:216; Gray, *Priory of Saint Radegund*, pp. 3–15, 74–79.

41. Nothing is known about the women who began Ankerwyke Priory, but the name suggests that anchoresses started it. Documents exist for the priory from the end of the twelfth century when a nun, "A., the daughter of W. Clement," left the priory fifteen years after she had made her profession. Controversy ensued when "A." claimed a share of her father's property on the grounds that "she had

been forced into the monastery against her will by a guardian who wished to secure the whole inheritance; and this roused her own relations against her. They appealed to no less a person than the pope himself." "A." was ordered to return to Ankerwyke or be excommunicated. *VCH*, Buckingham, 1:355–56; *CRR*, 5:123, 133, 162, 171, 183–86, 293. Earlier records of the house are sparse. See also *MRH*, p. 255.

42. *MRH*, p. 263. The poor documentation for monasteries like these is discussed in Thompson, "Why English Nunneries Had No History."

43. The charters of Wix Priory are numerous, but their authenticity is in question. For a discussion of forgeries in the records of this and other priories, see Brooke, "Episcopal Charters for Wix Priory." The family of the founder of Wix Priory is discussed in Dodwell, "Honour of Bacton," esp. pp. 150–57.

44. *VCH*, Cambridgeshire, 2:223; *MRH*, p. 259.

45. *VCH*, Hertfordshire, 4:434; *Monasticon*, 4:343.

46. *VCH*, Somerset, 2:109; *MRH*, p. 257.

47. *VCH*, Northampton, 2:101; Peck, *Academia tertia Anglicana*, p. 53.

48. *VCH*, Cambridgeshire, 2:226; Palmer, "Swaffham Bulbeck," pp. 30–31.

49. *VCH*, Kent, 2:144. *MRH*, p. 258 says that Davington was originally for twenty-six nuns, an unusually large house.

50. *VCH*, Oxford, 2:103. Goring may have been Augustinian, although it is more likely that it was Benedictine in the twelfth century.

CHAPTER 5

1. *MRH*, pp. 262, 280–81. See Table 1.

2. Farrer, *Yorkshire*, 1:278–81. See Table 1.

3. *MO*, p. 229.

4. Kapelle, *Norman Conquest of the North*, esp. pp. 191–236.

5. *Vita*, pp. v–vi. The *Vita* in *Monasticon* is based on Cotton MS, Cleop. B I, printed with many omissions and unmarked deletions. Cotton MS, Cleop. B I is one of three preserved manuscripts of Gilbert's *vita*, all of which are discussed in Foreville, *Un procès de canonisation*, pp. xiv–xxii. Composed originally before 1202 as part of the successful campaign to have Pope Innocent III canonize Gilbert, the *vita* was expanded in 1205, after Gilbert's canonization; it is this expanded version that is preserved in the manuscripts. For the most part, the *vita* better reveals end-of-the-century assumptions than Gilbert's own perspective or reliable history. Nonetheless, some of the biographical details it provides probably are accurate, for when it was written, people were still alive who had known Gilbert well.

6. See also Dyson, "Bishop Alexander," esp. pp. 14–24.

7. Ibid. For Markyate, Harrold, and Godstow, see above, Chapters 2 through 4.

8. The *Institutes* are preserved in an early thirteenth century manuscript, Douce 136, printed with no significant variations in *Monasticon*. The *Institutes* are introduced by a first-person narrative purporting to be by Gilbert: *Institutes*, pp. xix–xx; Douce 136, fols. xii–1.

Gilbert's recollections probably were recorded after the problems of the late 1160s because he states that the nuns' chapel was partitioned in a way that prevented the nuns from seeing or being seen by the canons. Undoubtedly, there had always been separate choirs for the nuns and canons, for in 1139, several years before Gilbert added canons, the Second Lateran Council had decreed that nuns could not join with canons or monks in church in one choir for singing the office. (Mansi, *Sacrorum Conciliorum*, vol. 21, col. 533.) But in the 1160s, the Gilbertines were criticized for the close proximity of nuns and canons in their monasteries, and they made some modifications as a result. The dividing partition in the main church, which prevented the nuns from even seeing the celebrating priest during mass, was apparently the compromise reached after the controversy in the 1160s. For more on this story, see Chapter 6.

Since Gilbert died in 1189, these reflections could date anytime between twenty and forty years after the final formation of his order. For a further discussion of this introductory portion, see Elkins, "Gilbertine Identity."

9. *Institutes*, p. xix; Douce 136, fol. xii. For a general treatment of the Gilbertines, still unsurpassed in detail and thoroughness, see Graham, *S. Gilbert of Sempringham*.

10. *Institutes*, p. xix; Douce 136, fols. xii–1.

11. The abbot of Rievaulx who advised Gilbert is identified as William in another section of the *Institutes*, p. xxxvi; Douce 136, fol. 38.

12. *Institutes*, p. xix; Douce 136, fols. xii–1.

13. *Institutes*, p. xix; Douce 136, fol. 1. In another section of the *Institutes* (p. xxxvi), the claim is made that the serving men themselves asked for austerities like those of the Cistercian lay brothers whom they saw accompanying the abbot of Rievaulx on his visit to Gilbert. This section could be considerably later than Gilbert's introductory recollection, so I have not set it on a par with his own account. (Compare the treatment in Golding, "St. Bernard and St. Gilbert," esp. p. 47; and in Giraudot and Bouton, "Bernard et les Gilbertins," esp. pp. 328–30.) Since Gilbert emphasized that the serving women desired a strict life, his failure to mention a similar wish by the serving men may reveal his later dissatisfaction with some of the first lay brothers after the lay brothers' revolt (see Chapter 6).

14. *Monasticon*, vol. 6, pt. 2, p. 947, no. 1.

15. *Monasticon*, vol. 6, pt. 2, p. 948, an accurate edition of Dods. MS. 144, a seventeenth-century transcription of a cartulary of Haverholme.

16. *VCH*, Lincolnshire, 2:187; *Monasticon*, vol. 6, pt. 2, pp. 948–49.

17. *Monasticon*, vol. 6, pt. 2, p. 948. Although this is a seventeenth-century transcription and not the twelfth-century original charter, there is no reason to assume a later altering of the original document. For a scribe to have interpolated this particular phrase at a later date would have served no purpose.

18. *Institutes*, pp. xix–xx; Douce 136, fol. 1.

19. Ibid. At this very chapter meeting in 1147, the Cistercians accepted into their order the monasteries in the congregation of Savigny, some of which included women. For recent literature on the Savigniacs and a discussion of the complexities of their incorporation in the Cistercian order, see Swietek and Deneen, "Episcopal Exemption of Savigny."

20. See Graham, *S. Gilbert of Sempringham*, pp. 10–14; *MO*, pp. 205–7; Golding, "St. Bernard and St. Gilbert," esp. pp. 42–54; and Giraudot and Bouton, "Bernard et les Gilbertins," esp. pp. 327–28. All these scholars accept the assertion made later in the *Vita* that the Cistercians were unwilling to undertake the supervision of women.

21. On the Augustinian canons in England, see Dickinson, *Origins of the Austin Canons*, esp. Chapter 2. See also the summary compiled in *MRH*, pp. 137–82. For perceptive studies of the canons and their understanding of their religious vocation, see Bynum, "Spirituality of Regular Canons," and her *Docere Verbo et Exemplo*.

22. *Institutes*, p. xx; Douce 136, fol. 1.

23. The Gilbertine priory of Sixhills may not have included all four groups from its inception; early donation charters mention only "the nuns"; canons may have been added when a church was given "for the support of thirteen canons" under King Henry II. Stenton, *Gilbertine*, pp. 1–5. Hence, Sixhills could have undergone a development paralleling that at Sempringham and Haverholme.

24. The three priories probably already present in the North are mentioned in Chapter 1. Usually said to have been founded around 1150, the Benedictine priory of Arden may have been begun somewhat later in the century; and if it had lay brothers, these were added later as well. (*MRH*, pp. 255–56.)

Stixwould Priory later added religious men but did not have them before 1147. (Stenton, *Danelaw*, pp. 281–88; *VCH*, Lincolnshire, 2:148.) Although Heynings Priory in Lincolnshire may have had lay brothers as well as nuns from its foundation around 1135, the men may have been added later. A confirmation charter from the time of King Henry III says that the earliest donations were to "fratribus et sororibus de Heyninges," but this report is too late to be trustworthy. (*Monasticon*, 5:723. Cf. *VCH*, Lincolnshire, 2:150; *MRH*, p. 247.)

25. If the Cistercian order recognized any of these English monasteries for women as officially Cistercian before the thirteenth century, no evidence survives. Precisely when Cistercian houses for women were first accepted as part of the Cistercian order is unknown. Cistercian legislation first referred to "incorporated" nuns in 1213, but Tart and some other Continental monasteries for women seem to have had some recognized status as Cistercians before this decree. For discussions of the problems in determining whether nuns were actually Cistercians, see Thompson, "Problem of the Cistercian Nuns"; and Connor, "First Cistercian Nuns." For particular attention to English nuns, see Graves, "English Cistercian Nuns," and Burton, "Yorkshire Nunneries," esp. p. 4.

26. Farrer, *Yorkshire*, 1:167–69.

27. *Monasticon*, 5:494.

28. *Close Rolls* for 1270, 14:301; *MRH*, p. 271. See discussion in Graves, "English Cistercian Nuns," pp. 495–99.

29. Hunt, *Cluny under St. Hugh*, esp. Chapter 4.

30. *MRH*, p. 270.

31. See Table 4 for a summary of my conclusions. In the table, I have marked with a "?" conclusions about the individual houses given in *MRH* that I have not been able to verify.

For early documentation on the presence of lay brothers, see for Greenfield

(present from 1160 on): Stenton, *Danelaw*, pp. 79, 92, 95–96. For Hutton/
Baysdale (first reference is beginning of thirteenth): *Monasticon*, 5:509; see
also a reference to "our brothers who have received our habits" in Farrer, *Yorkshire*, 1:443–44. For NunAppleton (at least one brother present by 1150): Farrer, *Yorkshire*, 1:419–21; *Monasticon*, 5:652–54. For NunCotham (present by
1170s): *Monasticon*, 5:676–77; *VCH*, Lincolnshire, 2:151. For Sinningthwaite
(present by 1172): Farrer, *Yorkshire*, 1:167–69. For Stixwould (present by 1160):
Stenton, *Danelaw*, pp. 281–88; *VCH*, Lincolnshire, 2:148. For Swine (at least by
1170): Farrer, *Yorkshire*, 3:75–78; *Monasticon*, 5:495.

32. The priories with virtually no documentation are Fosse and Ellerton. The
earliest in the shires were Kirklees and Keldholme in Yorkshire and Gokewell in
Lincolnshire. In addition to articles in *VCH*, for Kirklees see Chadwick, "Kirklees Priory."

33. Greenfield by the time of Henry II had a *prior* or *custos*—i.e., individual
charters mentioned either a *prior* or a *custos* but not both (Stenton, *Danelaw*,
pp. 94–96). Legbourne by 1200 had a *magister* or *prior* (*FOF*, pp. 99, 103;
CRR, 1:161, 164). NunCotham by the 1170s had a *magister* (*Monasticon*,
5:676–77); by the early thirteenth century, its constitution permitted a *magister*,
two chaplains, and twelve lay brothers (*Monasticon*, 5:677–78). Sinningthwaite
by 1172 was given permission to accept into membership *clerici* fleeing the
world, but since it is possible that these became lay brothers and not canons, I
have not listed canons at Sinningthwaite on Table 4 (Farrer, *Yorkshire*, 1:167–
69). Stixwould by 1160 had canons and a *magister* (Stenton, *Danelaw*, pp. 281–
88; *VCH*, Lincolnshire, 2:148). Swine by 1181 had a *magister* and canons; as
early as 1175, there is a reference to a *magister*, also called *prior* (Farrer, *Yorkshire*, 3:78). Wykeham by 1160–76 had a *magister* and a canon (Farrer, *Yorkshire*, 1:300).

Priors or masters were not typical in Cistercian monasteries for women, and
their presence in these English houses further indicates the unusual status of these
monasteries. On the men common in Cistercian monasteries for women, see
Connor, "First Cistercian Nuns," pp. 146–52.

34. In contrast to the nuns, canons, and lay brothers, the lay sisters were not
named as recipients in the gift formulae that provide the most information about
the composition of the priories. For instance, even the Gilbertines, who definitely
had lay sisters, received gifts "to the nuns and brothers, clerical and lay."

35. *Monasticon*, 5:676–77; *VCH*, Lincolnshire, 2:151.

36. Farrer, *Yorkshire*, 1:443–44.

37. *Monasticon*, 5:676–77; *VCH*, Lincolnshire, 2:151. For more on Nun-
Cotham, see Graves, "English Cistercian Nuns," p. 494, n. 15.

38. One of the few monasteries known not to have survived the century was
Tunstall. Sometime before 1164, Gilbert sent religious of both sexes to the island
of Tunstall to set up a monastery on land the baron Reginald de Crevequer
provided. Before the end of the century, Tunstall was united with Bullington by
the founder's son. *VCH*, Lincolnshire, 2:197; *Monasticon*, vol. 6, pt. 2, pp. 953–
54; *MRH*, p. 194.

39. On the early history of the Premonstratensians, see Lefevre and Grauwen,
Les statuts de Prémontré, and Petit, *S. Norbert*. On Premonstratensian sisters,

see Erens, "L'ordre de Prémontré," and de Fontette, *Les religieuses*, pp. 13–25. Since the original legislation on the separation of the male and female Premonstratensian no longer survives, the date of 1137 is only an approximation. For the English houses, see Colvin, *White Canons in England*, esp. pp. 327–36.

40. *MRH*, p. 238; Hodgson, et. al., *A History of Northumberland*, 5:477–79; *VCH*, Nottingham, 2:138.

41. *MRH*, p. 238; *VCH*, Nottingham, 2:138.

42. *MRH*, pp. 261–62; Farrer, *Yorkshire*, 1:328–30; *VCH*, 3:239. Later in the century, Marton became a house for canons alone, and the nuns were moved to nearby Moxby Priory. On this later development, see Chapter 6.

43. *VCH*, Lincolnshire, 2:179; *MRH*, p. 280.

44. When Robert of Chesney, Bishop Alexander's successor to the see of Lincoln, sought to improve the care provided the sick and the poor in a hospital in Lincoln that had been founded by Bishop Robert Bloet, Gilbert agreed to staff a priory there with his canons soon after 1148. Shortly thereafter lay sisters joined the canons to help tend the ill and needy. *VCH*, Lincolnshire, 2:188; Foster and Major, *Registrum Antiquissimum*, 1:120–21.

45. *MRH*, p. 198.

46. The documentation for these later foundations is particularly poor, and Table 4 here has to rely primarily on information in *MRH*, which I have not been able to verify. (Such information I designate with "?".) According to *MRH*, these communities included men at least until the early fourteenth century, but whether they already had them in the twelfth century is uncertain. For the early-thirteenth-century prior of Stainfield, see *CCR*, 1:346.

47. Sixhills (Syriel): 120 sisters to 55 brothers; Haverholme, Bullington, and North Ornsby: 100 women to 50 men; Alvingham: 100 sisters to 40 brothers; Catley: 60 sisters to 35 brothers. *Institutes*, p. lviii; Douce 136, fol. 187.

48. *Monasticon*, 5:676–77; *VCH*, Lincolnshire, 2:151.

49. For the Gilbertine privilege: Holtzmann, *Papsturkunden in England*, 1:442; compare translation in Graham, *S. Gilbert of Sempringham*, pp. 111–12. "Possesion of a church" was the shorthand language used for the possession of its advowson and rights to all the tithes and gifts given to the church and its dependent chapels.

50. For Hutton/Baysdale, see *Monasticon*, 5:508–9; Farrer, *Yorkshire*, 2:91–92. For Rosedale: *Monasticon*, 4:317–19; *MRH*, p. 275. Knowles claims that Robert of Stuteville was not the founder, as Dugdale had thought, but just the confirmer of the gift of the founder, William of Rosedale. For Marrick, see *Monasticon*, 4:254. For a discussion of the economy of the Cistercian monasteries for women, see Burton, "Yorkshire Nunneries," pp. 11–27. In France around 1150, the Benedictine Herman of Tournai described eight monasteries for women, "three in the order of the monks of Clairvaux and five in that of the clerics of the Premonstratensians." Herman claimed, "They did not only women's work, such as spinning and weaving, but they went out and worked in the fields, digging, cutting down and uprooting the forest with axe and mattock, tearing up thorns and briers, laboring assiduously with their hands and seeking their food in silence." (See Herman of Tournai, *PL* 156, cols. 1001–2; translated with some discussion in Lekai, *Cistercians: Ideals and Reality*, pp. 349–50.) Considering

the grants the nuns received in England, it is highly likely that at times they too worked in the fields, aiding their lay brothers, although no evidence of this activity survives.

51. Stenton, in his introduction to *Danelaw* and *Gilbertine*, provides an excellent overview of the economy of the North. The great arable fields were divided into *culturae*; these consolidated areas of ploughland were usually held only by important men of considerable wealth. The peasant, knight, and free tenant had strips of ploughland, called *seliones*, which were scattered over several *culturae*. A typical peasant holding was the bovate or oxgang, the amount of land that could be ploughed in a season by one ox, which in Lincolnshire usually meant about twenty acres. A bovate was one-eighth of a carucate, the area of land that could be ploughed in a season by a plough-team of eight oxen.

A normal arable holding carried with it rights in a common pasture, some meadowland, and a toft—i.e., the plot containing the house and buildings that belonged to a farm. Although usually including a farmhouse, a toft could instead be an enclosure for sheep, with the only dwelling a shepherd's hut.

When a lord gave a farm or village, he usually transferred as well the services of the tenants living there. Only rarely does the gift charter specify whether the tenants owed labor or money rents. Often the tenants were indicated as "men" being given with the farm or village, with no clear line drawn between freedmen and serfs. See esp. Stenton, *Gilbertine*, pp. xxi, xxv–xxvii; and *Danelaw*, pp. xix–xx, xxxv–xxxix.

52. In addition to poorly endowed Haverholme (*Monasticon*, vol. 6, pt. 2, pp. 948–49), the Gilbertines agreed to begin a monastery on the island of Tunstall, a marshy site comprised of some sixteen acres and a meadow and common rights in pasture, marsh, water, and fish. Some years later Tunstall was united with Bullington. On Tunstall, see *Monasticon*, vol. 6, pt. 2, p. 954; *VCH*, Lincolnshire, 2:197. (See also n. 38 above.)

Better endowed than the other island sites of Haverholme and Tunstall, Catley Priory was given by its founder the island with all its appurtenances in wood, field, plain, meadow, feeding, marshes, and water; this was supplemented with 10 *culturae*, 2 carucates, and 12 bovates of land, at least half of which was arable; 5 tofts; a water mill; a grange; and pasture for 400 sheep. Stenton, *Gilbertine*, pp. 72–73.

53. To found Bullington, the Gilbertines received the church of Bullington with its park and woodlands, other land on which grange houses could be constructed, a mill, another church, and pastureland for 600 sheep. Stenton, *Gilbertine*, pp. 91–101; Stenton, *Danelaw*, pp. lv, 1–74.

54. Sixhills Priory has a virtually complete set of documents from before 1187. The confirmation charter of Henry II in 1187 confirmed the grants of some twenty-eight people to that house. (Stenton, *Gilbertine*, pp. 35–38.) Separate charters for the grants of seventeen of these people correspond almost exactly with the confirmation of Henry II. (Stenton, *Gilbertine*, pp. 1–35.) The eleven people whose donations Henry confirmed but whose gifts have not been independently preserved gave about one bovate each. For additional treatment of Stixwould, see Graves, "Stixwould."

55. *Monasticon*, 5:676–77. Many small gifts were omitted from Alexander's confirmation, as a comparison with Farrer, *Yorkshire*, shows.

56. In addition, NunAppleton received rents, a salt pit, and several dwellings. Stixwould similarly had extensive grants of land and at least four churches. For NunAppleton, see primarily Farrer, *Yorkshire*, 1:422–25; 3:290–91, 302–4, 373–74, 462–64; *Monasticon*, 5:653–54. For Stixwould: *Monasticon*, 5:725, a later and perhaps inflated confirmation. Cf. Stenton, *Danelaw*, pp. 279–84, 287–89.

57. *Monasticon*, 5:665.

58. Stenton, *Danelaw*, pp. 332–33; *VCH*, Nottingham, 2:89. *Monasticon*, 4:295. I have accepted the date in *MRH*, p. 267. Only rarely does one find a monastery like NunMonkton, apparently for nuns alone yet endowed at its foundation with four churches. For NunMonkton, see Farrer, *Yorkshire*, 1:414–15.

59. In addition to Gilbert, the only other churchman in these years to found a new monastery for women in the North was Bishop Alexander of Lincoln, who gave Haverholme to Gilbert and his followers. Alexander's successor as bishop, Robert of Chesney, also gave Gilbert property to found the priory serving the hospital in Lincoln, which I have not included in this count since it did not include nuns.

Even though Orford, Guyzance, and Broadholme were on land formerly given to canons, and even though Grimsby was aided by canons of Wellow, these four monasteries for women technically were lay foundations, for laity provided the grants. Swine, however, may also have had a religious founder because its establisher was identified as "brother *(frater)*" Robert. Farrer, *Yorkshire*, 1:414–15; 3:75–76.

60. For Stixwould: *VCH*, Lincolnshire, 2:146; *Monasticon*, 5:725. By two marriages, Countess Lucy, the foundress of Stixwould, was the mother of the earl of Lincoln and the earl of Chester. For Keldholme: *MRH*, p. 274. Robert de Stuteville, founder of Keldholme, was either himself the baron, or his namesake son, who fought in the battle of the Standard. King Henry II may have aided the foundation of Moxby Priory; see Chapter 6 and *MRH*, pp. 262, 282.

61. Tired of the "disaffection of the greater Norman nobles" and older Anglo-Saxon barons, King Henry I created "a party of nobles who owed their position in the upper reaches of society to him." Recently granted much land and the lordship of Malton, Eustace fitz John was one of the "three mainstays of Henry's new regime in the North." His wife Agnes was the daughter of the constable of Chester. Kapelle, *Norman Conquest of the North*, pp. 197–98. Cf. Graham, S. *Gilbert of Sempringham*, p. 36.

62. The de Arches family was generous both in its initial endowment and in later support of its monasteries. To found Nunkeeling, Agnes provided the church of Keeling, three carucates of land there, a croft, twelve *denarii* a year from another croft, and materials from the wood of Bewholme for making ploughs and harrows. Agnes's brother William gave to his NunMonkton six and a half carucates and three churches. Agnes's daughter Alice gave the women of NunAppleton the place that Juliana held next to Appleton, with all the land on both sides of the brook, partly improved and partly not, along with three other

bovates of land. Nor did Alice's investment end with the foundation; she increased the endowment of NunAppleton with four more bovates, two dwellings, several messuages, a salt pan, and two churches. Sensitive to family ties, Alice added two bovates to her mother's Nunkeeling, while her son Robert granted NunAppleton another church and pasture for four hundred sheep with other animals. See the Chart on the de Arches. For NunAppleton, see Farrer, *Yorkshire*, 1:419–25. For Nunkeeling: Farrer, *Yorkshire*, 1:420; 3:53–59, 219. For Nun-Monkton: Farrer, *Yorkshire*, 1:414–15. For Bullington: Stenton, *Gilbertine*, p. 91; Graham, *S. Gilbert of Sempringham*, pp. 33–34. For projected foundation at Royton: Farrer, *Yorkshire*, 1:426, dated c. 1150–70; *VCH*, Yorkshire, 3:170–71.

Apart from Agnes de Arches and her family, the only women mentioned as foundresses were the woman who established Yedingham and another who co-founded Hampole with her husband. For Yedingham, see Farrer, *Yorkshire*, 1:483; Hampole: *Monasticon*, 5:487.

63. Agnes de Arches held the land for Nunkeeling from William de Aumale, earl of York, also the superior lord of North Ormsby's establisher, Gilbert of Ormsby. Agnes's daughter was the widow of the steward of William de Percy. One of William de Percy's men was also an endower of Wilberfoss. For North Ormsby, see *VCH*, Lincolnshire, 2:195; Stenton, *Gilbertine*, p. 39. For Wilberfoss: *Monasticon*, 4:355.

64. For Catley, see *VCH*, Lincolnshire, 2:196; Stenton, *Gilbertine*, pp. 72–73. For Fosse: *VCH*, Lincolnshire, 2:157; *Monasticon*, 4:293; *MRH*, p. 273. For Gokewell: *VCH*, Lincolnshire, 2:156; *MRH*, p. 273; Farrer, *Yorkshire*, 3:281. For Greenfield: *VCH*, Lincolnshire, 2:155; *Monasticon*, 5:579–80. For Hampole: *Monasticon*, 5:487. For Heynings: *MRH*, p. 274. For Marton: Farrer, *Yorkshire*, 1:329. For Yedingham: Farrer, *Yorkshire*, 1:483.

65. After 1154, there apparently was more similarity between the founders of male and female Cistercian houses, for Hill claims that during "the second Cistercian generation," the patrons of the monks were "from the broad class of knights." Hill, *English Cistercian Monasteries*, Chaps. 2 and 3, esp. pp. 30, 37, 38, 60, 64, 70, 75.

66. Even political strategies seem unlikely motives. If the founder's prestige was enhanced locally, other acts of public beneficence would have brought greater glory than a new monastery for women. Moreover, it may not have been politically astute to introduce one of Gilbert's unusual priories or a monastery that called itself Cistercian but was not recognized by Cîteaux. Although a desire for prestige encouraged the foundation of genuine Cistercian monasteries for men, it did not necessarily foster these forms of female monasticism.

67. Peter de Hoton, traditionally called the founder of Arden, had as his lord Roger de Mowbray, earl of Northumbria and the first northern Norman baron to revolt against central rule at the end of the eleventh century. On the other side, a firm backer of King Henry I was William of Warenne, earl of Surrey and the superior lord who confirmed the foundation of Kirklees by Reyner of Flanders. For Arden, see *Monasticon*, 4:285; for Kirklees: *Monasticon*, 5:739.

68. Of 107 grants to Gilbertines during the reign of Henry II, less than 20 percent had any discernible dues, services, or payments attached. Although in the

last third of the century, duties were more frequently attached to grants, even then most gifts apparently were free of obligations. If a few donors late in the century profited, the typical founders of the midcentury cannot be shown to have benefited materially from their grants.

69. For instance, even the great barons, Countess Lucy and Robert de Stuteville, provided generously for their foundations at Stixwould and Keldholme either with large tracts of land or an assortment of land and rights in one place. For Stixwould, see VCH, Lincolnshire, 2:146; Monasticon, 5:725. For Keldholme: MRH, p. 274.

Agnes and her husband Eustace fitz John, the justiciar of Henry I, gave the Gilbertines the entire vill of Watton, with all its land, water, pasture, and marches, plus a man and all his land (three bovates with his messuage). For Watton's original donation, see Farrer, Yorkshire, 2:404. The knight's service owed on Watton was considerable. When Eustace's superior lord William Fossard I quitclaimed the knight's service owed him for the vill, he expected Watton to be able to support thirteen canons on the savings. Yet one need not surmise that Agnes and Eustace were trying to rid themselves of unprofitable land; they had only recently acquired the vill by using some of Agnes's marriage lands. (Farrer, Yorkshire, 2:405–6.) See also n. 62 for gifts from the de Arches family.

70. Alvingham had multiple founders, and it received the daughters of two of the cofounders as well as one of the founders himself. In one of the few references to a reception of a man, the priest Hamelin gave up his rights in the church of Alvingham, several tofts, a few acres of land, a salt pan, and other grants before himself becoming a canon there. VCH, Lincolnshire, 2:192; Stenton, Gilbertine, pp. 103–7.

71. For NunMonkton, see Farrer, Yorkshire, 1:414–15. For Marrick: Clay, Early Yorkshire Charters, 5:77–78. For Wykeham: Farrer, Yorkshire, 1:300. Two of Gilbert of Sempringham's nephew's daughters also joined one of the Gilbertine monasteries. Stenton, Gilbertine, pp. 17, 82.

72. I have found only two records of lay advowsons definitely being retained by the founders, and both of these references are late, from the turn of the century. The heir of the founder of Handale gave "the advowson of the house of religious nuns" to a certain man "for his homage and service." (Monasticon, 4:75.) A relative of the founder of Yedingham was called "our advocate" by the prioress Beatrice. (Farrer, Yorkshire, 1:469.) Although references to advocates could simply be missing from other records, both Yedingham and Handale were Benedictine houses, with no canons affiliated. Perhaps the absence of priors encouraged laymen to perform the function of advocate. Otherwise, control of the monastery does not appear to have been a major consideration of the lay founders. One of the very few records of rights being reserved was when the mother of the king's steward retained the right to fatten forty swine in her woods after she had given Arthington Priory the land. (Farrer, Yorkshire, 3:472–73.) Also, when Sixhills was given land in the last decade of the century, the prior promised the donor a corrody in the house for life. (Stenton, Gilbertine, p. 18.) Such provisions were rare.

73. For a consideration of which donations and payments were considered simony, see Lynch, Simoniacal Entry. On entrance donations to Cistercian mon-

asteries for women, see Burton, "Yorkshire Nunneries," pp. 20–24. For Sixhills, see Stenton, *Gilbertine*, p. 30.

74. For instance, when the two daughters of Roger Musteile entered Sixhills, Roger gave the whole village of Legsby, complete with arable lands, meadows, feedings, woods, water, mill, churches, paths and ways, reserving for himself six marks a year. Roger also gave to Sixhills his entire fee in Willingham, reserving twenty shillings a year. On both, the nuns owed the knight's service, estimated as the fee of half a knight. Such grants are unusual both because of their size and their requirement of payments from the monastery. To consider such gifts as entrance grants would, however, be misleading, for Roger's grant was in part motivated by the fact that Gilbert of Sempringham was his uncle. Stenton, *Gilbertine*, p. 17. Another entrance gift that was disproportionately large and had an atypical stipulation also would unjustly skew the averages: a woman, whose husband and son were also donors to Alvingham, gave one-half her demesne in two villages, including thirty acres of arable land and ten acres of pasture, when her daughter joined Alvingham. However, this woman added that since the monastery "saw and knew that with a great debt I and my [husband] and my son John were obliged to the Jews, they aided us and acquited us of 87½ marks of silver." *Monasticon*, vol. 6, pt. 2, p. 958.

75. For instance, Heloise's father Supir (mentioned in text above) gave to Sixhills at another time a half church in East Wykeham. Hence, her family alienated more property than her entrance gift implies. Stenton, *Gilbertine*, p. 5; from before 1162, possibly 1155.

76. Stenton, *Gilbertine*, pp. 25–26, 30, 51, 55, 62–63, 75–76, 80, 82, 83; Stenton, *Danelaw*, pp. 63–64; *Monasticon*, vol. 6, pt. 2, p. 959.

77. Farrer, *Yorkshire*, 3:83.

78. Stenton, *Danelaw*, pp. 288–89.

79. Stenton, *Gilbertine*, pp. 17, 75–76, 80. Poynton, "Priory of Sempringham," 16:31.

80. See Chapter 7.

81. Aelred, "Wattun," col. 791–92. This text is a reprint of Twysden, *Historiae anglicanae*, 10:415–22, an edition of the only known manuscript—Cambridge MS. 139, fols. 149r–151v—with only minor variations. The recipient is mentioned at the end of the letter, col. 796.

82. Ibid. The location of the vision, on the step before the altar, suggests that until 1165 the Gilbertine nuns still had a clear view of the altar when the canons celebrated mass. Such was not the case later in the century. For Aelred on friendship, see especially *Spiritual Friendship*.

83. Aelred, "Sermones de Oneribus," cols. 370–72.

84. Ibid.

CHAPTER 6

1. Knowles, "Revolt," p. 481. For the discussion of this "revolt," see below.

2. The affair of the nun of Watton forms the substance of the letter Aelred wrote his "dearest friend who is far removed from these parts," the first part of

which was cited at the end of the previous chapter. (Aelred, "Wattun.") Aelred wrote this letter sometime before his last illness in December 1166, which incapacitated him until his death in January 1167. Since Aelred said the story had taken place long before, the latest possible years for the affair were the early 1160s. In the narrative (col. 791), Aelred relates that Henry Murdac had asked Watton to receive the girl for raising (*nutrienda*) when she was about four years of age. Since Henry was archbishop of York from 1147 to his death in 1153, and since Watton was founded in 1150, the four-year-old child was received sometime between 1150 and 1153, in the early days of the priory's history. At the earliest, she would have therefore entered puberty about 1160, so the pregnancy must have occurred between 1160 and 1165. See also Daniel, *Life of Ailred*, p. xcix, and cf. the treatment in Constable, "Aelred of Rievaulx."

3. Aelred, "Wattun," col. 793–94.

4. Ibid. As Biblical precedents, Aelred cited Simeon and Levi's revenge for the rape of their sister Dinah even after Hamor had married her (Gen. 34:25); the time Israel was spared God's vengeance because Phinehas, grandson of Aaron, killed a Midianite woman pregnant with an Israelite child (Num. 25:7–110); and Solomon's killing of his brother Adonijah, who sought to wed Abishag (I Kings 2:13–35). These Scriptural antecedents let Aelred argue that bloody vengeance was sometimes mandated when sexual liaisons violated God's will. Perhaps because these instances of violence all concerned sexual acts, they were not the ones typically used to justify war; for instance, none of them appear in the Biblical justifications Bernard of Clairvaux used for the Templars in the Holy Land. See Bernard, "Praise of the New Knighthood."

5. Aelred, "Wattun," cols. 794–96.

6. Ibid.

7. Aelred, "Wattun," cols. 791–92. In part, Aelred could blame the difficulties on the custom of child oblation, a practice the Cistercians no longer endorsed. Yet Aelred could not criticize the Gilbertines too severely for accepting the girl: child oblation was a long-standing custom, and the man who had requested the girl's admission was the saintly Henry Murdac, one of the leading Cistercians in England and at that time abbot of Fountains and archbishop of York. Perhaps in response to this episode, by the early thirteenth century the Gilbertines had legislated against receiving child oblates. On Cistercian attitudes, see Lynch, "Cistercians and Underage Novices."

Although the girl is called a nun in the title given Aelred's letter and although Aelred said she wore a veil, he never referred to her as a nun in his story. Hence, it is not clear if the girl had formally made her profession. Nonetheless, because she wore the habit and lived as if she were a nun, she was bound by the rule of celibacy according to the archbishops' decisions at the end of the eleventh century; see Chapter 1.

8. Aelred, "Wattun," cols. 791–92. Because the man was performing some manual labor, he probably was a lay brother. But canons may also have had some chores that brought them into the nuns' quarters. See also Constable, "Aelred of Rievaulx," pp. 218–19.

9. Aelred, "Wattun," cols. 791–92. The passage Aelred quoted is from Psalms 126.

10. Ibid.

11. Ibid.

12. Aelred, "Wattun," cols. 792–93.

13. A number of letters describing these charges and the responses to them were included in the *Vita* composed at the beginning of the thirteenth century for Gilbert's canonization. Dugdale omitted them from his rendition of the *Vita* in *Monasticon*, but two excellent editions of the letters have since been published, along with reconstructions of the events: Knowles, "Revolt," pp. 465–87, and Foreville, *Un procès de canonisation*, pp. 83–110, in an appendix entitled "Lettres relatives à la rébellion des frères lais de l'ordre de Sempringham."

14. Foreville, *Un procès de canonisation*, pp. 90–92. Only Foreville published the letters from Archbishop Thomas and Pope Alexander. Whenever the letters appear in both Foreville and Knowles, I have cited Knowles, for his article is more readily available. For earlier relations between the Gilbertines and Thomas Becket, see Graham, *S. Gilbert of Sempringham*, pp. 16–19.

Although Foreville and Knowles basically agree on the dates and authorship of the letters written about the lay brothers' revolt, some uncertainties remain. Foreville believes Becket's first letter to Gilbert about the revolt was written in 1165, with May 1166 the latest likely date. With little explicit consideration of this letter, Knowles agrees that the terminus a quo for the troubles is 1165; but he thinks the following year, or even 1167, is the earliest certain reference to the revolt. In either case, the nun of Watton episode would have occurred and probably been resolved by then, for Aelred of Rievaulx had seen the nun sometime "long before" his mortal illness at the end of 1166. See note 2 above.

15. Knowles, "Revolt," pp. 478–79.

16. Knowles, "Revolt," pp. 479, 483–85.

17. Knowles, "Revolt," pp. 475–86.

18. Knowles, "Revolt," pp. 481–82. For an argument that this letter, attributed in the manuscript to "R., bishop of York" and by Knowles to Roger of York, was actually from Robert of Chesney, see Foreville, *Un procès de canonisation*, pp. 87–88, 96. I have accepted Knowles's attribution.

19. Knowles, "Revolt," pp. 480–81.

20. Knowles, "Revolt," pp. 478–79, 482–85. Repeatedly, the discussion returned to whether the nuns and canons shared one chapel for praying and meditating. According to the decree of the Second Lateran Council in 1139, it was prohibited "for nuns to come together with canons or monks in church in one choir for singing psalms." (Mansi, *Sacrorum Conciliorum*, 21: col. 533.) Technically, this did not rule out sharing the church for mass, although it did prohibit using one choir for the offices.

21. Knowles, "Revolt," pp. 478, 483. Knowles notes how difficult this letter is to date, and Foreville claims that it was written a decade later, between 1175 and 1176, when Hugh was known to have been in England. (Foreville, *Un procès de canonisation*, pp. 108–9.) If Foreville is correct, the investigation continued to plague the Gilbertines for many years. According to the phrasing used in the letters, Pope Alexander III originally wanted the male and female Gilbertines to celebrate even the mass in separate churches. Before his death in 1181, he relaxed this strict demand and allowed them to share a common church for mass if

it was divided with a partition that prevented either gender from seeing or being seen by the other. If Foreville's later date for Hugh's letter is accepted, the report from Hugh would have been instrumental in the pope's revision of his earlier decision.

22. Knowles, "Revolt," pp. 479–80, 482–83. According to Cardinal-legate Hugh (p. 483), Pope Alexander had earlier approved the statutes of the Gilbertine order, as had his predecessors, including Pope Eugene. Although Bishop William's letter mentions predecessors, Hugh's is the earliest independent confirmation of the claim in the *Institutes* that Pope Eugene approved Gilbert's plan shortly after it was devised. (In Dugdale's version of the *Institutes*, p. xx, "Papae memoriae" is a misprint for "Papae Eugenio." See Douce 136, fol. 1.)

23. Knowles, "Revolt," pp. 481–82.

24. Knowles, "Revolt," p. 484.

25. Knowles, "Revolt," pp. 480–81, 483–85. Cardinal-legate Hugh noted the order's good reputation and rapid expansion to "around fifteen hundred members, they say." In his view the only discord came from one of the lay brothers, Ogger, whom Gilbert had sentenced for trying to change the order's statutes.

26. Knowles, "Revolt," pp. 477–80. Foreville believes the inquiries were held in 1166, after the January 1166 death of the bishop of Lincoln, who otherwise should have been a participant, and before the death of Robert of Chesney in January 1167. In her opinion, the entire affair was resolved by the end of 1167. (Foreville, *Un procès de canonisation*, pp. 86–88.) Knowles thinks the troubles may have continued until 1169, with the inquiries conducted sometime from 1166 to 1169. (Knowles, "Revolt," pp. 467–70.)

27. Knowles, "Revolt," pp. 469–73, 477–80; and Foreville, *Un procès de canonisation*, pp. 83–85. Neither scholar explained why an accusation might have been made concerning a vow to Savigny (called *Sabaneia* in the manuscript but identified as Savigny by Knowles on p. 470, n. 1). One likely explanation is that such a vow had been required some years earlier. In 1147, the Cistercians accepted into their order the monasteries in the reform congregation of Savigny, probably at the very chapter meeting where they refused Gilbert's request to accept responsibility for his priories. Perhaps there was an intermediate stage, otherwise unrecorded, in which Gilbert tried to gain Cistercian supervision by affiliating his priories with Savigny, a congregation that included women.

28. Knowles, "Revolt," p. 475. In this account, Gilbert provides the most detailed surviving picture of a "lay order family." Initially in desperate circumstances, needing material help as much as spiritual sustenance, the entire family then became connected with the Gilbertine order for years.

29. Knowles, "Revolt," pp. 475–77.

30. Ibid. Apparently the lay brothers had continued a custom, probably introduced in the early days of the order, of hearing the night office in the nuns' church. Note that the demand for separate churches was later modified; see above, n. 21.

31. Knowles, "Revolt," p. 481. By attributing this letter to Robert of Chesney, Foreville suggests that this letter actually concerned the diocese of Lincoln. (See n. 18 above.) Whether or not this particular letter was from Archbishop Roger of York, in another letter he cleared the Gilbertines of all charges even though

Watton Priory was the only Gilbertine house for both sexes in his diocese. (Knowles, "Revolt," pp. 477–78.)

32. Foreville, *Un procès de canonisation*, pp. 102–7.

33. For Foukeholme, which was also called Thimbleby, see *MRH*, p. 258; Brown, "Thimbleby." For Armathwaite, see *VCH*, Cumberland, 2:189–90. The charter (printed as *Monasticon*, 3:271, no. 1) crediting the foundation to William Rufus is spurious; see *MRH*, p. 256. For Lambley, see Hodgson, *History of Northumberland*, vol. 3, pt. 2, pp. 92–93; *Monasticon*, 4:306; *MRH*, p. 260. For Seton, see *VCH*, Cumberland, 2:192; *MRH*, p. 265.

34. Farrer, *Yorkshire*, 1:328–30; *VCH*, Yorkshire, 3:239; *MRH*, pp. 262, 282.

35. Also in these years there was discord at Grimsby Priory between male and female religious. Before 1184, the women of Grimsby in Lincolnshire complained to Pope Lucius II that brethren in the nearby canonry of Wellow had compelled them by threats to sell some property the women owned. By 1232 friendly relations with Wellow had been restored, for one of Wellow's canons became Grimsby's prior. It is interesting that the disagreement between the men and women dates from this inhospitable period. *VCH*, Lincolnshire, 2:179.

36. See Table 6. For references, see individual houses in *MRH* and in this chapter.

37. Abbot Warin had built the church to honor the relics of St. Amphibalus because of a vision a local man had reported to him. Only after he had built and dedicated the church to St. Amphibalus did the abbot decide to install in it the leprous women. See Riley, *Gesta Abbatum*, 1:199–204. Stubbs, *Chronicle*, 1:175–77, reports the miraculous discovery of St. Amphibalus's relics but does not include the later events: the building of a church in Amphibalus's honor and the introduction of leprous women. See also *VCH*, Hertfordshire, 4:429.

38. Bateson, "Crabhouse Nunnery," pp. 2–7, 12–13. Quote is from p. 2. Bateson admirably reconstructs the complicated history of Crabhouse.

39. Bateson, "Crabhouse Nunnery," pp. 3–5. Early in the thirteenth century, the women gained control of Crabhouse after (1) the canons of Ranham Priory gave up rights in the chapel and hermitage, and (2) the monks of Castle Acre permitted the women's own chaplains to celebrate the divine service there upon payment of an annual fee of six *denarii*.

40. *MRH*, p. 284; *VCH*, Somerset, 2:148; Hugo, *Mediaeval Nunneries*, pp. 6–13, 213–19; Weaver, *Buckland Priory*, pp. 1–9.

41. The sisters introduced at Buckland were Milsant from the preceptory of Standon in Hertfordshire, Johanna from Hampton in Middlesex, Basilia from Carbrooke in Norfolk, Amabilia and Amicia from Shingay in Cambridgeshire, Christina from Hogshaw in Buckingham, and Petronilla and Agnes from Clamfield and Gosford, both in Oxfordshire. Some of these preceptories are first known from this list. Hugo, *Mediaeval Nunneries*, pp. 6–13, 213–19; Weaver, *Buckland Priory*, pp. 1–9.

42. After Prior Garner's commitment, it is surprising that the laywoman Margaret de Lacy founded Aconbury Priory for Hospitaller sisters in the reign of King John. According to Margaret's plan, the sisters served a hospital for the poor and sick at Aconbury and were attached to the preceptory of Dinamore. Some years after she began Aconbury, however, Margaret de Lacy claimed she

had been unaware of the implications of placing the sisters under the Hospitaller Rule.

Margaret's views are expressed in a letter she wrote to the pope in the 1230s. Margaret said that when she had "wished to build a house for religious women," she acquired a site from the king and founded the priory without consulting her husband or the diocesan. She had put Aconbury "into the hands of the Hospitallers at their request, believing that colleges of women could be established under their rule." Bringing the women to Aconbury, she had them professed and given habits by the brethren. Margaret became dissatisfied later when she learned that the Hospitallers could move the sisters anywhere they wished, and the hospital could be deprived of their services. It is instructive that a foundress could act so independently in beginning a house, and that she could be so unaware of the special characteristics of an international order.

The Hospitallers contested Margaret's plea that the pope release Aconbury from their rule. Despite the Hospitallers' defense, Margaret's appeal was successful. Aconbury was released from the Hospitaller order and became an Augustinian priory. Buckland remained the only place for Hospitaller sisters in England. *MRH*, pp. 278–79; Bliss and Twemlow, *Papal Letters*, 1:134.

43. *VCH*, Bedfordshire, 1:388. Fowler, "Records of Harrold Priory," pp. 9–10, 54–59.

44. Woodcock, *St. Gregory, Canterbury*, pp. 6–7. Cf. *VCH*, Sussex, 2:63.

45. *Monasticon*, 7:974–75; *VCH*, Norfolk, 2:412. Graham, *S. Gilbert of Sempringham*, pp. 40–41.

46. For the cartulary of Walden Abbey, see *Monasticon*, 7:975, no. 2. The founder of Walden Abbey was Geoffrey de Mandeville, a previous earl of Essex; Beatrice de Say was the daughter of William de Say, nephew or brother of Geoffrey de Mandeville. Some years earlier, Walden Abbey was in a similar feud with the Gilbertine priory of Chicksands, also founded by a relative of Geoffrey de Mandeville; Chicksands was begun by Geoffrey's former wife Countess Roaise of Bedford, with her husband Payn de Beauchamp. On Chicksands, see Chapter 3.

47. *MRH*, pp. 197–99.

48. *MRH*, p. 105.

49. For Bristol, see *VCH*, Gloucester, 2:93. For Bungay: *VCH*, Suffolk, 2:81; *Monasticon*, 4:338. For Campsey Ash: *VCH*, Suffolk, 2:112. For Castle Hedingham: *VCH*, Essex, 2:122; *Monasticon*, 4:437. On Lucy's death, a mortuary roll was circulated asking for prayers; this roll still exists, with more than a hundred signatures, as Eg. MS. 2849. For Cheshunt, see *VCH*, Hertfordshire, 4:426. For Cook Hill: *VCH*, Worcester, 2:156. For Sewardsley: *VCH*, Northamptonshire, 2:125. For Studley: *VCH*, Oxford, 2:77–78; a descendant of the man on whose land Godstow had been built began Studley. For Tarrant: *VCH*, Dorset, 2:87; Tarrant is no longer thought to be the community that received the *Ancrene Riwle*; nor are the Cistercians thought to have formally recognized it as one of their houses in the twelfth century: see Thompson, "Problem of the Cistercian Nuns," pp. 243–44. For Wintney, see *Calendar of Charter Rolls*, 4:391–93. See the individual houses in *MRH* for the little information that survives about the other monasteries: Barrow Gurney, Brewood White Ladies, Broomhall, Limebrook, and Rusper.

50. For Catesby, see *VCH*, Northampton, 2:121–23; *Monasticon*, 4:637–38; and Thompson, "Problem of the Cistercian Nuns," p. 247. In a summary of a charter of Wintney entered in the calendar of charter rolls in 1337, a donor to Wintney is said to have demanded that the nuns perform (*persolvere*) three masses a week for the absolution of his and his wife's sins; the donor then stated that "the convent of Waverley, who founded the said nuns in their order, forbids on the authority of the whole order under an anathema, any nun of the order from breaking this agreement." (*Calendar of Charter Rolls*, 4:391–93.) Since no other English Cistercian abbey is said to have founded a daughter house in the twelfth century, it is unlikely that this claim in a fourteenth-century charter means that Cistercian monks of Waverly originally founded Wintney. Probably the monks sponsored Wintney's later acceptance into their order. Nonetheless, this chance remark does suggest that Cistercian monks may have assumed more responsibilities for Cistercian nuns than has otherwise been recorded. See also Thompson, "Problem of the Cistercian Nuns," p. 250, who places the foundation a few years earlier.

CHAPTER 7

1. *Vita*, p. xv.

2. *MRH*, pp. 491–93 provides a reliable estimate. The female religious probably outnumbered the men two to one.

3. For a discussion of the manuscript tradition of the *Vita* and the identification of Ralph as the likely author, see Foreville, *Un procès de canonisation*, pp. xiv–xxii. For more on the *Institutes*, see above, Chapter 5, n. 8.

4. Gilbert's canonization is the first complete surviving account of the procedures being developed at Rome to determine a person's sanctity. Foreville, *Un procès de canonisation*, pp. xiii–xiv, xxxi–xli, 33.

5. The edition of the *Vita* printed in the *Monasticon* omitted both the letters written on behalf of Gilbert's canonization and the miracles presented as evidence. Foreville has, however, provided a critical edition of this portion of the *Vita*. For the letters, see Foreville, *Un procès de canonisation*, pp. 5–42, esp. 11, 22, 31, 35.

6. Ibid., esp. pp. xxxv–xxxvii, 15.

7. Ibid., pp. 30–32.

8. Because the childless couple had a son after Gilbert slept in their bed, they named him Gilbert. In response, Gilbert sent the couple a cow to provide milk for the child. Gilbert's resistance to natural forces was shown when he refused to leave an inn where he was staying even though the building beside it was on fire. On another occasion, when Gilbert was impatient for a storm to end so that he could cross the Humber River, it calmed long enough for his safe passage. Ibid., pp. 75, 79–81.

9. Ibid., pp. 76, 79.

10. On another occasion, Albinus was amazed when he was able to shake off a fever in obedience to Gilbert's command. Ibid., pp. 49, 74.

11. I have used the translation in Gerald of Wales, *Jewel of the Church*, p. 188.

For the Latin text, see Gerald of Wales, *Gemma Ecclesiastica*, pp. 247–48. Also treated by Constable, "Aelred of Rievaulx," p. 222.

12. Gerald of Wales, *Jewel of the Church*, p. 321, n. 6.

13. Foreville, *Un procès de canonisation*, pp. 42–59. Sometimes nuns received emergency cures, as when Emcina, a nun of Haverholme, choked on a fish bone stuck in her throat, drank the wash water from Gilbert's corpse, and was saved. Other nuns were cured of infirmities they had suffered for years. Juliana, a nun of Sempringham, "received into the order by master Gilbert himself," had leprosy. After a complicated dream-vision, Juliana was healed—a miracle attested to by Claricia, the nun who had nursed her; the nun Lecelina; and "the prioress and greater part of the convent of Sempringham." Even relatively minor problems could be entrusted to Gilbert, as when Mabilia, a nun of Chicksands, injured her foot while rushing to the kitchen to carry out her prioress's command; a linen cloth which had lain on Gilbert's corpse brought this obedient nun's recovery.

14. *Vita*, pp. v–vi. Since Gilbert was at the episcopal court for eight years, this girl must have been in her late teens or early twenties by the time Gilbert provided her and the other six women with Sempringham Priory.

15. *Vita*, p. x.

16. *Vita*, p. xvi. Agnes's dream indicates that a prioress of a Cistercian monastery knew Gilbert by sight. NunAppleton was one of the houses with nuns and lay brothers, somewhat like the early arrangement Gilbert had designed for Sempringham. For the Biblical reference on the relationship between John and Mary, see John 19:25–27.

17. *Vita*, p. vii. Cf. John 4:34–38.

18. *Vita*, p. vii.

19. *Vita*, p. viii.

20. Because Gilbert had acknowledged Cistercian inspiration for the lay sisters and brothers, the decision to go to Cîteaux had been logical in his account. However, because the *vita* never mentioned Cistercian influence on the lay brothers or sisters, it needed to explain Gilbert's choice. So the *vita* claimed, "Gilbert had more familiarity of these than of others, having received frequent hospitality." Moreover, "he judged them more religious than others because they were more recent and stricter of rule. Therefore he believed it safer to give them command of his work, because the rigor of the order and newness of their conversion made them guard that way of life which he considered the stricter." Ibid.

21. Ibid. For a fuller account of the differences between the *Vita* and the *Institutes*, see Elkins, "Gilbertine Identity."

22. *Vita*, pp. viii–ix. The conclusion that Gilbert would have had to stay at Cîteaux a year was correctly reached by Giraudot and Bouton, "Bernard et les Gilbertins," pp. 331–32. See also Golding, "St. Bernard and St. Gilbert," pp. 42–47. The story of the visit was probably added to the original edition of the *vita*. Foreville reasons that the few references to Gilbert in the *vita* as *beatus*, instead of his usual designation as *magister*, were inserted after the canonization. (Foreville, *Un procès de canonisation*, pp. xvii–xviii.) The paragraph about the extended stay with the Cistercians is one such passage.

About the same time as the *vita* was being composed, William of Newburgh wrote that Bernard had aided Gilbert on his trip to Cîteaux. William Parvi de Newburgh, *Historia Rerum Anglicarum*, 1:45–46. Probably a tradition was developing that Bernard had collaborated with Gilbert early in his career, and hence the *vita* included this story in its expanded edition.

23. The *vita* explained that the canons were ideal additions since they could rule by church law, protect the women, and show the way of salvation to all. *Vita*, p. ix.

24. Ibid., For Peter's vision, see Acts 11:4–10.

25. *Vita*, p. x. The *vita* paraphrased Gal. 1:11–13 in which Paul claimed he received his gospel through a revelation, not from men.

26. To facilitate access to the lengthy manuscript of the *Institutes*, I have footnoted both the printed text in *Monasticon* and the corresponding section in Douce 136. Additional details about the workings of the Gilbertine order can be found in Graham, *S. Gilbert of Sempringham*.

27. Although the manuscript proceeds without a break from the autobiographical section into elaborate rules for the selection of a new master general, the introductory section has a distinctive tone, style, and content that sets it apart. See also Chapter 5, n. 8.

28. *Institutes*, pp. xxxi, lvi; Douce 136, fols. 27, 83.

29. *Institutes*, pp. xx–xxi; Douce 136, fols. 3–6. Gilbert clearly wished his office of master general to continue, for he personally designated a successor. Although the master general held extensive authority within the order, he was not mitred, so a bishop gave the benediction to all new Gilbertines.

30. *Institutes*, pp. xxi–xxiv; Douce 136, fols. 6–11. To prevent the scrutinizers from burdening their host communities, they were instructed to eat in common with the others and to bring all their own essential clothes, with a needle and thread for repairs. In case gifts might tempt scrutinizers to modify their judgments, their luggage was examined to insure that nothing new had been acquired.

31. *Institutes*, p. xxiii; Douce 136, fols. 8–9.

32. *Institutes*, p. xlvi; Douce 136, fols. 61–62. Graham suggested that the prioresses rotated their office weekly. Graham, *S. Gilbert of Sempringham*, p. 68.

33. *Institutes*, p. xxiv; Douce 136, fols. 11–12.

34. *Institutes*, pp. xxix–xxx, 1, liii; Douce 136, fols. 21–24, 71, 77. In assigning penances for most faults, the prioress was following a long-standing monastic tradition. However, increasingly during the twelfth century, absolution for sins was reserved to the clergy. In 1210 Innocent III ruled that abbesses could not exercise the "clerical" roles of hearing confessions or preaching. (Innocent III, "Nova quaedam nuper.") Since the *Institutes* permitted prioresses to perform these roles, they may have been written before 1210, perhaps about the same time as the canonization of Gilbert.

35. *Institutes*, pp. xxi, lvii–lviii; Douce 136, fols. 5–6, 86–87. The only lay brother and sister present were the general scrutinizers. Claiming to imitate the Cistercians, the *Institutes* excluded all "grangers"—lay brothers in charge of the monasteries' granges or farms—from the annual chapter in what it claimed was an attempt to avoid "useless speech and evil communication." After the rebellion

of the lay brothers in the mid-twelfth century, their position and influence in the order appear to have continued to decrease.

36. *Institutes*, p. xx; Douce 136, fols. 2–3. One other potential difference in representation from the annual general chapter was that the cellarer did not have to be one of the three canons from each house. Elaborate precautions were legislated to enable the nuns to attend the elections and the general chapters and to permit the female scrutinizers to travel from house to house. Riding in covered carriages, the women were to be accompanied by men of the order; for example, a canon and a lay brother from the monastery the female scrutinizers had just visited accompanied them to the next house. Instructed never to talk or communicate by eye with these brothers, the nuns could speak indirectly to them, in the third person, only in situations of manifest danger. Concerned about gossip, the *Institutes* legislated that the women could lodge only in female religious houses, unless necessity demanded spending one night in a Gilbertine grange. Probably because travel was so complicated, the female scrutinizers made their rounds only once a year, less frequently than the male scrutinizers. *Institutes*, pp. xxii–xxiii, lvii; Douce 136, fols. 7–10, 86–87.

37. Like the Cistercians, the Gilbertines were forbidden "to sing" the melismatic polyphony popular among some Benedictines. The nuns' *magistra* instructed them in the offices. "Nun" and "literate female" were usually synonyms in the *Institutes*, although at some point a hybrid group was formed, "lay nuns," or "illiterate nuns," unable to read because of their late conversion to religious life. *Institutes*, pp. xlviii–l; Douce 136, fols. 65–71.

38. Ibid.

39. *Institutes*, pp. li–liv; Douce 136, fols. 72–79. Under the supervision of two or three nuns, the guest hospice for women was tended primarily by the lay sisters, who were to discourage long-term residence. The prioress's permission was needed for a guest to stay more than one night, receive a bath, or be given meat. If any male child entered the female hospice, even the lay sisters were not allowed inside the building.

40. *Institutes*, pp. lii–liv; Douce 136, fols. 74–79. Because of their strenuous labor, concessions were made for the lay sisters attending the offices; they were allowed to sit when they prayed and they were not required to be as punctual.

41. *Institutes*, pp. xxxvi–xliv; Douce 136, fols. 37–55. Some lay brothers appear to have been enthusiastic about their duties for legislation forbade them to lift things too heavy or hurt themselves through immoderate labor.

42. *Institutes*, pp. xxvii–xxxvi; Douce 136, fols. 16–37. Admitted to the novitiate at fifteen years of age, a man could become a canon at twenty. A bishop ordained the men the Gilbertines recommended. Only houses with abundant resources were permitted to have more than thirteen canons.

43. *Institutes*, xlviii, l; Douce 136, fols. 65, 71. In an acknowledgment that the rules could be violated, the *Institutes* provided instructions for disciplining those who communicated improperly with the opposite sex. If a man and a woman were found to have written each other, they suffered fasts, flogging, and a transfer to another convent. A man who actually committed a "sexual sin" was incarcerated or dismissed from the order. Fearing that a scandal would result if a

"licentious" woman was allowed to wander freely, the *Institutes* required that she be imprisoned in the nuns' section, isolated far from the others, and made to perform penances with fasts and prayers. *Institutes*, pp. xxxi, xliii; Douce 136, fols. 27, 53. When the nuns in the 1160s imposed this very penalty on the nun of Watton, they said they were abiding by the legislation of the order, an indication that this regulation may have been included in the earliest versions of the *Institutes*. For the story of the nun of Watton, see Chapter 6.

44. *Institutes*, pp. xxix–xxxi, xlviii–xlix; Douce 136, fols. 21–26, 65–69. Only on Sundays and feast days did the entire community enter the large church for mass. Since the days of Pope Alexander III the common church had been divided so that the women on their side could only hear the two or three canons who daily celebrated mass for them on the other side of the partition, at the canons' altar. For an intriguing consideration of the role of visual understanding in fourteenth-century Christianity, see Miles, *Image as Insight*, esp. pp. 63–75.

45. *Institutes*, pp. xlv–xlvi, liii; Douce 136, fols. 58–60, 77–78. The nuns may have been reminded of the emphasis on listening in the opening passage in *St. Benedict's Rule* (pp. 6–7), which they would have repeatedly heard: "Hearken, my son, to the precepts of the master and incline the ear of thy heart."

46. Another example of unseen hands was during Passion Week. Two canons entered the nuns' portion of the church when it was empty and placed the large painted wooden cross on the ground for the nuns' adoration; after the women had finished their devotions and had left the church, the two canons returned the cross to the altar. *Institutes*, pp. xlviii–l; Douce 136, fols. 65–70.

47. *Institutes*, pp. xxv, xxvii, xxxvi–xxxvii, xlv–xlvi, li–liii; Douce 136, fols. 13, 18–19, 38–40, 58–60, 74–77. Virtually the only other time the women were allowed to see men was when the master general, or some other visiting dignitary, preached a sermon, gave a speech, or administered a blessing in the nuns' chapter house. When such dignitaries visited, a number of witnesses were present to attest to all that was said and done.

48. *Institutes*, p. liv; Douce 136, fols. 79–80.

49. *Institutes*, pp. xxiv–xxvi, xliv–xlv; Douce 136, fols. 11–16, 57.

50. *Institutes*, p. xliv; Douce 136, fols. 55–57. Once the nuns decided what was needed to repair their church, tighten their security, or improve their cloister, they gave a detailed list to a canon and a lay brother who made the purchases for them at fairs and markets. On the obedientary system, see Knowles, *MO*, pp. 431–39.

51. *Institutes*, pp. xxvii–xxviii, xxxvi, xlvii–xlviii; Douce 136, fols. 19–20, 38, 64–65.

52. *Institutes*, pp. xxxii–xxxiv, xl–xlii, l–li; Douce 136, fols. 28–32, 48–50, 70–72.

53. *Institutes*, p. xx, col. 1, lines 11–13 should read, according to Douce 136, fol. 1, "inter fratres laicos et canonicos, vel inter canonicos et moniales, vel inter moniales et fratres laicos." In this section, where Gilbert reveals the groups between whom he fears discord, he does not include the lay sisters.

CHAPTER 8

1. For Amesbury, see below. For Winchester and Wherwell, *VCH*, Hampshire, 2:122, 132; *VCH*, Derby, 2:43; *Monasticon*, 2:452.

2. John of Salisbury, *Letters*, 1:111.

3. The other preconquest abbeys rarely appear in the earlier twelfth-century documents. For occasional new grants or confirmations of possessions, see individual abbeys in *RRAN*. In her study of royal alms, Warren notes that Henry II instituted new permanent grants for only three Benedictine female monasteries—Moxby, Thetford, and Polsloe—none of which were preconquest abbeys. (Warren, *Anchorites*, p. 145, n. 23.)

4. Stubbs, *Chronicle*, 1:135–36, 165. No other source provides such a detailed account of the events at Amesbury. A confirmation charter from the time of King John summarizes the same charges given in the chronicle; it reported that "on account of the turpitude of their lives" about thirty nuns were dismissed from Amesbury and their order dissolved before the nuns from Fontevrault were introduced. Landon, *Cartae Antiquae Rolls*, pp. 23, 90–91.

5. A nun of Wilton Abbey was also said to have had a child. Between 1198 and 1204, it was argued in the court of the bishop of Winchester that a certain Henry was the son of a professed nun of Wilton Abbey and should therefore be considered a bastard. When the case was appealed to Archbishop Hubert Walter, however, it was decided that Henry was legitimate, for his mother Eve had legally married his father. The new verdict was based on the argument that, although Henry's mother Eve had lived for a time at Wilton, she had neither worn a habit nor made a profession. Hence, Eve was not a nun and she had been free to marry Henry's father. Cheney, *Hubert Walter*, p. 74.

6. Round, *Calendar*, pp. 378–79. Although Round only suggested—and did not attempt to prove—that this bull of Pope Alexander III was from 15 September 1176, its content establishes that it predated the investigation of the bishops at Amesbury.

7. John of Salisbury, *Letters*, 1:187–89.

8. A bitter battle between the nuns of Elstow and the monks of Newhouse over rights to a church plagued their ecclesiastical superiors for years. Holtzmann, *Papal Decretals*, pp. 12–15.

9. Osbert of Clare, *Letters*, pp. 9–17, 89–96, 135–79. Osbert of Clare was prior of Westminster Abbey when it gave Kilburn to three women. Osbert's letters were addressed to his nieces Margaret and Cecilia, nuns at Barking; their abbess Adelidis/Alice; Ida, a nun, perhaps also at Barking; and the "virgin Matilda of Darenth," who was in daily communication with the women of Malling and perhaps a nun there herself. In flowery images and glowing hyperboles, Osbert lauded the love of Christ and the superiority of virginity to marriage. See also J. Robinson, "Westminster in the Twelfth Century," esp. pp. 346–47, 352–53.

10. Osbert of Clare, *Letters*, pp. 153–79.

11. John of Salisbury, *Letters*, 1:111. See also Saltman, *Theobald*, pp. 49, 89, 155.

12. John of Salisbury, *Letters*, 1:238–39. See treatment of this case in Salt-man, *Theobald*, p. 155.

13. John of Salisbury, *Letters*, 1:111.

14. Knowles, *Heads of Religious Houses*, p. 208.

15. Ibid.

16. Sodergärd, *Vie D'Edouard le Confesseur*, esp. pp. 16–27, 34–35, 273, 304–7. One of the few included details of life at Barking Abbey was a miracle story: to be cured of a burning fever that had raged for two years, a nun at Barking reenacted an episode she had seen in a dream, with successful results.

17. In a recent paper, William MacBain, the editor of Clemence's life of St. Catherine, has raised questions about the long-standing assumption that Clemence was also the translator of the life of St. Edward. Clemence was so innovative in form and content in her life of St. Catherine that MacBain questions whether the less sophisticated life of St. Edward was also by her. Hence, although the life of St. Edward may be an earlier work by Clemence, it may instead have been written by another nun, perhaps one who was attempting to imitate Clemence's style. MacBain, " 'Courtly Echoes.' "

18. In her life of St. Catherine, Clemence had Emperor Maxentius confront the limits of earthly power. In obedience to his own law forbidding conversion to Christianity, Maxentius was forced to acquiesce to his wife's execution after Catherine converted her to Christianity. While the *Longer Vulgata* presented Emperor Maxentius as an angry lord concerned primarily with his wife's lack of loyalty, Clemence's Maxentius was passionately in love with his wife and distraught that her death, on his orders, would make him lose what mattered most. Clemence of Barking, *St. Catherine*, pp. 69–70, 74–75; MacBain, " 'Courtly Echoes.' "

19. Either Mary was not suited for religious life or, as the only surviving child of King Stephen, she had to bow to political pressures, for around 1160 she left Romsey to marry Matthew, son of the count of Flanders. An uproar ensued, so heated that, according to Matthew Paris, Romsey later received back the penitent Mary. Financially, Romsey profited from Mary's presence there since her uncle, Henry of Blois, the bishop of Winchester, facilitated the construction of new buildings at the abbey. *Monasticon*, 2:506. See also Saltman, *Theobald*, pp. 52–53, and *VCH*, Hampshire, 2:126–27.

20. Fox, "Mary, Abbess of Shaftesbury."

21. If Marie de France could reliably be shown to have been a nun, her works would be marvelous sources for exploring the assumptions of these literary nuns. Although some have argued that Marie de France was a nun, neither internal evidence in her writings nor external evidence from other sources proves that hypothesis. Scholars have long discarded the forced arguments identifying her with Mary, abbess of Shaftesbury. Despite the suggestion repeated in the most recent translation of her *Lais*, Marie could not have been the abbess of Reading, for Reading was a house of Cluniac monks whose abbots are known. Marie's interests did become increasingly religious; she followed her *Lais* with the moral animal fables, and later still she translated *St. Patrick's Purgatory*. This development has led some to suppose that Marie became a nun at some later point in her life, perhaps after a period in close affiliation with Henry and Eleanor's court

as an English female troubador. Her status, however, is too uncertain to risk stretching the portrait of late twelfth-century female monasticism to include such an anomalous woman. The literature on Marie de France is vast. Especially useful is Mickel, *Marie de France*, and the recent translation of her *Lais* by Hanning and Ferrante.

22. In Clay's list of more than three hundred religious solitaries from the twelfth and thirteenth centuries, the "hermits" whose sex is known were always men, whereas women were called "anchoress" twice as often as men were called "anchorite." Published as an appendix to Clay's book, the original list is now Lambeth Palace Library MS. 1970. Clay lists a Matilda who was an anchoress at Belchford in Lincolnshire in 1183; before 1228 an anchoress Sarah was at Loose and another was at Sutton, both in Kent; six *inclusae* were at Ely in 1169; at Oxford before 1225 there was an anchoress Basilia; and in Wiltshire lived the anchoress Eve and, separately, the anchoress Alice. Under King John, a "Dame Lucy" living as an anchoress in the churchyard of Bury St. Edmunds was given a garment, evidence that female religious solitaries remained connected with that monastery a half century after it had endowed women with the cell of Thetford. Since six of the *inclusae* lived together, they may have been solitary women who had gathered together in a community. Clay, *Hermits and Anchorites*, pp. 206–7, 222–27, 242–43, 248–49, 252–53.

23. In a work written in the latter part of the century, John of Ford referred to a female "friend of God" named Odolina, an anchoress in the vill of Crewkerne; and he retold a story from Aldida, a venerable *"inclusa"* from Sturminster Newton. (John, Abbot of Ford, *Wulfric of Haselbury*, pp. 90, 110–11.) The monk of Evesham Abbey's *Revelations* in 1196 included a vision of an anchoress who was being purged on her journey to heaven. (Salter, *Eynsham Cartulary*, 2:334–35.) Among the anchoresses Warren mentions are a female recluse who lived at Newnham in Gloucestershire for forty-four years, beginning in 1158; an anchoress already living at Pevesia in Berkshire in 1156, who was succeeded by another woman there for five years in the mid-1160s; a recluse of Cookham, Berkshire, from 1171 to 1214; an anchoress of St. Audoneus in Herefordshire, from 1193 to 1201; and the *inclusa* Margaret at St. Sepulchre, Herefordshire, from 1203 to 1212. Warren, *Anchorites*, pp. 135–39, 149, 154.

24. Stenton, *Gilbertine*, p. 65; *Monasticon*, vol. 6, pt. 2, pp. 961, 963.

25. See Warren, *Anchorites*, esp. pp. 19–28, 292–93; she concludes that in the twelfth century, female anchorites outnumbered men roughly five to three; in the thirteenth century, women outnumbered men four to one. (Ibid., p. 19.) Although Warren does not focus on many issues concerning gender, her treatment is the fullest on anchorites in England. See also her article, "Nun as Anchoress"; Dauphin, "L'érémitisme en Angleterre"; Ward, "Hermits and Communities"; and Mayr-Harting, "Twelfth Century Recluse."

26. This is the earliest service for enclosing a recluse found in an English manuscript, and it is the only one from before 1225. Cotton MS D XV, a twelfth-century manuscript in excellent condition, is printed as "Seruicium Recludendi," in Wilson, *Pontifical*, pp. 243–44. Although there are two types of writing in the manuscript, Wilson's italics do not always correspond to the manuscript variations; otherwise his printed text is accurate. According to instructions in the

preface, the enclosure ceremony was for either a man or a woman; hence, although the pronouns in the manuscript are masculine, I have used feminine forms for this discussion.

27. Wilson, *Pontifical*, pp. 243–44. Precisely when the recluse was raised from her prone position and led to the altar is unclear in the liturgy. The Isaiah passage that was read was Isa. 26:20 to 27:4.

28. The recluse's petition, Ps. 119:116, was the traditional Benedictine petition for joining a monastery. On the development of profession, see Leclerq, "Profession."

29. The choir chanted the rest of Ps. 132, which in part pleaded, "Yahweh, go up to your resting place, . . . For Yahweh has chosen Zion, desiring this to be his home, 'Here I will stay for ever, this is the home I have chosen.'" Wilson, *Pontifical*, pp. 243–44.

30. Ibid. For a discussion of the recluse's life as "the permanent institutionalization of the liminal state," see Warren, *Anchorites*, pp. 95–96.

31. The critical edition is Aelred, "De Institutione Inclusarum," pp. 637–82. A fine translation is Aelred, "Rule," which I use throughout this section. Although Aelred said he was writing this tract for young girls less wise and accomplished than his sister, he included a number of biographical references that reveal his particular concern for her. For his recommendations for her *horarium*, see Aelred, "Rule," pp. 54–59.

32. Aelred advised his sister to earn just enough by the labor of her hands to support only herself, even if she thereby risked "scandalizing people" because she neither gave alms to the poor nor received guests. Although Aelred criticized recluses who held classes or were too concerned with business, he never specified what type of labor his sister should undertake. Aelred, "Rule," pp. 45–49.

33. Aelred, "Rule," pp. 46–47, 51–53, 67–68.

34. No other twelfth-century English writer claimed that contemporary women were *virgines subintroductae*. In France earlier in the century, Robert of Arbrissel was said to have slept chastely with his female converts; and a mid-twelfth-century English author thought an Anglo-Saxon saint had tested his chastity in this way. See Gougaud, "Mulierum consortia." For an earlier period, see Reynolds, "*Virgines subintroductae* in Celtic Christianity."

35. One possible explanation for Aelred's strong opinion could have been his experiences in helping Gilbert of Sempringham resolve the affair at Watton. (See Chapter 6.) But already, in his *Mirror of Charity*, Aelred had warned about friendships between holy men and women, for he claimed he had known chaste men who had fallen in love with young nuns. Initially attracted by reports of a nun's virtues, a man might feel a reasonable love toward her and develop a friendship with her; but then this friendship eventually could degenerate into carnal lust. Aelred, "De Speculo Caritatis," 1:120.

36. Aelred, "Rule," pp. 46–52.

37. Ibid., pp. 48–49.

38. Ibid., pp. 50–53. Usually Aelred was such an exponent of spiritual friendships that two recent books on him have chapters entitled "God is Friendship": Chapter 2 of Hallier, *Monastic Theology*; and Chapter 5 of Squire, *Aelred of Rievaulx*. In his *Mirror of Charity*, Aelred considered love of neighbor an essen-

tial prerequisite for the love of God. See Aelred, "De Speculo Caritatis," esp. pp. 82–83. In *Spiritual Friendship*, Aelred made it clear that he was not rhapsodizing merely about intellectual love or about the *agape* that Christians were supposed to offer all people, for he described close friendships, of great intimacy, which were based on both reason and affection. According to Aelred, Jesus showed that it was all right to have special friendships when he let John, his beloved disciple, rest his head on Jesus' breast. See Aelred, "De Spiritali Amicitia," esp. pp. 344–45.

39. Aelred, "Rule," pp. 76–78.

40. Ibid., p. 102.

41. Ibid., p. 59.

42. Ibid., p. 85.

43. Ibid., p. 73. On the image of Jesus as mother, see Bynum, "Jesus as Mother." Aelred never intended or imagined that virginity was a virtue appropriate primarily for women, for the models he proposed for virginity were the virgin Mary and the disciple John. John, the example par excellence of human friendship in Aelred's *Mirror of Charity* and *Spiritual Friendship*, was in the "Rule" (p. 87) said to be close to Jesus as a result of his virginity.

44. Aelred, "Rule," pp. 90–92.

45. Ibid., p. 101.

46. Ibid., p. 96.

47. Ibid., p. 63. In part Aelred emphasized his sister's virginity because he had lost his own, having been enticed by "wicked men" in his youth. Ibid., pp. 93–94. Aelred's virginity was the subject of an exchange of letters between Walter Daniel, Aelred's friend and biographer, and a certain Maurice. See Daniel, *Life of Aelred*, p. 76. By virginity Aelred did not mean just chastity or technical virginity. Even if the recluse escaped defilement from the touch of a man or woman, virginity could be lost if a strong heat subdued the will and seized the members. Aelred, "Rule," p. 64. In his other works, Aelred usually praised chastity, not virginity per se, and love was the virtue stressed above all others. See, for instance, Aelred, "Sermones de Tempore," cols. 304–5. See also Renna, "Virginity," pp. 89–92.

48. The *Ancrene Riwle*'s importance for female religious is attested by its numerous versions in French, English, and Latin, which are a sign of its popularity and influence as late as the sixteenth century. (The *Ancrene Riwle* and the *Ancrene Wisse* are nearly identical versions of the same urtext.) Early in this century, Godwyn, the hermit of Kilburn, was thought to have written it for the three women under his guardianship there. (Allen, "Author of the 'Ancrene Riwle.'") But on the basis of references, liturgy, and language, it is now dated at the earliest late in the twelfth century. See Talbot, "Dating of the Ancrene Riwle"; Dobson, "Date and Composition," esp. p. 206; Dobson, *Origins*, pp. 48–50; Ackerman and Dahood, *Ancrene Riwle: Introduction*, pp. 4–6. On the manuscript tradition, see Dobson, "Affiliations."

49. I quote from *Ancrene Riwle*, a translation by Salu of *Corpus Christi College*, Cambridge MS. 402, later published in a critical edition by Tolkien, *English Text of the Ancrene Riwle*. Passages cited are from Salu, *Ancrene Riwle*, pp. 44–45, 174.

50. Bugge, *Virginitas*, pp. 96–110, has some particularly intriguing conclusions. Arguing that the *Ancrene Riwle* is an example of "virginity sexualized" to the point of "erotic spirituality," he asserts, "Christ begins to compete for the love of the English nun solely as a man." Bugge continues, "As [Christ] grows more masculine and more sexually susceptible, the figure of the nun or anchoress becomes more realistically feminine." The result of this tendency, Bugge claims, was "an unavoidable distinction as to gender in respect of Christ's love for the human race, his motive for undertaking redemption. The effect was in some sense to disqualify male monasticism from the fullest measure of that love." Bugge, *Virginitas*, pp. 98, 107–9.

In underscoring the intense emotionality of the recluse's love for Christ, Bugge is indeed correct. However, it is unwarranted to assume that medieval men felt excluded by references to Christ as bridegroom. The soul—both of men and women—had long been referred to in feminine terms. To assume that medieval people identified as exclusively with one gender as we tend to do seems unwise, especially since heroic holy women thought of themselves and were considered "manly." An excellent study on twelfth-century uses of what we consider gender-specific words is Bynum, "Jesus as Mother."

51. Virginity, once lost, could even be restored: "This kind of break may be mended afterwards, so that there is as much wholeness as before, through the medicine of Confession and repentance." Salu, *Ancrene Riwle*, pp. 72–73.

52. In a well-known passage, Christ is compared to a powerful knight rescuing a damsel in distress. Ibid., pp. 172–73. See also Frost, "Attitude to Women," pp. 242–45.

53. Salu, *Ancrene Riwle*, p. 162.

54. Ibid., pp. 14, 180.

55. Ibid., pp. 102, 175, where Christ is also compared to a mother playing with her "darling child." Passages like these could invite men as well as women to a deeper love of Christ.

56. Love is the heading for only one chapter, but the penitential life is developed in chapters on "The Custody of the Senses," "Regulation of the Inward Feelings," "Temptations," "Confessions," "Penance," and "External Rules."

57. Death imagery abounds. The *Ancrene Riwle* asks, "What is her anchorhouse but her grave?" Should the recluse eat with her guests? "One has often heard of the dead speaking with the living but I have never found that they ate with the living." Salu, *Ancrene Riwle*, pp. 47, 183. Cf. pp. 51, 155–56, 167.

58. Ibid., pp. 107–8. Cf. pp. 47, 54, 57.

59. Ibid., pp. 62, 161.

60. Ibid., pp. 22, 27, 28, 31.

61. "Keep your hands inside your windows," the cleric railed. "Touching with the hands, or any other kind of touch between a man and an anchoress is a thing so anomalous, an action so shameful . . . that . . . I would far rather see all three of you, my dear sisters, to me the dearest of women, hanging on a gibbet in order to avoid sin, than see one of you giving a single kiss to any man on earth in the way I mean." Ibid., pp. 23–25, 27, 51, 152. For an argument that comments like these indicate that the author has "adopted, probably unconsciously, the dichotomy in the medieval Church's view of women" as either "wicked temp-

tresses" or "redemptive saints," see Frost, "Attitude to Women," esp. pp. 237–39.

62. Salu, *Ancrene Riwle*, p. 112. Cf. p. 84.

63. Because of their common language, Tolkien linked the Corpus manuscript of the *Ancrene Wisse* with Bodley 34, a manuscript that contains the lives of three female saints—Juliana, Katherine, and Margaret (the "Katherine Group") —and the homilies *Hali Meidenhad* and *Sawles Warde*. Arguing that the language of the two manuscripts was identical, even in minute details and spelling, Tolkien enabled both to be dated and placed. Both were penned between 1224 and 1230, in the western midlands, probably Herefordshire, and both were slight reworkings of an urtext from at most a decade or two earlier. Tolkien, " 'Ancrene Wisse.' " Cf. Dobson, "Date and Composition," p. 206.

Although the similarities have suggested to some scholars that all the works had a single author, the current assessment is instead that the texts reveal "a common religious feeling and literary tradition," but "common authorship need not of necessity be assumed." (See Mack, *Seinte Marherete*, p. xxiii.) In the words of d'Ardenne, the editor of the life of St. Juliana, "We are in the presence of a tradition, with one specially active and influential centre or school, rather than with one busy author and universal provider of devotional literature." *Seinte Iuliene*, pp. xli–xliii. Edited for the Early English Text Society, all three female saints' lives in "the Katherine Group" have been published with the Latin texts that were either the likely source of the translation/adaptions or a parallel stemma. By comparing the Early Middle English and Latin versions, the peculiarities of the early-thirteenth-century renditions can be discerned.

64. I have followed the translation of Cockayne (*Seinte Marherete*, pp. 64–66), who identified the scene as unique (p. vii). For the critical edition, see Mack, *Seinte Marherete*, esp. pp. xix, xxx–xxxii.

65. Riley, *Gesta Abbatum*, 1:98–99. Matthew Paris, the author of most of the early part of the *Gesta*, was not the author of the portions concerning Roger, but either Walsingham or his anonymous predecessor made the additions.

CONCLUSION

1. Power, *Medieval English Nunneries*, p. 3, n. 2.
2. MO, p. 690.
3. Graham, *S. Gilbert of Sempringham*, pp. 98–104.
4. Graves, "Stixwould in the Market-Place," p. 228.
5. Power, *Medieval English Nunneries*, pp. 213–14.
6. Ibid., p. 234.
7. Nichols, "English Cistercian Nunneries," pp. 28–30.
8. Power, *Medieval English Nunneries*, p. 236.

BIBLIOGRAPHY

PRIMARY SOURCES

Manuscripts

Original Charters
  Bodleian Library, Oxford
    MS Eng Hist a 2
  British Museum
    Cotton Charter XI, 6, 8, 36, 66
    Cotton Charter XXVIII, 56

Other Twelfth- and Thirteenth-Century Manuscripts
  Bodleian Library, Oxford
    Digby 36
    Douce 136
    Bodley 285
    MS Lincoln College Latin 27
  British Museum
    Egerton MS. 2849
    Cotton MSS
      Cleopatra B I
      Vespasian D XV
  Corpus Christi College, Cambridge MS. 139

Charters in Thirteenth- and Fourteenth-Century Registers
  Bodleian Library, Oxford
    MS Topography, Lincs. d 1
  British Museum
    Cotton MSS
      Claudius A VIII
      Faustina A III
      Faustina B II
      Vespasian B XXIV
      Vespasian E XXII
    Harley MSS. 743, 2044, 2101

Dodsworth's Seventeenth-Century Transcriptions
  Bodleian Library, Oxford
    Dodsworth MSS. 32, 59, 63, 75, 79, 102, 144

Printed Sources

Ackerman, Robert, and Dahood, Roger, eds. and trans. *Ancrene Riwle: Introduction and Part I.* Binghampton, N.Y., 1984.

Aelred of Rievaulx, "De Institutis Inclusarum." Edited by Charles H. Talbot. In Aelredi Rievallensis, *Opera Omnia*, edited by Anselm Hoste and C. H. Talbot, pp. 636–82. Corpus Christianorum Continuatio Mediaevalis 1. Turnholt, Belgium, 1971.

————. *The Mirror of Charity.* Translated by Geoffrey Webb and Adrian Walker. London, 1962.

————. "Rule of Life for a Recluse." In *Works*, vol. 1: *Treatises; The Pastoral Prayer*, translated by Mary Paul Macpherson, pp. 43–102. Cistercian Fathers Series 2. Spencer, Mass., 1971.

————. "De Sanctimoniali de Wattun." *PL.* 195: cols. 789–96.

————. "Sermones de Oneribus." *PL.* 195: cols. 361–500.

————. "Sermones de Tempore et de Sanctis." *PL.* 195: cols. 210–360.

————. "De Speculo Caritatis." Edited by C. H. Talbot. In Aelredi Rievallensis, *Opera Omnia*, edited by Anselm Hoste and C. H. Talbot, pp. 2–161. Corpus Christianorum Continuatio Mediaevalis 1. Turnholt, Belgium, 1971.

————. "De Spiritali Amicitia." Edited by A. Hoste. In Aelredi Rievallensis, *Opera Omnia*, edited by Anselm Hoste and C. H. Talbot, pp. 352–634. Corpus Christianorum Continuatio Mediaevalis 1. Turnholt, Belgium, 1971.

————. *Spiritual Friendship.* Translated by Mary Eugenia Laker. Cistercian Fathers Series 5. Washington, D.C., 1974.

Anselm, Archbishop of Canterbury. *Sancti Anselmi Opera Omnia.* 6 vols. Edited by Franciscus S. Schmitt. Edinburgh, 1946–61.

Bateson, Mary. "The Register of Crabhouse Nunnery." *Norfolk Archaeology* 11 (1892): 1–71.

Baudri de Bourgueil. *Les oeuvres poétiques de Baudri de Bourgueil (1046–1130).* Edited by Phyllis Abrahams. Paris, 1926.

Benedict, St. *The Rule of Saint Benedict.* Edited and translated by Abbot Justin McCann. London, 1952.

Bernard of Clairvaux. "In Praise of the New Knighthood." In *Treatises III*, translated by Conrad Greenia, pp. 125–67. Kalamazoo, Mich., 1977.

Bliss, William Henry, and J. A. Twemlow, eds. *Calendar of Entries in the Papal Registers Relating to Great Britain and Ireland: Papal Letters (1198–1492).* 14 vols. London, 1893–1960.

Calendar of Charter Rolls Preserved in the Public Record Office. 6 vols. London, 1903–27.

Clark, Andrew, ed. *The English Register of Godstow Nunnery, near Oxford, Written About 1450.* EETS, o.s. 129, 130, 142 (1905–11).

Clay, Charles Francis, ed. *Early Yorkshire Charters.* Vols. 4–12. Yorkshire Archaeological Society Record Series, extra series 1–10 (1935–65).

Clemence of Barking. *The Life of St. Catherine.* Edited by William MacBain. Anglo-Norman Texts 18. Oxford, 1964.

Close Rolls of the Reign of Henry III Preserved in the Public Record Office. 14 vols. London, 1902–38.

Cockayne, Oswald, ed. *Seinte Marherete, The Meiden ant Martyr*. EETS, o.s. 13 (1866).

Colker, Marvin. "Texts of Jocelyn of Canterbury Which Relate to the History of Barking Abbey." *Studia Monastica* 7 (1965):383–460.

Crossman, William. "A Bull of Adrian IV Relating to Neasham Priory, Co. Durham." *Archaeologia Aeliana*, n.s. 16 (1894):268–73.

Curia Regis Rolls of the Reigns of Richard I and John Preserved in the Public Record Office. 7 vols. London, 1922–35.

Daniel, Walter. *The Life of Ailred of Rievaulx*. Edited and translated by F. M. Powicke. London, 1960.

d'Ardenne, S. R. T. O., ed. *The Liflade ant te Passiun of Seinte Iuliene*. EETS 248 (1961 for 1960).

Davis, H. W. C. et al., eds. *Regesta Regum Anglo-Normannorum, 1066–1154*. 4 vols. Oxford, 1913–69.

Dobson, E. J., ed. *The English Text of the Ancrene Riwle*. EETS 267 (1972).

Dugdale, William. *Monasticon anglicanum*. Edited by John Caley, Henry Ellis, and Bulkeley Bandinel. 6 vols. in 8. London, 1817–30, 1846.

Eadmer. *Historia Novorum in Anglia*. Edited by Martin Rule. Rolls Series 81. London, 1884.

Eadmer's History of Recent Events in England. Translated by Geoffrey Bosanquet. London, 1964.

Esposito, Mario. "Analecta Varia (II)." *Hermathena* 36 (1910):86–90.

———. "La vie de Sainte Vulfhilde par Goscelin de Cantorbéry." *Analecta Bollandiana* 32 (1913):10–26.

Farrer, William, ed. *Early Yorkshire Charters*. 3 vols. Edinburgh, 1914–16.

Foliot, Gilbert. *The Letters and Charters of Gilbert Foliot*. Edited by Adrian Morey and C. N. L. Brooke. Cambridge, 1967.

Foreville, Raymonde. *Un procès de canonisation à l'aube du XIIIe siècle (1201–1202); Le livre de saint Gilbert de Sempringham*. Paris, 1943.

Foster, C. W., and Kathleen Major, eds. *The Registrum Antiquissimum of the Cathedral Church of Lincoln*. 9 vols. Lincoln Record Society 27 (and eight other vols.) (1931–68).

Fowler, G. Herbert. "Early Charters of the Priory of Chicksand." *Publications of the Bedfordshire Historical Record Society* 1 (1913):101–28.

———. "Records of Harrold Priory." *Publications of the Bedfordshire Historical Record Society* 17 (1935):1–252.

Geoffrey, Abbot of Vendome. "Epistolae." *PL*. 157 (1898): cols. 33–210.

Gerald of Wales. *Gemma Ecclesiastica*. Vol. 2, *Giraldi Cambrensis Opera*. Edited by J. S. Brewer. London, 1862.

———. *The Jewel of the Church; A Translation of "Gemma Ecclesiastica" by Giraldus Cambrensis*. Translated by John J. Hagen. Leiden, The Netherlands, 1979.

Goscelin. "The Liber confortatorius of Goscelin of Saint Bertin." Edited by C. H. Talbot. In *Analecta Monastica*, edited by M. M. Lebreton, J. Leclercq, and C. H. Talbot, 3:1–117. Studia Anselmiana 37. Rome, 1955.

Gray, Arthur. *The Priory of Saint Radegund, Cambridge*. Cambridge Antiquarian Society 31 (1898).

Hassall, William O., ed. *Cartulary of St. Mary Clerkenwell.* Camden Society, 3d ser. 71. London, 1949.

Herman of Tournai. "De Miraculis S. Mariae Laudunensis. Libri Tres." Appendix ad Librum III Guiberti de vita sua. *PL.* 156: cols. 961–1018.

Hilary. *Versus et ludi.* Edited by J. J. Champollion-Figeac. Paris, 1838.

Holtzmann, Walter. *Papal Decretals Relating to the Diocese of Lincoln in the Twelfth Century.* Lincoln Record Society 47 (1954 for 1951).

———, ed. *Papsturkunden in England.* Abhandlungen des Gesellschaft der Wissenschaften zu Göttingen. 3 vols. Berlin, 1930–52.

Horstmann, Carl. *The Life of St. Werburga of Chester by Henry Bradshaw.* EETS, o.s. 88 (1887).

Innocent III. "Nova quaedam nuper." *PL.* 216: col. 356.

"The Institutes of the Gilbertine Order." In William Dugdale, *Monasticon anglicanum,* edited by John Caley, Henry Ellis, and Bulkeley Bandinel, vol. 6, pt. 2, insert after 945, pp. xix–lviii. London, 1846.

Jeayes, Isaac Herbert. *Descriptive Catalogue of Derbyshire Charters.* London, 1906.

John, Abbot of Ford. *Wulfric of Haselbury.* Edited by Maurice Bell. Somerset Record Society 47 (1933 for 1932).

John of Salisbury. *The Letters of John of Salisbury.* Vol. 1, edited by W. J. Millor and H. E. Butler. London, 1955. Vol. 2, edited by W. J. Millor and C. N. L. Brooke. Oxford, 1979.

Landon, Lionel, ed. *The Cartae Antiquae Rolls 1–10.* Publications of the Pipe Rolls Society 55, n.s. 17. London, 1939.

Lanfranc, Archbishop of Canterbury. *Opera quae supersunt omnia.* Edited by J. A. Giles. 2 vols. Oxford, 1844.

———. *The Letters of Lanfranc Archbishop of Canterbury.* Edited and translated by Helen Clover and Margaret Gibson. Oxford, 1979.

"The Life of St. Gilbert of Sempringham." In William Dugdale, *Monasticon anglicanum,* edited by John Caley, Henry Ellis, and Bulkeley Bandinel, vol. 6, pt. 2, insert after 945, pp. v–xix. London, 1846.

Mack, Frances, ed. *Seinte Marherete, The Meiden ant Martyr.* EETS, o.s. 193 (1934).

Mander, Gerald. "The Priory of the Black Ladies of Brewood, Co. Stafford." In *Collections for a History of Staffordshire,* edited by the Staffordshire Record Society. (1940 for 1939):177–220.

Mansi, Johannes D. *Sacrorum Conciliorum Nova et Amplissima Collectio.* Vol. 21. Venice, 1776. Reprint. Paris, 1903.

Marie de France. *The Lais of Marie de France.* Translated by Robert Hanning and Joan Ferrante. Durham, N.C., 1978.

Massingberd, W. O., and Boyd, W., eds. *Abstracts of Final Concords Temp. Richard I, John, and Henry III.* Lincolnshire Records 1. London, 1896.

Milis, Ludo, ed. *L'ordre des chanoines réguliers d'Arrouaise; Constitutiones canonicorum regularium Ordinis Arroasiensis.* Corpus Christianorum Continuatio Mediaevalis 20. Turnholt, Belgium, 1970.

Orderic Vitalis. *The Ecclesiastical History.* Edited and translated by Marjorie Chibnall. 6 vols. Oxford, 1969–80.

Osbert of Clare. *The Letters of Osbert of Clare, Prior of Westminster.* Edited by E. W. Williamson. Oxford, 1929.

Peck, Francis. *Academia tertia Anglicana; or the Antiquarian Annals of Stanford.* London, 1727.

Phillimore, W. P. W., and Davis, F. N., eds. *Rotuli Hugonis de Welles, episcopi Lincolniensis.* 3 vols. Lincoln Record Society 3–5 (1912–14).

Placitorum in Domo Capitulari Westmonasteriensi asservatorum abbreviatio temporibus regum Ric. I, Johann., Henr. III, Edw. I, Edw. II. (no place), 1811.

Poynton, E. M., ed. "Charters Relating to the Priory of Sempringham." *The Genealogist,* n.s. 15 (1899):158–61, 221–27; n.s. 16 (1900):30–35, 76–83, 153–58, 223–28; n.s. 17 (1901):29–35, 164–68, 232–39.

Reginald, monk of Durham. *Libellus de Vita et Miraculis S. Godrici, Heremitae de Finchale.* Edited by Joseph Stevenson. Surtees Society 20. London, 1847.

Riley, Henry Thomas, ed. *Gesta Abbatum Monasterii Sancti Albani.* Rolls Series 28–30. London, 1867–69.

Roffensi, Monacho. "De Vita Gundulfi Episcopi Roffensis." In *Anglia Sacra,* edited by Henry Wharton, vol. 2. London, 1691.

Round, John Horace, ed. *Calendar of Documents Preserved in France, Illustrative of the History of Great Britain and Ireland.* London, 1899.

———. "The Foundation of the Priories of St. Mary and St. John, Clerkenwell." *Archaeologia* 56 (1899):223–28.

Rye, Walter, ed. *The Norfolk Antiquarian Miscellany* 2 (1883):465–67, 500–501.

Ryland, John William. *Records of Wroxall Abbey and Manor.* London, 1903.

Salter, H. E., ed. *Eynsham Cartulary.* 2 vols. Oxford Historical Society 49 (1907) and 51 (1908).

Salu, Mary B., trans. *The Ancrene Riwle (The Corpus MS.: Ancrene Wisse).* London, 1955.

Serlo. "Poemata." In *The Anglo-Latin Satirical Poets and Epigrammatists of the Twelfth Century,* vol. 2, edited by Thomas Wright. Rolls Series 59. London, 1872.

Shepherd, Geoffrey, ed. *Ancrene Wisse, Parts Six and Seven.* London, 1959.

Sodergärd, Osten, ed. *Vie D'Edouard le Confesseur: Poème Anglo-Normand du XIIe Siècle.* Uppsala, 1948.

Stenton, F. M., ed. *Documents Illustrative of the Social and Economic History of the Danelaw from Various Collections.* Records of the Social and Economic History of England and Wales 5. London, 1920.

———. *Transcripts of the Charters Relating to the Gilbertine Houses of Sixle, Ormsby, Catley, Bullington, and Alvingham.* Publications of the Lincoln Record Society 18 (1922 for 1920).

Stubbs, William, ed. *The Chronicle of the Reigns of Henry II and Richard I* AD *1169–1192; Known Commonly under the Name of Benedict of Peterborough.* Vol. 1. Rolls Series 49. London, 1867.

Talbot, C. H., ed. and trans. *The Life of Christina of Markyate: A Twelfth-Century Recluse.* Oxford, 1959.

Tolkien, J. R. R., ed. *The English Text of the Ancrene Riwle: Ancrene Wisse.*

EETS 249 (1962 for 1960).

Twysden, Roger. *Historiae anglicanae scriptores 10*. London, 1652.

Walker, Margaret S., ed. *Feet of Fines for the County of Lincoln for the Reign of King John 1199–1216*. Publications of the Pipe Roll Society 67, n.s. 29. London, 1954 for 1953.

Weaver, F. W., ed. *A Cartulary of Buckland Priory in the County of Somerset*. Somerset Record Society 25. London, 1909.

William of Malmesbury. *Chronicle of the Kings of England*. Translated by J. A. Giles. London, 1847. Reprint. New York, 1968.

———. *Gesta Regum Anglorum*. 2 vols. Edited by Thomas D. Hardy. Rolls Series 13. London, 1840.

———. *De Gestis Pontificum Anglorum*. Edited by N. E. S. A. Hamilton. London, 1870.

———. *The Vita Wulfstani*. Edited by Reginald Darlington. Camden Society 3d ser. 40. London, 1928.

William Parvi de Newburgh. In *Historia Rerum Anglicarum*. Edited by Hans Claude Hamilton, vol. 1. London, 1856.

Wilmart, André. "La légende de Ste Édith en prose et vers par le moine Goscelin." *Analecta Bollandiana* 56 (1938):5–101, 265–307.

Wilson, H. A., ed. *The Pontifical of Magdalen College*. Henry Bradshaw Society 39. London, 1910.

Woodcock, Audrey M., ed. *Cartulary of the Priory of St. Gregory, Canterbury*. Camden Society 3d ser. 88. London, 1956.

Woolley, Reginald Maxwell, ed. *The Gilbertine Rite*. 2 vols. Henry Bradshaw Society 59. London, 1921.

SECONDARY SOURCES

Manuscript

Lambeth Palace Library MS. 1970: Rotha Mary Clay's early-twentieth-century list of hermits and anchoresses.

Printed Sources

Allen, Hope Emily. "The Author of the 'Ancrene Riwle.'" *Publications of the Modern Language Association* 44 (1929):635–80.

Baker, Derek, ed. *Medieval Women*. Oxford, 1978.

Barlow, Frank. *William I and the Norman Conquest*. London, 1965.

Bateson, Mary. "Origin and Early History of Double Monasteries." *Transactions of the Royal Historical Society*, n.s. 13 (1899):137–98.

Bell, H. E. "Esholt Priory." *The Yorkshire Archaeological Journal* 33 (1936):5–33.

Berlière, Ursmer. *Les monastères doubles aux XIIe et XIIIe siècles*. Académie royale de Belgique. Classe des lettres et des sciences morales et politiques: Mémoires in 8 vols. 2d ser. 18. Brussels, 1923.

Bernards, Matthäus. *Speculum virginum; Geistigkeit und Seelenleben der Frau im Hochmittelalter.* Cologne-Graz, 1955.

Bishop, Edmund. "Origins of the Feast of the Conception of the B.V.M." *The Downside Review* 5 (1886):107–19.

Bolton, Brenda M. "Mulieres Sanctae." In *Women in Medieval Society*, edited by Susan Mosher Stuard, pp. 141–58. Philadelphia, 1976.

Bouton, Jean de la Croix. *Histoire de l'order de Cîteaux.* Westmale, 1959.

Boyd, Catherine. *A Cistercian Nunnery in Mediaeval Italy: The Story of Rifreddo in Saluzzo, 1220–1300.* Harvard Historical Monographs 18. Cambridge, Mass., 1943.

Brett, Martin. *The English Church under Henry I.* Oxford, 1970.

Brooke, Christopher. "Episcopal Charters for Wix Priory." In *A Medieval Miscellany for D. M. Stenton*, edited by Patricia Barnes and C. F. Slade, pp. 45–63. Publications of the Pipe Roll Society 76, n.s. 36. London, 1962 for 1960.

———. "Princes and Kings as Patrons of Monasteries, Normandy and England." In *Il Monachesimo e la Riforma Ecclesiastica (1049–1122)*, pp. 125–44. Milan, 1971.

Brown, William. "The Nunnery of St. Stephen's of Thimbleby." *Yorkshire Archaeological and Topographical Journal* 9 (1886):334–37.

Brundage, James. "Concubinage and Marriage in Medieval Canon Law." In *Sexual Practices and the Medieval Church*, edited by Vern L. Bullough and James Brundage, pp. 118–28. Buffalo, N.Y., 1982.

Bugge, John. *Virginitas: An Essay in the History of a Medieval Ideal.* The Hague, 1975.

Burton, Janet. "The Yorkshire Nunneries in the Twelfth and Thirteenth Centuries." *Borthwick Papers* 56. York, 1979.

Bynum, Caroline Walker. *Docere Verbo et Exemplo: An Aspect of Twelfth-Century Spirituality.* Harvard Theological Studies 31. Ann Arbor, Mich., 1979.

———. "Jesus as Mother and Abbot as Mother; Some Themes in Twelfth-Century Cistercian Writing." Chap. 4 in *Jesus as Mother: Studies in the Spirituality of the High Middle Ages.* Berkeley and Los Angeles, 1982.

———. "The Spirituality of Regular Canons in the Twelfth Century." Chap. 1 in *Jesus as Mother: Studies in the Spirituality of the High Middle Ages.* Berkeley and Los Angeles, 1982.

Chadwick, S. J. "Kirklees Priory." *Yorkshire Archaeological Journal* 16 (1902):319–68, 464–69.

Cheney, C. R. "Harrold Priory: a Twelfth Century Dispute." *Publications of the Bedfordshire Historical Record Society* 32 (1952):1–26.

———. *Hubert Walter.* London, 1967.

———. *Pope Innocent III and England.* Stuttgart, 1976.

Chettle, H. F. "The English Houses of the Order of Fontevraud." *The Downside Review* 60 (1942):33–55.

Chibnall, Marjorie. *Anglo-Norman England 1066–1166.* Oxford and New York, 1986.

Clark, Elizabeth. "John Chrysostom and the *Subintroductae*." *Church History* 46 (1977):171–85.

Clay, Rotha May. *The Hermits and Anchorites of England.* London, 1914.

Colvin, H. M. *The White Canons in England.* Oxford, 1951.

Connor, Sister Michael [Elizabeth]. "The First Cistercian Nuns and Renewal Today." *Cistercian Studies* 5 (1970):131–68.

Constable, Giles. "Aelred of Rievaulx and the Nun of Watton: An Episode in the Early History of the Gilbertine Order." In *Medieval Women*, edited by Derek Baker, pp. 205–26. Oxford, 1978.

_____. *Medieval Monasticism: A Select Bibliography.* Toronto and Buffalo, 1976.

Cronne, H. A. *The Reign of Stephen, 1135–54: Anarchy in England.* London, 1970.

Darby, H. C. *The Domesday Geography of Eastern England.* Cambridge, England, 1971.

Darby, H. C., and Campbell, Eila, eds. *The Domesday Geography of South-East England.* Cambridge, England, 1962.

Darby, H. C., and Maxwell, I. S., eds. *The Domesday Geography of Northern England.* Cambridge, England, 1962.

Darby, H. C., and Terrett, I. B., eds. *The Domesday Geography of Midland England.* Cambridge, England, 1971.

Darwin, Francis D. S. *The English Mediaeval Recluse.* London, [1944].

Dauphin, Hubert. "L'érémitisme en Angleterre aux XIe et XIIe siècles." In *L'eremitismo in Occidente nei secoli XI e XII*, pp. 271–310. Milan, 1962.

Davis, R. H. C. *King Stephen: 1135–1154.* Berkeley and Los Angeles, 1967.

de Fontette, Micheline. *Les religieuses à l'âge classique du droit canon: Recherches sur les structures juridiques des branches féminines des ordres.* Paris, 1967.

Dickinson, J. C. *The Origins of the Austin Canons and Their Introduction into England.* London, 1950.

Dictionary of National Biography. Edited by Leslie Stephen and Sidney Lee. New edition in 22 vols. London, 1908–9.

Dijk, S. J. P. van. "The Origin of the Latin Feast of the Conception of the Blessed Virgin Mary." *The Dublin Review* 228 (1954):251–67, 428–42.

Dimier, Anselme. "Chapitres généraux d'abbesses Cisterciennes." *Cîteaux* 11 (1960):268–75.

Dobson, E. J. "The Affiliations of the Manuscripts of *Ancrene Wisse*." In *English and Medieval Studies Presented to J.R.R. Tolkien on the Occasion of His Seventieth Birthday*, edited by Norman Davis and C. L. Wrenn, pp. 128–62. London, 1962.

_____. "The Date and Composition of the *Ancrene Wisse*." *Proceedings of the British Academy* 52 (1966):181–208.

_____. *The Origins of 'Ancrene Wisse.'* Oxford, 1976.

Dodwell, Barbara. "Some Charters Relating to the Honour of Bacton." In *A Medieval Miscellany for Doris Mary Stenton*, edited by Patricia Barnes and C. F. Slade, pp. 147–65. Publications of the Pipe Roll Society 76, n.s. 36. London, 1962 for 1960.

Donnelly, James S. *The Decline of the Medieval Cistercian Laybrotherhood.* New York, 1949.

Dyson, A. G. "The Monastic Patronage of Bishop Alexander of Lincoln." *Journal of Ecclesiastical History* 26 (1975):1–24.

Eckenrode, T. R. "The English Cistercians and Their Sheep during the Middle Ages." *Cîteaux* 24 (1973):250–66.

Elkins, Sharon. "The Emergence of a Gilbertine Identity." In *Medieval Religious Women.* Vol. 1, *Distant Echoes,* edited by John A. Nichols and Lilian Thomas Shank, pp. 169–82. Kalamazoo, Mich., 1984.

———. "Nunneries Founded by Monks in Twelfth-Century England." In *Benedictus; Studies in Honor of St. Benedict of Nursia,* edited by E. Rozanne Elder, pp. 71–80. Kalamazoo, Mich., 1981.

Erens, A. "Les soeurs dans l'ordre de Prémontré." *Analecta Praemonstratensia* 5 (1929):5–26.

Fairweather, F. H. "The Abbey of St. Mary, Malling, Kent." *The Archaeological Journal* 88 (1932 for 1931):175–92.

Fox, John Charles. "Mary, Abbess of Shaftesbury." *English Historical Review* 26 (1911):317–26.

Frost, Cheryl. "The Attitude to Women and the Adaption to a Feminine Audience in the *Ancrene Wisse.*" *AUMLA: Journal of the Australasian Universities Language and Literature Association,* no. 50 (1978):235–50.

Gibson, Margaret. *Lanfranc of Bec.* Oxford, 1978.

Gies, Frances and Joseph. *Women in the Middle Ages.* New York, 1978.

Giraudot, Francis, and Bouton, Jean de la Croix. "Bernard et les Gilbertins." Chap. 18 in *Bernard de Clairvaux,* pp. 327–38. Paris, 1953.

Gold, Penny Schine. *The Lady and the Virgin; Image, Attitude, and Experience in Twelfth-Century France.* Chicago, 1985.

———. "Male/Female Cooperation: The Example of Fontevrault." In *Medieval Religious Women.* Vol. 1, *Distant Echoes,* edited by John Nichols and Lillian Thomas Shank, pp. 151–68. Kalamazoo, Mich., 1984.

Golding, Brian. "St. Bernard and St. Gilbert." In *The Influence of Saint Bernard,* edited by Sister Benedicta Ward, pp. 42–54. Oxford, 1976.

Gougaud, Louis. *Ermites et reclus.* Ligugé, 1928.

———. "*Mulierum consortia*: Étude sur le Syneisaktisme chez les ascètes Celtiques." *Ériu* 9 (1921):147–56.

Graham, Rose. "The Finance of Malton Priory 1244–1257." *Transactions of the Royal Historical Society,* n.s. 18 (1904):131–56.

———. *S. Gilbert of Sempringham and the Gilbertines.* London, 1901.

Graves, Coburn. "English Cistercian Nuns in Lincolnshire." *Speculum* 54 (1979):492–99.

———. "Stixwould in the Market Place." In *Medieval Religious Women.* Vol. 1, *Distant Echoes,* edited by John A. Nichols and Lillian Thomas Shank, pp. 213–36. Kalamazoo, Mich., 1984.

Grundmann, Herbert. *Religiöse Bewegungen in Mittelalter.* Berlin, 1935. Reprint. Hildesheim, 1961.

Hallam, H. E. *Rural England, 1066–1348.* Atlantic Highlands, N.J., 1981.

Hallier, Amédée. *The Monastic Theology of Aelred of Rievaulx.* Translated by

Columban Heaney. *Cistercian Studies* 2. Spencer, Mass., 1969.

Hentsch, Alice. *De la littérature didactique du moyen âge s'adressant spécialement aux femmes.* Halle, 1903.

Hill, Bennett. *English Cistercian Monasteries and Their Patrons in the Twelfth Century.* Urbana, Ill., 1968.

Hilpisch, Stephanus. *Die Doppelklöster: Entstehung und Organisation.* Münster i. W., 1928.

Hodgson, John Crawford. *History of Northumberland.* 7 vols. Newcastle-upon-Tyne, 1820–58.

———— et al. *A History of Northumberland.* 2d. ed. 12 vols. Newcastle-upon-Tyne, 1893–1926.

Holdsworth, Christopher J. "Christina of Markyate." In *Medieval Women,* edited by Derek Baker, pp. 185–204. Oxford, 1978.

Hollingsworth, T. H. *Historical Demography.* Ithaca, N.Y., 1969.

Hoste, Anselm. *Bibliotheca Aelrediana.* Steenburgis, 1962.

Hugo, Thomas. *The Mediaeval Nunneries of the County of Somerset and Diocese of Bath and Wells.* London, 1867.

Hunt, Noreen. *Cluny under St. Hugh, 1049–1109.* Notre Dame, Ind., 1967.

Husain, B. M. C. *Cheshire under the Norman Earls, 1066–1237.* Chester, England, 1973.

Iogna-Prat, Dominique. "La femme dans la perspective pénitentielle des ermites du Bas-Maine." *Revue d'histoire de la spiritualité* 53 (1977):47–64.

Kapelle, William. *The Norman Conquest of the North; The Region and its Transformation, 1000–1135.* Chapel Hill, N.C., 1979.

Knowles, David. *The Historian and Character.* Cambridge, England, 1963.

————. *The Monastic Order in England.* 2d ed. Cambridge, England, 1966.

————. "The Revolt of the Lay Brothers of Sempringham." *English Historical Review* 50 (1935):465–87.

Knowles, David; Brooke, Christopher; and Londan, Vera. *The Heads of Religious Houses: England and Wales, 940–1216.* Cambridge, England, 1972.

Knowles, David, and Hadcock, Neville. *Medieval Religious Houses, England and Wales.* 2d ed. London, 1971.

Krenig, Ernst. "Mittelalterliche Frauenklöster nach den Konstitutionen von Cîteaux." *Analecta Sacri Ordinis Cisterciensis* 10 (1954):1–105.

Kroll, H. *Analecta Praemonstratensia* 56 (1980):21–38.

Leclercq, Jean. "Consciousness of Identification in Twelfth-Century Monasticism." *Cistercian Studies* 14 (1979):219–31.

————. "Profession According to the Rule of St. Benedict." In *Rule and Life: An Interdisciplinary Symposium,* edited by M. Basil Pennington, pp. 117–50. Spencer, Mass., 1971.

Lefevre, Pl. F., and Grauwen, E. M. *Les statuts de Prémontré au milieu du XIIe siècle.* Averbode, 1978.

Lekai, Louis. *The Cistercians: Ideals and Reality.* Kent, Ohio, 1977.

Lynch, J. H. "The Cistercians and Underage Novices." *Cîteaux* 14 (1973):283–97.

————. *Simoniacal Entry into Religious Life from 1000–1216; A Social, Economic, and Legal Study.* Columbus, Ohio, 1976.

MacBain, William. " 'Courtly Echoes' in Clemence's *Life of St. Catherine*." Unpublished paper delivered at the Fourteenth International Congress on Medieval Studies, Kalamazoo, Mich., 1979.

McLaughlin, Eleanor C. "Equality of Souls, Inequality of Sexes: Women in Medieval Theology." In *Religion and Sexism: Images of Women in the Jewish and Christian Traditions*, edited by Rosemary Radford Reuther, pp. 233–51. New York, 1974.

Madan, Falconer. *A Summary Catalogue of Western Manuscripts in the Bodleian Library at Oxford*. Oxford, 1897.

Mayr-Harting, H. "Functions of a Twelfth-Century Recluse." *History* 60 (1975):337–52.

Meyer, M. A. "Women and the Tenth Century English Monastic Reform." *R. Ben.* 87 (1977):34–61.

Mickel, Jr., E. J. *Marie de France*. New York, 1974.

Miles, Margaret. *Image as Insight: Visual Understanding in Western Christianity and Secular Culture*. Boston, 1985.

Millinger, Susan. "Anglo-Saxon Nuns in Anglo-Norman Hagiography: Humility and Power." In *Medieval Religious Women*. Vol. 1, *Distant Echoes*, edited by John A. Nichols and Lillian Thomas Shank, pp. 115–30. Kalamazoo, Mich., 1984.

Nicholl, Donald. *Thurstan, Archbishop of York (1114–1140)*. York, 1964.

Nichols, John A. "The Internal Organization of English Cistercian Nunneries." *Cîteaux: Commentarii Cistercienses* 30 (1979):23–40.

Nichols, John A., and Shank, Lillian Thomas, eds. *Medieval Religious Women*. Vol. 1, *Distant Echoes*. Kalamazoo, Mich., 1984.

Pächt, Otto; Dodwell, C. R.; and Wormald, Francis. *The St. Albans Psalter (Albani Psalter)*. London, 1960.

Palmer, W. M. "The Benedictine Nunnery of Swaffham Bulbeck." *Proceedings of the Cambridge Antiquarian Society* 31 (1931):30–65.

Petit, F. S. *Norbert et l'origine des Prémontrés*. Paris, 1981.

Platt, Colin. *The Abbeys and Priories of Medieval England*. New York, 1984.

Power, Eileen. *Medieval English Nunneries, c. 1275 to 1535*. Cambridge, England, 1922.

Raison, L., and Niderst, R. "Le mouvement érémitique dans l'ouest de la France à la fin du XIe siècle et au début du XIIe siècle." *Annales de Bretagne* 55 (1948):1–46.

Renna, Thomas. "Virginity in the *Life* of Christina of Markyate and Aelred of Rievaulx's *Rule*." *American Benedictine Review* 36 (1985):79–92.

Reynolds, Roger. "*Virgines subintroductae* in Celtic Christianity." *Harvard Theological Review* 61 (1968):547–66.

Robinson, J. Armitage. *Gilbert Crispin, Abbot of Westminster*. Cambridge, England, 1911.

————. "Westminster in the Twelfth Century: Osbert of Clare." *Church Quarterly Review* 68 (1909):336–56.

Roisin, Simone. "L'efflorescence cistercienne et le courant féminin de piété au XIIIe siècle." *Revue d'histoire ecclésiastique* 39 (1943):342–78.

Round, John H. *Feudal England*. London, 1895.

———. *Geoffrey de Mandeville*. London, 1892.

Saltman, Avrom. *Theobald, Archbishop of Canterbury*. London, 1956.

Schmitz, Philibert. *Histoire de l'ordre de Saint-Benoît*. 7 vols. Maredsous, 1948–56.

Schulenburg, Jane Tibbetts. "Sexism and the Celestial *Gynaeceum* from 500 to 1200." *Journal of Medieval History* 4 (1978):117–33.

———. "Strict Active Enclosure and Its Effects on the Female Monastic Experience, ca. 500–1100." In *Medieval Religious Women*. Vol. 1, *Distant Echoes*, edited by John A. Nichols and Lillian Thomas Shank, pp. 51–86. Kalamazoo, Mich., 1984.

Smith, Jacqueline. "Robert of Arbrissel: Procurator Mulierum." In *Medieval Women*, edited by Derek Baker, pp. 175–84. Oxford, 1978.

Southern, Richard W. "The English Origins of the 'Miracles of the Virgin.'" *Mediaeval and Renaissance Studies* 4 (1958):176–216.

———. *Western Society and the Church in the Middle Ages*. Harmondsworth, 1970.

Squire, Aelred. *Aelred of Rievaulx: A Study*. London, 1969.

Steele, F. M. *Anchoresses of the West*. London, 1903.

Stuard, Susan Mosher, ed. *Women in Medieval Society*. Philadelphia, 1976.

Swietek, Francis R., and Deneen, Terrence M. "The Episcopal Exemption of Savigny, 1112–1184." *Church History* 52 (1983):285–98.

Talbot, C. H. "Godric of Finchale and Christina of Markyate." In *Pre-Reformation English Spirituality*, edited by James Walsh, pp. 39–55. London, [1966].

———. "Some Notes on the Dating of the Ancrene Riwle." *Neophilologus* 40 (1965):38–51.

Tatlock, J. S. P. "Muriel: the Earliest English Poetess." *Publications of the Modern Language Association of America* 48 (1933):317–21.

Thompson, Alexander Hamilton. "Double Monasteries and the Male Element in Nunneries." *The Ministry of Women: A Report by a Committee Appointed by His Grace the Lord Archbishop of Canterbury*, pp. 145–64. London, 1919.

Thompson, Sally. "The Problem of the Cistercian Nuns in the Twelfth and Early Thirteenth Centuries." In *Medieval Women*, edited by Derek Baker, pp. 227–52. Oxford, 1978.

———. "Why English Nunneries Had No History: A Study of the Problems of the English Nunneries Founded After the Conquest." In *Medieval Religious Women*. Vol. 1, *Distant Echoes*, edited by John A. Nichols and Lillian Thomas Shank, 131–50. Kalamazoo, Mich., 1984.

Tolkien, J. R. R. "'Ancrene Wisse' and 'Hali Meidhad.'" *Essays and Studies by Members of the English Association* 14 (1929):104–26.

Van Engen, John. "The 'Crisis of Cenobitism' Reconsidered: Benedictine Monasticism in the Years 1050–1150." *Speculum* 61 (1986):269–304.

Varin, M. "Mémoire sur les causes de la dissidence entre l'Eglise bretonne et l'Eglise romaine," *Mémoires présentés par divers savants à l'Académie des Inscriptions et Belles Lettres*, Paris, 1858, pp. 165–205.

Vaughn, Sally. *The Abbey of Bec and the Anglo-Norman State 1034–1136*. Bury St. Edmunds, Suffolk, 1981.

Ward, Sister Benedicta. *The Influence of Saint Bernard*. Oxford, 1976.
―――. "The Relationship between Hermits and Communities in the West with
Special Reference to the Twelfth Century." In *Solitude and Communion*,
edited by A. M. Allchin, pp. 54–63. Oxford, 1977.
Warren, Ann K. *Anchorites and Their Patrons in Medieval England*. Berkeley,
Calif., 1985.
―――. "The Nun as Anchoress: England, 1100–1500." In *Medieval Religious
Women*. Vol. 1, *Distant Echoes*, edited by John A. Nichols and Lillian
Thomas Shank, pp. 197–212. Kalamazoo, Mich., 1984.
Werner, Ernst. *Pauperes Christi*. Leipzig, 1956.
The Victoria History of the Counties of England. Edited by H. A. Doubleday,
William Page, L. F. Salzman, and R. B. Pugh. Westminster, etc., 1900 +.
Wilmart, André. "Ève et Goscelin." *R. Ben.* 46 (1934):414–38; 50 (1938);42–
83.
―――. "Une lettre inédite de S. Anselme à une moniale inconstante." *R. Ben.*
40 (1928):319–32.
Wood, Susan. *English Monasteries and Their Patrons in the Thirteenth Century*.
Oxford, 1955.